Praise for *The Great Divorce*

"*The Great Divorce* is much more than a fascinating account of a woman's trailblazing battle for her children. . . .Woo brings the past to life in all its wonderful strangeness, complexity, and verve. This is what history is all about."
—Nathaniel Philbrick,
National Book Award–winning author of *In the Heart of the Sea*

"*The Great Divorce* is a superb book—masterfully written, deeply suspenseful, and filled with fascinating facts and insights. American history would be everyone's favorite subject if more historians wrote like this. Woo is a writer to watch."
—Debby Applegate, winner of the Pulitzer Prize for
The Most Famous Man in America: The Biography of Henry Ward Beecher

"A writer of extraordinary empathy and great resourcefulness, Ilyon Woo has transformed a neglected historical record into a vivid evocation of an era and an amazing tribute to a remarkably tenacious woman, Eunice Chapman. Meticulously researched and compellingly narrated, *The Great Divorce* will stand in the pantheon of American women's history writing."
—John Matteson, Pulitzer Prize–winning author of *Eden's Outcasts*

"Ilyon Woo has taken the stuff of obscure history and transformed it into a gripping drama that resonates with our own world. Though she lived in the nineteenth century, Eunice Chapman reminded me of Erin Brockovich—a woman on a mission who fights like a tigress for what she believes in. Woo has an eye for the telling detail, and a prose style as elegantly spare as a Shaker chair."
—Simon Worrall, author of *The Poet and the Murderer*

"In addition to providing an enthralling account of Eunice's early life, marriage, and legislative campaign, Woo offers a detailed look at the Shakers' communal way of life . . . Wo writes with verve."
—Pamela H. Sacks, *Worcester Telegram & Gazette*

"Woo captures the drama and many ironies of Eunice's story, admiring her courage without adopting her view of the Shakers as unmitigated villains." *he New Yorker*

"Modern Am   rity divorces,
probably assu   omenon. This
lively, well-wri

es Book Review

"American history, law, religion, and politics all come alive in this poignant account of an abandoned woman's rescue of her children in the first decades of the nineteenth century. Ilyon Woo gives us the unfolding drama of the first and only legislative divorce in the history of New York as part of a larger struggle for civil identity and women's rights. It is not enough to say that this story of Eunice Chapman's fight against injustice is well told. Ilyon Woo tells a story that every American should want to read."
—Robert A. Ferguson, George Edward Woodberry
Professor of Law, Literature, and Criticism, Columbia
University and author of *The American Enlightenment, 1750–1820*

"Provocative . . . Woo vividly tells the story of the Chapmans' broken family, beginning with a dramatic sentence worthy of Stephen King. . . . Woo tells [this story] in nuanced and absorbing detail."
—Elaine Showalter, *The Washington Post*

"Neglected history comes alive in this meticulously researched and compelling story of one tenacious woman. Strongly recommended to all interested readers."   —*Library Journal* (starred review),
Nancy Richey, Western Kentucky Univ. Lib., Bowling Green

"Ilyon Woo presents the earliest child custody laws of this country with vivid relevance. . . . Eunice has all the splash and charisma of a modern celebrity."   —Holly Silva, *St. Louis Post-Dispatch*

"This biography makes a movie-worthy story of [Chapman's] struggle to reclaim her children and her destiny."   —Meredith Maran, *More*

"A smooth narrative and revealing debut . . . Full of information about women's lives and status at the time, the book makes the case that Eunice's charisma and obsessive determination helped her overcome the usual rejection of women in the public sphere. Both Eunice's struggle and the Shakers' story fascinate equally while dispelling romanticized myths of utopian societies in the tumultuous post–revolutionary period."
—*Publishers Weekly*

"Woo weaves a tale of high drama, religious extremism, legal battles, scandalous allegations, and midnight raids carried out on behalf of tiny, ferocious Eunice Chapman, who was a woman ahead of her time. . . . *The Great Divorce* is vivid and evocative, full of informed conclusions, with a well-executed dramatic arc. . . . Eunice Chapman is a character for the ages."
—*The Santa Fe New Mexican*

Ilyon Woo

THE GREAT DIVORCE

A Nineteenth-Century Mother's Extraordinary Fight Against Her Husband, the Shakers, and Her Times

Grove Press
New York

Published simultaneously in Canada
Printed in the United States of America

ISBN-13: 978-0-8021-4537-6

Grove Press
an imprint of Grove/Atlantic, Inc.
841 Broadway
New York, NY 10003

Distributed by Publishers Group West

www.groveatlantic.com

11 12 13 14 15   10 9 8 7 6 5 4 3 2 1

To my parents

*Live with me, my child! The foxes have holes and the birds of
the air have nests, but I have not where to lay my head.
Go child, and I will go with you; if you go through the waters,
the floods shall not overflow you; and if you go through the fire,
it shall not kindle upon you; and if you go to the ends of the earth,
I will never leave you nor forsake you.*

—Mother Ann Lee

CONTENTS

THE GREAT
DIVORCE

PROLOGUE
Enfield, New Hampshire
May 1818

Five years after the children first disappeared, it had come to this: a hundred strangers circling the Shaker village, torches lit. It was an unseasonably cold night for May, with snow on the ground for reasons no one could explain. The intruders crouched along the trim white fences, hovered by the low stone walls, and rode their horses around the village's periphery, marring the strange spring snow. It was said that five hundred more might come by morning.

Leading the mob was the mother of the missing children, Eunice Chapman, a woman so small that she might have been mistaken for a child herself, her eyes scanning the darkened village. Somewhere here—in one of the closed workshops or barns, or perhaps in the looming, four-story dwelling where the Shakers spent their nights—was her former husband, James, and with him, the children he had stolen from her: Julia, Susan, and George.

The Shakers were saints, James had declared, but to her, these so-called Believers were as far from holy as they could be: They were responsible for separating her from her family, and for hiding her children. Now, after a long search and years of legal warfare, she was closer than she had ever been to bringing her children home. She would do whatever was required. As she had warned the Shakers two days before, "I will scare you yet and make you tremble."

But James was equally resolute. He had once declared that he would sooner kill himself than give up his children, and days earlier had announced that he would rather send his children floating down the river than see them reunited with their mother. By law, children rightfully belonged to their father, and James Chapman had no intention of surrendering his kin.

There had never been much love between the Chapmans, not even when they were courting more than fifteen years earlier. Yet even when the gulf between them had been widest— when the two would sleep on separate floors of their home or James would sleep with other women, when Eunice would threaten James and he would spit into her face—they had never imagined that they would come to blows like this, with hundreds gathered on either side of them, and with everything between them distorted by the glare of torchlight.

The story leading to this standoff begins with America in a time of revolution. The United States was at war with the British during the so-called "Second American Revolution," or the War of 1812. The government was nearly bankrupt and a spirit of speculation was running high, propelling the country toward its first financial crash, the Panic of 1819. Gleaming new steamboats dotted the nation's harbors, and freshly paved roads led the way out West, testament to the transportation revolution then under way. Even legal tradition was coming unmoored as Americans, newly released from the constraints of British rule, sought to define justice in their own terms. And all across the country, religious revivalism raged, stoked by the hopes and anxieties of a people who yearned for something definitive, if not in this life, then in the hereafter.

It was during this period of unrest and discovery that Eunice Hawley Chapman—a woman born two years into the War for Independence, on November 22, 1778—began a revolution of her own, one that eventually made her known across the country. It started when her husband, a troubled merchant named James Chapman, sought to join the Shakers near Albany, New York, and resolved to take his children with him.

Today, the Shakers are remembered mainly for their handiwork —oval boxes, straight-back chairs, and spare, modern-looking furniture that has sold for hundreds of thousands of dollars apiece. Other products of Shaker culture are also familiar, if not always recognized as Shaker, such as the song "Simple Gift," popularized in Aaron Copland's *Appalachian Spring*. In contrast, the people behind these objects have largely been forgotten. As Shaker Sister Mildred Barker once remarked, she "almost expect[ed] to be remembered as a chair or a table." In the second decade of the nineteenth century, however, the Shakers were a vibrant order, several thousand strong and growing, with sixteen communities stretching across eight states—from Maine to Indiana and down to Kentucky. And they were hardly the exemplars of American culture they are now. Even then, the Shakers were known for their excellent wares, but they also aroused deep controversy on account of their radical religious beliefs.

Brought to America by the charismatic English visionary Ann Lee, the Shakers believed in the continuing revelation of Christ—that one's relationship with God was determined not by books or creeds but by the present experience of the divine. They believed in perfectibility, that as Believers they could overcome sin, and that together they could create a heaven on earth. What made the Shakers radicals, however, was not merely their religious "enthusiasm," or their belief that salvation could be guaranteed, but the extreme mandates of their faith. All Shakers were required to renounce their sexuality, property, and family as the first step toward being liberated from earthly sin.

When James Chapman decided to bring his children into this unorthodox society, there was little that his wife could do to oppose him. By law, the Chapman children were considered the exclusive property of their father, valued as his heirs, as well as sources of social security. Decades would pass before mothers like Eunice had any rights to their children, let alone custodial preference in the eyes of the law. Wives, too, belonged to the husband and had few legal rights. Given James's decision, Eunice's only real options were to join the Shakers to be with her children or to give up her family and prepare to live alone.

But Eunice Chapman was an uncommon woman. Famously seductive, willful, and canny, she learned through difficult experience what was expected of her as a woman and how to exploit those expectations. She turned feminine weakness into a source of political strength, using every strategy available to her—including some forbidden ones—in her quest for her children.

From 1814 to 1819, this determined mother—a "modern enchantress," as she was called by some, or an "ornament to her sex," as she was known to others—waged a war against her husband, the Shakers, and the law and culture of her times. Rather than stay out of the public sphere, as women were supposed to do, she fought her way through courtrooms, wooing politicians and drawing the attention of such luminaries as Thomas Jefferson and Martin Van Buren. She whipped up a mob, staged a kidnapping of her own, and—perhaps most skillfully—penned thrilling tales of Shaker bondage that sensationalized her story. Throughout, she succeeded in making her case about much more than herself, convincing the leaders of her state and the public beyond that freedom of religion, the sanctity of marriage, feminine virtue, and even democracy were at stake. This, in the end, enabled her to achieve a landmark legal victory that granted her unprecedented rights as a wife and mother and put her more than a century ahead of her time.

Witnesses were often baffled by how this tiny woman managed to accomplish all that she did. Some were certain that a kind of witchery or magic was at play. The truth is that Eunice Chapman was far more savvy and capable than she appeared. Publicly, she may have played up her helplessness, but privately she imagined herself as a warrior, Moses leading his people or Abraham put to the test—nothing short of a divine instrument. At the height of her battles, and on the brink of conquest, she taunted the Shakers with these formidable words:

Think not that the battle is over after such a victory is gained—I am consulting my friends, COLLECTING MY FORCES FOR A NEW INVASION. You see what I, as an instrument in the hands of God, have brought to pass— You see that all your money and lawyers, nor your Gods could not save you—You have fallen before a poor weak woman. You will soon see what will become of your boasted Military law,—I shall yet convince you that my children is my object—And my children I will have.

It has been said that well-behaved women seldom make history. This is the story of one woman who expressed herself unabashedly—and made history bow to her.

PART I
FAITH

I know how to pray,
I know how to be thankful,
For God has blessed me
With a broken heart.

—*Shaker hymn*

1

A CIVIL DEATH

In 1802 Eunice Hawley should have been married. She was twenty-four years old and single at a time when women tended to wed much earlier. Her two elder sisters—one of whom was only a year older than Eunice—had been married off years ago to good men near their age. Both now had several children, and Eunice had often cradled their babies in her arms. Eunice, however, showed no signs of starting a family of her own.

It was not that she lacked physical charm. Unfortunately, no images exist to show precisely what Eunice looked like, but eyewitnesses recounted that she was strikingly fair and unusually small—and in possession of a powerful allure that would now be called sex appeal. While her tiny frame enhanced her appearance of innocence and defenselessness (both considered feminine virtues), there was something about Eunice that led men to impure thoughts—or so it would later be alleged.

If Eunice had looks, however, she also had a powerful temper, which might have affected her marriage prospects had she developed a reputation for being outspoken or mean. Practical factors might also have accounted for her single status. Eunice was the middle of eight children born to Elijah and Mercy Hawley. With their two older girls married off, the Hawleys may have wanted to hold on to their next-born daughter a little longer, to help keep house and care for their younger ones. Financial troubles might have been another consideration. Eunice's father was an entrepreneurial character, a dry-goods merchant and skilled carpenter in Bridgeport, Connecticut, who ran a boarding-house for sailors on the side. His business failures, though common in this era, would blight Eunice's prospects in the years to come: It is possible that he had already failed in Bridgeport, further diminishing Eunice's chances of marrying well.

Then again, Eunice herself may have been holding out for something better or simply different. She may also have made and lost a match. In any case, when her parents, like so many of their Yankee neighbors, decided to move to the frontiers of New York State in search of better land and fortunes, Eunice, too, seized upon the adventure—she was single and ready to begin her life again.

The Hawleys left behind a well-settled world in Bridge-port. Their family had lived in the area for generations, arriving as Puritan dissenters and later serving as sergeants and constables, surveyors and bell-ringers, reverends, and justices of the peace. Elijah himself was a deacon of the Presbyterian Church. The family lived off of Main Street, not far from Bridgeport Harbor, where a fine breeze came off Long Island Sound and tall ships arrived from Boston, New York, and as far away as the West Indies.

As they journeyed west (slowly, with all of their belongings in tow), the Hawleys encountered a terrain that was far more primitive. The deeper they moved inland, the less likely they were to see church spires and the more likely they were to encounter taverns instead—mean-looking hovels, as one fellow New Englander described them, where "rude" and "clownish" people would congregate, drinking during all hours of the day. For Elijah and Mercy Hawley, who attended worship meetings during the week, as well as on Sundays, the sight of these churchless settlements was surely discomforting.

Then they reached Durham. Located in the heart of Catskill country, forty miles southwest of the New York State capitol in Albany and settled by Connecticut natives like themselves, this community of more than two thousand people stood as an orderly sanctuary in a landscape of disarray. The homely barrenness of the land all around gave way to an undulating terrain of gentle slopes and open valleys, with loamy, clay-rich fields yielding golden crops of grass and wheat, as one eyewitness observed. The town itself was high on a hill, with a Congregational meetinghouse taking a prominent place at its center. There were several schools, and shops carrying such niceties as chocolate and indigo. Here, in short, was every semblance of home.

Equally promising, Durham fell along the route of the brand-new Susquehanna Turnpike, which was crowded, day and night, with all manner of men—homesteaders and farmers, peddlers and grave diggers, itinerant preachers and traveling portrait painters, as well as herds of cattle, turkeys, and other beasts being driven farther west. It was said of this road that dust never settled, and in the evenings, the fields glowed with the makeshift hearths of campers stopping to rest.

This vibrant town was the perfect place for an enterprising merchant to start a business, and it should also have been an ideal location for his daughter to find a husband. But two years after her arrival, Eunice Hawley was still without a partner—a serious situation for a woman of twenty-six, in an era when a woman's future lay largely with the fortunes of the man she married. Were she to remain single, Eunice might support herself as a teacher, passing on the same basic lessons she had learned at home, or perhaps by taking in sewing. But her income would be meager, and she risked becoming a burden to her family. If her parents had not been worried before, they were certainly anxious now. Years later, when Eunice's youngest sister remained unmarried at the younger age of twenty-three, her nephew would regretfully report back to her kin: "Aunt Sally has been here three months, and is still in a state of celibacy."

By this time, Elijah Hawley's financial troubles had become a determining factor in his daughter's lack of prospects. His business with his oldest son, Jesse, was failing, and though the Hawleys were innocent of wrongdoing, they would soon face prosecution from their creditors. With pressure mounting, Eunice now had to reexamine her options with a more practical eye and consider candidates whom she may have overlooked—withered bachelors, widowers, fathers with children, and men she simply did not like. Eventually, for security's sake, she chose to do what many others in her position had done before: she settled.

Life had not begun well for James Chapman. In an era when the brand of bastard was borne for life, he was barely born into legitimacy on October 28, 1763, just one month after his parents, Phineas Chapman and Mary Hillier, were wed.

The mere fact that James's parents had had sexual contact prior to marriage was not such a shock for the times. (Indeed, they were hardly alone: The bridal pregnancy rate rose to nearly 30 percent by the last quarter of the eighteenth century.) In Connecticut, where the Chapmans lived, courting couples often "bundled" together for the night; that is, they slept in the same bed, fully clothed, with extra cloth "bundled" around one or both of them as further defense against temptation. Bundling was in many ways a practice of convenience, since beds were scarce, the weather was cold, and travelers were numerous, but it was also meant to give young people the chance to make sure they shared a "spark" before they became bound to one another for good. Sometimes the spark could be too strong, as a popular "Bundling Song" tells:

> *A bundling couple went to bed,*
> *With all their clothes from foot to head,*
> *That the defence* [sic] *might seem complete,*
> *Each one was wrapped in a sheet.*
> *But O! this bundlin's such a witch*
> *The man of her did catch the itch,*
> *And so provoked was the wretch,*
> *That she of him a bastard catch'd.*

Phineas Chapman and Mary Hillier, however, were hardly the kind of people who were sung about in bawdy ballads. Puritan descendants like the Hawleys, they were the children of leading members of their community in Saybrook, Connecticut. Phineas's father was the deacon of their town church. By their community's standards of propriety, James's birth was a very close call.

Phineas and Mary Chapman had four more children, three sons and a daughter. Within this brood, James had difficulty standing out. By custom, a firstborn son like himself should have received the greater share of his family's resources, while his younger brothers were expected to seek their own fortunes —in trade, for instance, or on the sea. But in the Chapman family, James's younger brother Asa was taken up by a popular pastor, was groomed for Yale College, and shone as an attorney and judge, while James, the eldest, became a merchant.

In at least one area of his life, however, James fulfilled his family's expectations. At twenty-six, he married a distant cousin named Temperance. A daughter, Fanny, was born, and on the same day that she was baptized, April 3, 1791, James and Temperance were both admitted with full communion to the Saybrook Congregational Church. This was a high honor: In order to take communion, congregants had to have experienced a conversion, a "born-again" moment by which they knew they had been touched by God. Perhaps the birth of their daughter had brought the young couple to this awakening. But a year later, James encountered a tragedy that was all too common in this era. His wife died at only twenty-three, probably while giving birth to another child, who was laid to rest beside her. James was left to raise his young daughter alone.

It was around this time that James decided to move to New York State, where by all reports he prospered. He built one of the first houses in Durham and ran a successful business, most likely a store. Apparently, he found little need to remarry. Indeed, if the later confidences of a troubled young ex-Shaker by the name of Josiah Terry are to be believed, James had sworn that his first wife would never find a replacement. That, however, was before he met Eunice Hawley. From the first, James felt the telltale spark, a feeling of intense sexual excitement, as he would later recall. On some level, James considered a connection with Eunice beneath him, given her family's financial situation, but he was deeply aroused by her presence.

A popular conduct manual, John Gregory's *A Father's Legacy to His Daughters*, provides insight into how a woman was expected to exert her appeal in this era. The manual stresses that a woman should not put herself out forcefully, that she should leave the greater part of herself to be imagined. On speaking with men, Gregory advises: "The great art of pleasing in conversation consists in making the company pleased with themselves." On dress, he counsels: "A fine woman shows her charms to most advantage, when she seems most to conceal them. The finest bosom in nature is not so fine as what imagination forms." On the whole, a woman should appear blushing and meek. Eunice may have adopted such strategies as Gregory suggests, although they were hardly intended to promote coquetry.

Whatever techniques Eunice Hawley employed to capture James Chapman's attention, they were effective. According to the later testimony of Josiah Terry, Eunice seemed to know just what to say, just how to look to make him feel important, to make him believe that what she wanted was what he wanted, too. In 1804, James Chapman had been alone for well over a decade. With a little encouragement, he became determined to end his bachelorhood and make Eunice Hawley his wife.

For Eunice, however, the decision to accept James Chapman as her husband had not come easily. To his credit, he came from a good family and had a successful business, but he was also a forty-one-year-old widower, fifteen years her senior. On a personal level, Eunice found him old, disagreeable, and repulsive. Not long after she had first arrived in Durham, she had felt his eyes on her. Nevertheless, it took two years for her to decide to catch—and return—his gaze.

Marriage, moreover, was not a commitment to be considered lightly. To Protestants like the Chapmans and Hawleys, marriage was both a public compact and a covenant with God: a total, eternal commitment that would merge their identities in all ways, one that would determine not only their social standing in the present but their status in the hereafter—and one that could not be revoked.

For a woman like Eunice, the consequences of entering this everlasting union were especially grave, because from the moment she wed, she became "civilly dead," and her legal identity vanished. As the English jurist William Blackstone stated in his *Commentaries,* which provided the foundation for American marital law, "By marriage, the husband and wife are one person in law," which is to say, the husband. The legal term for this process was called coverture. A wife could not own her own property, earn her own wages, sue or be sued, make a will, or sign any other contract by herself. So wholly did the law consider man and wife united that spouses were not allowed to testify against each other, on the grounds that to do so would be an act of self-incrimination. By the same logic, a man marrying his deceased wife's sister was said to commit incest. Even in spiritual matters a wife was expected to defer to her husband, to assume his religious views and practice his faith. Only when her husband died, or in the rare case of divorce, could a married woman recover her legal identity.

Naturally, there was a trade-off. In return for her submission, a woman received social security: food, clothing, shelter, and a lifestyle befitting her social position. And, while a man was considered the ruler of his home, there were some ground rules for his leadership. He could strike his wife, but he was not supposed to abuse her. The difference could be subtle, as demonstrated by the "rule of thumb." This expression originates in the legal argument that a man could beat his wife with a stick the width of a finger but not as wide as a thumb. Finally, a woman was supposed to have some access to marital assets upon her husband's death, retaining dower rights that entitled her to one-third of the land he owned. (These rights, however, were rarely enforced.)

To Eunice, who faced the prospect of spinsterhood, whose family was in a financial crisis, and who yearned for a family of her own, these assurances were enough, in the end, to induce her to accept James's hand. His ability to provide her with the status and security she craved outweighed her instinctive dislike for him. If she refused him, moreover, she might never have another opportunity to have children of her own.

And so, on a chilly February day in 1804, Eunice Hawley and James Chapman faced each other many miles south from where they originally met. Their marriage took place across the shores of bustling Manhattan, in a quiet suburb called Brooklyn, New York, where they perhaps hoped to settle. Here, as they took each other's hands to wed before God, Eunice Hawley died a "civil death," and James Chapman and his wife merged as one.

2

ARDENT SPIRITS

The Chapmans seemed to prosper. In Durham, to which they returned soon after their wedding, they moved into a commodious two-story house, whose centerpiece was the nuptial bed that Eunice's family had given her for her wedding. There, she bore three children in quick succession: George in 1805, Susan in 1806, and Julia in 1809. At a time when many children did not live past infancy, the presence of these healthy youngsters signaled good fortune. There were material comforts, as well. The Chapmans owned at least two large farms in Durham, and they could afford hired help. James, as Eunice later boasted, never even fed his own pigs, while Eunice had servants to help her with the housework. And, in perhaps one of the most telling signs of their prosperity, Eunice had a doctor and a nurse, rather than a midwife, to assist her when she gave birth.

As a couple, however, the Chapmans were in conflict. Some of their differences were generational. James had come of age in the eighteenth century, when a man was considered the supreme governor of his home. He expected total acquiescence from Eunice, not to mention gratitude, given her family's poor circumstances. Instead, two months after the wedding, James was stunned as the tiny, entrancing creature he had so long desired was transformed into a temperamental shrew who sassed him and acted as if *she* were in charge. James finally went to Eunice's parents, complaining that they had advertised false goods, only to be told that Eunice had suffered a head injury as a child and that he should live with her as best he could. Disgusted, he withdrew.

But Eunice, too, had reason to complain. Born in the midst of the War for Independence, a decade and a half after James, Eunice had come of age in an era when women were gaining more power in the home as "Republican Mothers," or nurturers of future citizens. Her expectations were also shaped by a growing popular emphasis on romantic love, as opposed to order, as the basis for a marital relationship. To Eunice, James's arbitrary exercise of power—his insistence, for example, that she give birth in a particular room, one that reeked of plaster—was brutal and tyrannical.

Yet there was more to the Chapmans' marital problems than differences in generation and personality. If Eunice had masked her true, rebellious nature, as James complained to her parents, James had also failed to make a full disclosure. He was, Eunice soon learned, an alcoholic.

To be considered an excessive drinker at this time was no small thing. Americans—women and children, as well as men, and Shakers too, for that matter—guzzled hard cider as they would water, drinking it with every meal. Average yearly consumption was more than three and a half gallons of 200-proof liquor *per person*. In cities and towns across the land, there were more taverns than churches. For men, tavern-going was a source of both business and bonding. Country bars were rough, heady places that reeked of spilled spirits and other smells of the day—the stench of fish oil and sundry fats rubbed into sweat-softened, weather-hardened leather, the acrid tang of animal sweat emanating from dirty horse blankets and old buffalo hides. In these dusky barrooms, men would drink while trading news of fugitive slaves and errant apprentice boys, crop prices and election tallies. They would chat with their neighbors and ask questions of travelers. They would share newspapers and scan announcements pinned to the wall. Here, in short, they gained access to a world larger than their own.

A stiff drink would have been a comfort to a man like James Chapman in this frenetic age, when everything, it seemed, was changing at a bewildering pace and so much seemed uncertain. No one would have begrudged him a drink or even several drinks during daylight hours, but somewhere along the way James Chapman crossed the line. He drank so much that he could not sit up straight in his own wagon. He drank so much that he could not run his shop. James would later claim that his wife had driven him to excess, but his former business partner, Benjamin Chapman (who was also his first wife's brother) testified that James was an alcoholic well before he married Eunice. It was because of James's drinking, he added, that their partnership finally ended.

Under the influence of "ardent spirits," James became abusive, and Eunice feared for her life. Once she awoke to the sound of metal scraping a smooth, stiff surface: a blade against leather. She could smell James in all his vulgar familiarity—his sweat, the ale on his breath, his unwashed clothes—and she was certain that he was preparing to cut her with his razor. With her eyes closed, trying her best not to betray her alertness to her husband, Eunice prayed hard, until suddenly and inexplicably, James left.

By the time their youngest child was a year old, the Chapmans were living separate lives. While Eunice remained in Durham with the children, James rented a shop in Schoharie, a town twenty miles away, where he would play cards, drink, and lie with other women in a back-room bed. Eunice was well aware of her husband's philandering, which surely seemed all the more cruel and perplexing given his oddly prudish behavior toward her. James and Eunice rarely slept together, but when they did, James seemed tormented with guilt. The morning after sharing her bed, James would drop to his knees and beg God for forgiveness. Occasionally, when Eunice could catch him in a sober moment, she would plead with James to stop his reckless behavior, and for a moment, he would seem overcome with regret—but then he would run to the alehouse and the cycle would recommence.

Eunice did her best to keep her troubles hidden from public view, anxious to preserve her husband's reputation, which directly affected her own. Any bad behavior or moral laxness on James's part reflected badly on her, too, and it was very important to her to appear "respectable." Thus she watched what she said to her neighbors and tried to cover for her husband's erratic behavior. She told her children to mind their manners and to heed their father. She even went to Schoharie and quietly ran James's shop in his absence.

Nevertheless, there came a point when the Chapman's troubles became obvious to everyone. This was an era when business was still personal, when credit was tracked in storeroom ledgers and bills could be paid with handwritten promissory notes.

James became known for his excesses, and those excesses were intruding upon his ability to operate a business. Soon, creditors were calling in their loans and threatening to sue.

Debt is an unpleasant matter in any age, but in the early nineteenth century it was especially fearsome, because debtors could be sent to prison. The Chapmans knew this consequence firsthand, since, not long after they were married, Eunice's father and brother had been given jail time on account of their debts. Apparently, a third business partner ran off with a large sum of their money, leaving them ten thousand dollars short and overrun with creditors. Fortunately, the Hawleys had connections, so they were kept "on the limits," which meant that instead of doing time in a cell, they were confined within their community—a reprieve, to be sure, but still a disgrace.

Well aware of the dangers he faced, and miserable in his marriage to Eunice, James decided in June 1811 to move out of the family home and in with his father. James's daughter from his first marriage had just been married, so at least there was one less child to worry about. After a month away from his family, he decided that what he needed was a clean start, and he resolved to leave for good the wife he blamed for all of his troubles.

At summer's peak, with James's mind made up to leave, notices appeared in taverns and papers, announcing a sheriff's sale at the Chapman residence. On the appointed day in July, Eunice was forced to watch as every last pig, sheep, and cow was trotted out from her yard, and everything she owned was removed in payment of her husband's debts—from the table where she fed her children to the fine wooden bureaus her mother had given her before moving away. All that remained was her marriage bed, the sole item that was conceded as hers. Buyers received a bargain. The entire Chapman estate, which was worth $6,000—roughly $84,000 today—was auctioned for $1,500—or $21,000 now.

At the conclusion of the sale, James departed from the premises along with everyone else, leaving Eunice alone with her three children, aged two, five, and six, in the empty house that she could no longer call her own. Two months later, he came by to tell her that he was leaving for New York City, where he had to settle some further debts, and that he did not plan to come back soon, if ever.

When the Chapmans parted ways, informally and without a legal agreement, they followed a common pattern. Most Americans of this era never considered divorcing, not just because divorces were seen as a source of terrible shame, but also because in most places they were difficult to obtain—above all in New York State, which had some of the most stringent family laws in the country. In New York, only adultery, the sole cause that was explicitly named in the Bible, was considered just grounds for terminating a marriage. This meant that not even a woman who had been abused or deserted for years or one whose children had been harmed by her husband was guaranteed a way to end her marriage, go on with her life, and if she chose, marry again.

Divorce proceedings, moreover, were expensive, time-consuming, and inevitably humiliating, given the kinds of evidence required. In the case of *Cock v. Cock*, for instance, a witness testified that he saw, with his own eyes, a man named John Youngs "in bed with the said Eliza E. Cock[,] she being undressed and he having his breeches unbuttoned and down about his feet." Likewise, in the case against Aaron Burr, the infamous Founding Father, a servant deposed that she had seen "Jane McManus with her clothes all up and Coln Burr with his hands under them and his pantaloons down."

Given the difficulties and the costs of obtaining a divorce, most couples simply separated without a formal agreement—even in cases like the Chapmans, where one spouse had reason to charge the other with adultery. Many went on to find new partners and start second families, despite the fact that any children they then bore would be considered illegitimate. But such informal arrangements left women especially vulnerable. For, as long as her husband was alive and she had no divorce, a woman remained civilly dead. As far as the law was concerned, her identity remained one with her husband's, whether she lived with him or not. Any wages she earned, property she inherited, or life she subsequently built for herself was subject to his authority. Thus in theory, a man could return to his wife years after he abandoned her, to lay claim to her and to any and all of her worldly possessions, as well as the children she had raised alone. This was the precarious situation in which Eunice found herself when James left her—not knowing how, when, or with whom, if ever, he might return.

3

A BETTER MAN

James himself had no idea where he was headed when he left his wife and children in the fall of 1811. For about a year, he idled in New York City, indulging in all the pleasures the city had to offer, in brothels, gambling houses, and taverns. Then came the war, and if rumors at the time are to be believed, he signed up to work aboard a privateering ship (a private vessel that was encouraged to raid enemy ships) but deserted once he was paid. Finally, in October 1812, he traveled back north to Troy, near Albany, to start a business with his brother Nathaniel.

James's spirits could not have been lower. When he abandoned his family, he became not just a deadbeat but a failure in the eyes of the world. Without property, he could no longer vote, and without his family, he could claim no public standing. What James Chapman lost, in essence, was his claim to manhood. As he described his outlook at this time, "I felt myself unfit either to die or to live." He was in this vulnerable frame of mind when he came across an unusual settlement inhabited by a people who considered themselves God's chosen.

The Shakers offered a radically different perspective from that of the religion with which James and Eunice had been raised. In the predominant Calvinist way of thinking, man was naturally depraved, tainted by original sin, and fully deserving of every bit of misery that came his way. Only God could save him or elect him to eternal life—and only if God chose to do so. Herein lay the problem. As the famous theologian Jonathan Edwards expressed it before a weeping, hysterical congregation:

> The bow of God's wrath is bent, and the arrow made ready on the string, and justice bends the arrow at your heart, and strains the bow, and it is nothing but the mere pleasure of God, and that of an angry God, without any promise or obligation at all, that keeps the arrow one moment from being made drunk with your blood.

God in his mercy *might* decide to save a soul, but he could just as well shoot it down, and there was nothing that anyone could do to stop him. What is worse, there was no way for a person to know, beyond a doubt, what God had in store. Even the converted, who had experienced a crisis of awakening and felt God's light, could not be sure of their eternal fate. To presume knowledge was in itself blasphemy. To traditionalists, both the idea that salvation could be earned and, another extreme, the idea that it was freely accessible were equally sinful.

The uncertainty was enough to drive some to madness or even suicide. What, after all, was the point of being good—of doing anything at all—if salvation was predetermined? In one particularly horrific example from 1806, a woman from Westmoreland, New York, neatly prepared five sets of burial clothes before killing her four daughters and herself. She preferred to die than to endure the torment of not knowing whether she was destined for hell or heaven. At least death was definitive.

Others, however, were starting to reject such hopelessness for a more sustaining vision of God. Methodists, Baptists, and similarly "enthusiastic" groups were gaining currency as they spread the word that you could *choose* the right way and that salvation was available to all. A lesser-known group of evangelicals took this message even further. From their base in New Lebanon, New York, and in settlements across New England and the West, the Shakers offered the ultimate promise: Not only was there a sure way to heaven, but it could be experienced in the present.

Heaven, as the Shakers saw it, came not to those who waited but to those who embraced it. God himself was an immediate, palpable presence—one that was to be feared, to be sure, but also to be known and loved in every aspect of daily life. To men and women who were anguished over their fate, to those who were converted but unsure of their next steps, or to those who simply did not know what to believe, the Shaker message could not have been more reassuring. It offered a clear direction and absolute guarantees at a time when nothing seemed secure.

What is more, the Shakers seemed to have proof of their godliness. "By their fruits ye shall known them," was one of their favorite biblical lines, and they quoted it often as they pointed to their idyllic communities. By the 1810s, the Shakers had sixteen settlements in Connecticut, Indiana, Kentucky, Maine, Massachusetts, New Hampshire, New York, and Ohio. In contrast to the ragged hamlets that lined the way out West, these communities were models of self-reliance and order. Even the Shakers' critics were impressed. James Fenimore Cooper, who dismissed the Shaker religion as one "founded on fanaticism and folly," remarked that he had "never seen, in any country, villages so neat, and so perfectly beautiful."

Within each Shaker village, all Believers, from the newest novice to the highest Elder, labored side by side to produce nearly everything their society needed—food, clothing, furniture, tools, and more—and sold their surpluses at a profit. With such a large collective workforce, and their religion to motivate and organize them, the Shakers achieved a level of material prosperity that was seldom seen. They boasted extensive orchards and fertile farms, whose fruits were reputed to be sweeter than those from anywhere else, and impeccable dwellings, where everyone seemed to live in harmony. In this Arcadia, no one was excluded, and everyone's needs were met. As the reformer Horace Greeley rhapsodized years later:

> Here are no pampered and purse proud nobles—no famished and pining beggars. Here no widow clasps in anguish her shivering babes, and looks despairingly to her empty cupboard and hearth; no slave of business, scarcely less to be pitied, hurries from hollow friend to friend, imploring, in a perspiration of agony, for the means of taking up the note which must be met before . . . he is a bankrupt. Here experiments have no potency, lawyers no business, sheriffs no terror. Happy happy community!

Here, in short, miseries such as those experienced by the Chapmans—Eunice's desperation as a single mother, James's struggles as a debtor fighting off creditors—were nowhere to be found. The community provided everyone with nourishment and shelter, in addition to salvation.

Of course, paradise did not come without a price. True Believers were expected to live a perfectly Christ-like life, forsaking all attachments that bound them to the world. Jesus himself had declared: "If any man come to me, and hate not his father, and mother, and wife, and children, and brethren, and sisters, yea, and his own life also, he cannot be my disciple" (Luke 14:26). In the same spirit, Shakers were required to give up their families, relinquish their private property, and, perhaps most controversially, embrace celibacy. As the Shakers believed, it was only by doing away with exclusive, personal attachments, whether to an object or to a person, that one could open oneself up fully to a greater, universal, divinely inspired love.

The Shakers' requirements were unorthodox, to say the least. There may have been precedents for celibacy and communalism in other religions—such as the chaste monastic life of Catholic monks and nuns—but for most Americans, these practices went against the natural order: against the spirit of capitalism, for one, and also against God's command to "go forth and multiply." In fact, these self-denying tenets were critical to the Shakers' success. By the middle of the nineteenth century communitarian experiments such as John Humphrey Noyes's Oneida Community, Bronson Alcott's Fruitlands, and Robert Owen's New Harmony would be in vogue. Most would fail, however, when their founders died or individualism and personal ties overcame communal bonds. The Shakers not only pioneered the communistic trend but also endured.

The Shakers knew that their orders were not easy to follow, and so when visitors such as James Chapman inquired about their faith, they tended not to flaunt their dogma. Instead, they quietly impressed their guests with their Christian love and hospitality. It was later, when an inquirer was in a receptive frame of mind, that the Shakers preferred to introduce their more contentious views. As they often said, to share everything of their religion was to cast pearls before swine.

James Chapman was not a stranger to Shakerism. He had done business with traveling Shaker salesmen in Durham. He had even hosted a Brother, as the men were called, overnight. But when James visited Watervliet one cool fall day in 1812 (possibly as a result of this acquaintance), he was in a very different situation, adrift from his family and from society at large. As he entered the Shaker world in this condition, feeling unfit for death as well as life, he became overwhelmed by all he saw— by the Shakers' warmth and generosity and by the beauty of their place in the autumn light. Long ago, beside his first wife, Temperance, James Chapman had been a God-fearing man: He had experienced a powerful conversion, whereby he was convinced of his own worthlessness before God and earned the blessings of his church. Now, in the presence of the Shakers, he believed that he could be with God once more.

Becoming a Shaker was a gradual process. In the first step, initiates made a full confession of their sins in order to purge themselves of the evils of "the world," as the Shakers referred to outsiders. They then entered a trial period, sometimes for years, to prove that they could "bear the cross," or take up the required Shaker burdens, such as celibacy. If all went well, novitiates would sign a covenant, agreeing to abide by the society's rules and consecrate all that they owned in joint interest with the Shakers.

Converts with children also relinquished their parental rights through agreements called indentures. As strange as it may seem today, this transfer of guardianship was not unusual in that

era. Children worked from a young age, and many were appren-
ticed or "bound" to masters in exchange for food, shelter, and
training. Shakers preferred not to specify a trade in their indentures, believing that youngsters needed time to identify their
talents, but they promised a basic education. Early Shaker indentures also included a unique provision that some considered
unfair: Parents had to promise not to remove their children for
any reason, whereas the Shakers could return children who were
badly behaved. This stipulation was a means of self-defense.
From early on, the Shakers were harassed with lawsuits, typically from ex-members seeking to recover property, family members, or wages for past labor. As a result the Shakers tried to
make the terms of their agreements irrevocable. Converts who
reneged could not retrieve anything—neither children, property, nor wages—and indentured children were expected to
remain in the society until they turned twenty-one. At that
point, they were free to choose whether to sign the Shaker covenant or leave for the world.

To James Chapman, Shakerism seemed well worth the price.
Then again, in practical terms, it would cost him almost nothing.
He had no property to consecrate and no family to disavow, since
he had already lost both. And, if his wife's reports are to be believed, he had deeply conflicted feelings about sexuality, an overwhelming sense of shame and guilt after the act. To make the
sacrifices demanded by the Shakers would merely be to formalize
his repudiation of what he had already abandoned. In exchange,
he would have instant access to everything that was then missing
from his life: a stable home, financial security, a supportive community, and more—a sense of acceptance and a reason to live.

James's dependence on alcohol may have given him reason to
pause before joining a sect where any excess (short of a religious

kind) was not tolerated, but he may also have seen joining the Shakers as an impetus for relinquishing a ruinous habit. Or perhaps he simply made a cognitive switch. In a song called "Spiritual Wine," the Shakers exulted:

> *I have found the true vine, and have tasted its wine*
> *Which has made me to stagger and reel;*
> *And to such it belongs to break forth in songs,*
> *To express how delightful they feel;*
> *By a bountiful use of this heavenly juice,*
> *I forget all my sorrows and woes;*
> *Give me plenty of this, I want no other bliss,*
> *And I care not much how the world goes—goes—goes,*
> *And I care not much how the world goes.*

Protestants in this era typically bridled at the thought of making a popish confession, but with the taste of this "heavenly juice" on his lips, James quickly swallowed any prejudices he may have had. He knelt before his Elder, and then, with great emotion, recounted every sinful act he could remember—how he had become an alcoholic, abused his wife, lost his business, and finally, deserted his family.

At once, James felt free. Not only did the Shakers declare him cleansed of his sins, but they said it was not too late for him to make amends, return to his family, and fulfill his obligations. Indeed, they informed him that he must, for they would not take him until he had first settled his outside affairs. James was deeply humbled. Until now, he had thought of himself as a man on his own. The Shakers showed him that he had to honor his word—that if he bound himself to a woman and brought children into the world, he was required "by the laws of God and man" to do justice to them. James realized, in short, that "to be a real good Shaker, was to be a better man than I had ever been, or expected to, in this world." Before he encountered the Shakers, James had no intention of returning to Eunice and the children: With their help, he embraced his duties as a man.

The Shakers deserve credit: They could easily have ignored James's obligations to a world that they actively renounced. But there were practical reasons for them to encourage a man like James to return to his wife and children. It made little difference that the Chapman family was already destroyed; in order to avoid charges that they wrecked homes, the Shakers needed to do their best to broker a peace. If James could persuade his family members to enter the society, then so much the better for everyone. His kinsmen would be saved, James himself would be more comfortable, and the Shakers would have new converts. Such was the peculiar plight of the celibate sect: The Shakers were dependent on the very world they renounced for the continuation of their society.

With the Shakers behind him, James wrote to Eunice to tell her that he was prepared, at last, to do right by her and the children and that he was coming home. Herein lies one of the terrible ironies of the Chapmans' story. Owing to the influence of a society that rejected family ties, James Chapman was reunited with his kin; after he vowed to honor his commitments to his wife and children, everything went wrong. One cannot help wondering what might have happened if the Shakers had simply accepted James Chapman as a man on his own.

4

A WOMAN ALONE

Durham was not an easy place for a woman to survive by herself, let alone with three children. The land that could appear so bounteous in the glow of the harvest season became unforgiving in the winter: windblown, lonesome, and brutally cold. Men heading out to the nearby town of Catskill were obliged to layer thick, blanket-like shawls over their heaviest coats, pull fur hats over their earmuffs, and wear mittens that were tightly cinched at the wrist to fend off the chill. Firewood, preserved foods, warm clothing, and coverlets all had to be in good supply. Eunice had none of these things. Her home had been cleared of every object except her bed, and even this was soon stripped. Shortly after James's departure, officers began raiding the house to seize whatever possessions Eunice might have had left, presumably as payment for her husband's debts. On the third such visit, as Eunice lay sick, an officer grabbed the very sheets upon her bed, tearing them out from under her body.

Alone with her children, Eunice faced what she had long considered her worst possible fate. But before, she had feared that her much older husband would leave her a widow, not that he would leave her behind—a situation that was far worse. At least as a widow, she could hold her head high, manage her own finances, perhaps even start up a small business, as widows often did, and if she was lucky, marry again. None of these options was open to a deserted wife, who suffered an added burden of shame. Common sense held that if a man was so dissatisfied that he would leave home, there must be something seriously wrong with his wife.

Many nights, past midnight, Eunice would ponder her uncertain future, pacing the floor while snowstorms raged and her children slept—warm for once, curled up together. Without candles or firewood, she moved about to create heat in the darkness. How was she to provide for her children, the youngest just a toddler, with no income and with officers coming by for whatever she managed to gather? For the time being, she was surviving on handouts from her sister Mary Spencer, who lived in Durham, and occasionally from her parents, who had left town after their business failures. She also had a place to live, thanks to a soft-hearted judge from Catskill, who allowed her to remain in the house he now owned. Still, Eunice knew she could not depend on such help for much longer.

By now, Eunice's health had deteriorated to the point where she could not recognize her image in the glass. Once flushed and full, her cheeks were pale and hollow—a "skeleton," she called herself. Then there were the children. During the day, as Eunice struggled to find enough for her children to eat or to keep them warm, she was all too aware of their anxious eyes, fixed on her for any sign of fear or distress. George was especially vulnerable. Although the eldest, he had become as needy as an infant and was prone to hysterics when he saw that his only remaining parent was in any kind of pain. For his sake especially, Eunice felt compelled to hold herself together. Only at this hour, alone in the darkness, would she finally allow herself to cry.

Under the kinds of pressures she faced, Eunice might easily have fallen apart. Or she might have given her children to others to raise, a common recourse in this era. Incidentally, many indigent children were taken to the Shakers under just these conditions. Although the Shakers preferred not to accept straightforward charity cases, they often did, unable to withstand the sight of a shivering, malnourished child coming through their doors with a desperate parent.

Eunice was fortunate that she had offers from her stepdaughter, Fanny, and from others to take in her children. She might well have let her youngest child go or hired out her eldest when he turned seven, the minimum age to begin an apprenticeship. But to Eunice, giving up any of her children—even to their well-meaning and well-married half sister—was never an option. Her children were her life's pleasure, and they gave her a reason to live. She delighted in caring for them and teaching them all she could, guiding Susan's hands as she learned to knit her first stitches or helping George as he stumbled over words in the Bible. And thus she refused to compromise, showing what would become her signature colors.

As her husband had already seen, Eunice was a fighter, and far hardier than her dainty proportions suggested—combative, outspoken, and stubborn. James had hated her for these qualities, which were also out of sync with the expectations of the times. But now, the very characteristics that her husband blamed for their failed marriage became Eunice's best tools for survival, as they would time and again.

Eunice was also sustained by her stalwart religious faith. Eunice was a deeply religious woman, raised in a strong Calvinist tradition that continually underscored man's sinfulness and the need to trust in an all-knowing, all-powerful God. In this tradition, the ability to endure any trial, even torture, was no mere test of personal fortitude, but a test of spirit. The truly faithful not only expected suffering but embraced it as an opportunity to demonstrate their worthiness to their Maker. Whenever she faced a crisis—whether it was when James seemed ready to strike her or as she wept at midnight—she called out to her Lord, spoke to him, and drew strength. She had to believe that her experiences were part of a larger plan, and that if she did not know what that plan was, there was someone greater who did.

That conviction remained even as Eunice became estranged from the religious society she had joined a year prior to James's departure. The Durham Presbyterian Church was a rigidly conservative organization—perhaps even as restricted, in some ways, as that of the Shakers. Congregants met weekly, beyond the Sabbath, to discuss one another's personal failings, and they watched one another vigilantly for all manner of sins—most commonly swearing, skipping church, and drunkenness, with some more unusual violations in the mix. One member was excommunicated for dancing at a tavern, another for saying "Damn you" to his horses.

Initially, Eunice appreciated her church's tough moral codes and predictable structure. All that changed, however, at the sheriff's sale at her home. When she was most in need of compassion, Eunice was outraged to see her fellow congregants seeking to profit from her loss, bidding low on her most intimate possessions, just like everyone else. This experience, as much as any other, toughened Eunice, teaching her that she could not rely on others, however much they professed their love and called themselves her "Brothers and Sisters," as her church fellows did. She also began to see her relationship to a church as separate from her relationship with God—a distinction that would prove fateful in her dealings with the Shakers. In spiritual matters, as well as practical ones, Eunice learned that she was on her own.

It is here that Eunice's remarkable resourcefulness first surfaces: her almost uncanny ability to obtain what she needed, seemingly out of nowhere. She foraged for firewood and other necessities and beseeched her friends and relatives for whatever they could spare. She probably hired herself out, bartering her services as a teacher or a seamstress for food. She also relied on the older children to do their part. Although George and Susan were only five and six when their father left, they were old enough to weed a garden plot or gather kindling and to watch over their younger sister. Somehow, by making the most of what little she had, Eunice managed to keep her children clothed and fed and her family intact.

This was a formative time for Eunice. Her experience of providing for her children as a single mother—and her awareness that she could live without a man—would empower her to reject what others offered and to create an alternative destiny for herself. Not everything, however, remained under her control. While Eunice succeeded in holding her family together, her troubles with her church spun out of bounds, teaching her more critical lessons that would prove instrumental years down the line.

After the sheriff's sale at her home, Eunice's relations with her church deteriorated. Feeling betrayed, Eunice lashed out against her fellow congregants. She admonished a man named John Adams for refusing to sell back her dressers for the same price he

had paid for them, and she charged another family with pilfering items at the sale. She also looked back to the days when her husband was present, accusing a neighbor of having stolen a piece of freshly slaughtered pork. More conflicts rose over a tin pan that Eunice reputedly borrowed and refused to return, and a set of misplaced quilting hoops. Throughout, Eunice addressed her neighbors in a manner that was deemed "unchristian," and at least once, she lied; she lamented that the dressers John Adams now possessed had belonged to her dead mother, when Mercy Hawley was alive and well in Schoharie.

Eunice's behavior toward her church fellows shows the strains of a woman who had lost nearly everything of value in her world—her husband, her property, and her social standing —and no longer had patience for social decorum. She had come far from the days when she had cared so much about others' opinions that she had tried to hide her husband's failings. Her skirmishes with her church also reveal the depths of her isolation. Eunice sought out other women to mediate her quarrels, as required by her church: None of them would help her.

But while James was learning to humble himself among the Believers, Eunice was learning to stand her ground. Even as her church brethren repudiated her for "evil" behavior and an "unbridled tongue," she remained uncowed. She refused to make the full apology her church demanded. In the end, her obstinacy did not serve her well, and here, Eunice may have learned her most valuable lesson to date: that the very quality that helped her survive—her forcefulness—could become a liability when directed outward, especially against tradition-minded authorities. Eventually, her church excommunicated her.

It was precisely at this time—when Eunice was struggling to support her family and chafing against the constraints of her religious community—that she heard from her husband. James wrote to say that he had found God and that he was coming home.

Eunice knew the Shakers by sight. Shaker Brothers often came through town on peddling excursions, their wagons bearing the freshest produce in the area—crisp russets, tender greens, and large, plump gourds—and all kinds of high-quality wares, such as combs, pails, brooms, and, perhaps most famously, storage boxes, medicines, and seeds. The Shakers' oval boxes, which have since become icons of their culture, were not entirely unique to the sect: Round storage boxes had been popular since the colonial era. However, the Shakers' boxes boasted delicate "fingers" at their joints—subtle additions that, by allowing the wood to expand and shrink with the elements, made the boxes famously airtight and durable. The community's fragrant herbal remedies, which were pressed into little cakes or extracted and poured into vials, were similarly known for their long-lasting effects. The Shakers also pioneered the practice of slipping their superior seeds into little packets—a method that proved to be much more practical than carrying seeds loose in boxes and measuring on the fly.

Shaker Brothers were easily distinguishable in their pegged pants, broad-waisted coats, and unfashionable wide-brimmed hats. They were peculiar in other ways, using antiquated terms like "yea" and "nay," and taking extreme pains to avoid physical contact with women—refusing even to take change from a woman's hand. Some Brothers would not utter a word in an exchange with a woman, allowing a housewife to lay down the amount of money she wanted to pay for an item, then taking it if he approved or walking away if he did not. Yet for all their idiosyncrasies, Shakers enjoyed a mostly positive reputation. They were known for being dependable trading partners, honest, hardworking, and kind to the poor—all of which meant a great deal in financially troubled times. From Eunice's perspective, James might well have found far worse company.

Not that she would have been exactly enthralled: As she read James's letter, Eunice certainly recalled that her husband had once invited a Shaker to take shelter in their house and stayed up talking all night with an unnervingly manic intensity. Still, James had remained home that night, instead of heading to the tavern as he so often did.

As for the particulars of Shakerism, Eunice knew very little, but she came from a family that was relatively open-minded in its religious beliefs, if fundamentally traditional. There had been a time in Bridgeport when people were not letting Methodists into their doors; such "New Light" preachers were known to "go on like madmen," beating their pulpits and foaming at the mouth, while exhorting their hearers to "come away to the Lord." Many considered the Methodists' emphasis on free will, as opposed to predestination, tantamount to heresy. Eunice's parents, however, welcomed at least one Methodist minister to hold services at their home. There was grace that day, with worshippers bursting into tears at the preacher's words. To a woman who had been raised in such a household, a man's interest in an unconventional religion was not reason enough to turn him away. On the contrary, Eunice hoped that under the Shakers' influence, James had been, as he promised, truly transformed.

She was soon disappointed. Eunice welcomed James home as a good wife should: She cooked his meals, washed and mended his clothes, and even sewed him a new suit to replace his Shaker outfit. James, however, would not do his part as a husband. He spoke rapturously of the Shakers—of how they would provide the family with all that they needed, including a glorious home —but when Eunice challenged him to provide for his family *himself*, he refused. He would give her no money or any other assistance, lived wherever he pleased, and for a short time took George and Susan to board elsewhere, over Eunice's protests.

It is unclear why James would pay for his children's room and board, yet refuse to assist Eunice directly. Eunice later suspected that the Shakers forbade him to give her anything, but he may simply have been trying to do his best to provide for his children while breaking down his wife's resolve. In any case, he soon returned the children, forcing Eunice to care for them by herself. To Eunice, it was evident that James was as unreliable as ever.

As the days grew colder, the family's needs grew more apparent. More and more they were forced to pass the time in dark, stuffy quarters, gathered around the sooty hearth or hunkered over bland, stewed meals. Thanksgiving passed, then Julia's third birthday in December, Christmas, and New Year's Day, 1813. Still, Eunice and James could not agree on how or where they should live. James wanted his family to move near the Shakers, but Eunice, unwilling to leave her home for a place and people she knew nothing about, demanded that her husband support them in Durham. Finally, in February, James decided that he had had enough. The time had come for him to return to the Shakers, whether his family joined him or not.

As he prepared for his departure, he made one final plea to Eunice: that she at least consider accompanying him to the Shaker village for a visit. Despite her lack of faith in her husband, Eunice consented, curious. The Shakers were rumored to be rich as well as charitable. Perhaps, if they were all that everyone said they were, she could persuade the Shakers to help her and her family. The only way to find out would be to go and see them for herself.

The Chapmans traveled to Watervliet with James's brother John. The children remained at home; the long journey would have been too much for them, particularly given the unpredictability of the February weather. Nestled under blankets, watching as the trees raced by above her, Eunice must have remembered with some mournfulness that it was precisely this time of year, nine years ago, that she and James had first braced against the chill together as husband and wife. Back then, even in her ambivalence about James, she had thrilled to the warmth they made together as they snuggled close. Now, they measured the empty space that lay between them, blinking hard at the distance ahead.

5

WATERVLIET

Eight miles outside Albany, in what were once wetlands between the Hudson and Mohawk rivers, was the site of the
first Shaker community, called Watervliet. Less than fifty years
before, this terrain had been dark with pines, swarmed over
with mosquitoes, and dismissed by most white pioneers. Now,
however, it was home to roughly 150 Shaker souls. The Believers remained isolated: The nearest settlement was a village
called Niskeyuna, hardly more than a sprinkling of dwellings
set back in the pine forest. In order to reach the Shakers, most
visitors traveled by way of Albany.

The Chapmans started off from the northern flats of the capital city, taking a narrow, winding road past the venerable Van
Rensselaer Manor, home of the "patroon," the Dutch-descended
landowner from whom the Shakers leased their two-thousand-
acre estate. The Chapmans encountered a series of low, frosted
hills before coming to the forest. Here they slogged through several miles of rutted old Indian trails, which in this season were
overlaid with snow, mud, and other debris. But then the scenery

around them became transformed: The road grew smooth and clear, and the looming pines made way for more diverse vegetation—low oaks and spindly willows, as well as small, unmarked pastures where animals calmly grazed.

All at once the visitors caught the brilliant shine of a frozen lake, which, as James probably boasted, was entirely man-made. Then the forest opened up, and before them was a fantastic clearing where a complex of bold-colored buildings—barns, workshops, and other houses in hues of blue, red, and marigold —glowed against the snow. At the highest point of this clearing, alone in its whiteness, was the great Shaker meetinghouse or church, whose broad tin roof glittered in the winter daylight.

This village was the seat of the Church Family, one of four Shaker orders in Watervliet. Practically speaking, the Families functioned independently, with separate finances, leaders and property. However, the lesser orders—the North, West, and South Families—ultimately looked to the Church for direction. The Church, in turn, reported to the head Church or Ministry in New Lebanon, New York, which provided leadership for the society nationwide.

To a Shaker, membership in the Church Family was a high honor. But James could not even dream of joining the elite, as long as Eunice and the children remained in the world outside. Only those who showed the greatest promise *and* had no external ties could be considered for election to the society's finest. And so James did not stop at the great white church: There would be time, he assured his wife and brother, to visit it tomorrow, when Sabbath Day services would be held for the public. Instead, he drove on for another mile or so, past a stretch of frozen pastures and then a Shaker cemetery, where the uniform graves of past Believers came up through the snow like even rows of teeth. Finally, as the visitors approached a second complex of buildings, much like the first, James slowed his team.

They had arrived at the West Family, the newest of the Families in Watervliet. This order had been created four years ago to relieve overcrowding in the South Family, also called the "Gathering Order." The West Family was considered a step above the South Family, the entry point for new converts, but the two orders remained linked in ways that would prove important for Eunice. The presiding Elder and Eldress of the West Family—a pair of middle-aged siblings named Seth and Hannah Wells—provided direction for those in the South Family, one of whom was their blood brother, Calvin.

As Eunice descended from the carriage—no doubt with assistance from her brother-in-law, since James was now forbidden to touch her—she looked out upon a village quite unlike any that she had ever seen. The Shakers' villages were always finely situated, and this one was no exception, founded on an even stretch of land, where the Shakers' workshops, barns, and enormous dwelling house were neatly arranged about an oblong clearing. The buildings were color-coded by function: the shops a dusky red, the farm buildings uniformly dark, the dwellings a golden ochre. They also stood nearer together than they might in a regular country town, since privacy was hardly an issue when everything was shared.

Any other village of this size would be filled with noise and commotion as people hailed one another in the streets, hurtled by in their wagons, or stopped in the shops to gossip. Here, however, the few Shakers who ventured outdoors went about their business in nearly complete silence, treading carefully along neat stone paths that crossed one another at perfect angles between the buildings. They might nod at one another as they passed, or pause to exchange a necessary word, but no one dawdled, and hardly any one Believer could be distinguished from the next, the Brothers uniformly clad in drab-colored overcoats and the women enshrouded in long, dark cloaks.

But what would have been most impressive to Eunice was the village's stunning neatness. In cities and countrysides alike, slops, refuse, and even human excrement were commonly thrown out of windows, making for slick, unsavory streets and foul-smelling yards. In nearby Albany, waste management was conducted by hundreds of roving pigs who feasted on the city's trash and were, in turn, devoured by its inhabitants. Among the Shakers, by contrast, there was not a stray stick or rock in sight. Every building appeared freshly painted, and not a nail head was out of line. Even nighttime chamber pots were tucked away in closed cabinets, and the swine did not wander. The smallest tasks were executed with equal care and ingenuity. Observing that firewood, when stacked horizontally, was susceptible to rot, the Shakers stood their logs upright so that rain would drain off the sides. No ornaments, moreover, adorned the buildings, inside or out: Every shape was simplified so that its form was one with its function.

Visitors, then and now, would often joke that the Shakers were able to achieve all that they did because they did not have sex. It is easy to make fun of the Shakers in this way—to conjure up a flushed Shakeress giving vigorous strokes to a butter churn and an agitated Brother rubbing away at the surface of a dovetailed box far longer than necessary in their efforts to subdue their carnal appetites. In fact, the Shakers did use physical work to purge their desires, but it was more than a simple matter of sublimation. The Shakers knew better than anyone else that pleasure in work itself could be taken too far and become an act of gratification. What the Believers sought instead was to overcome their desires, and they cherished orderliness as proof that the power of mind and spirit could prevail. For the Shakers, work was not just a means to an end or an end in itself but a form of worship that bound them closer to their community and God.

Once the Chapmans entered the village, James led his guests to the dwelling house, where he could introduce them to the leaders of his Family. It was there, as she looked up at the mammoth, four-story structure, built solidly of brick and stone, that Eunice first encountered a defining feature of Shaker architecture, one that graced nearly every other building in the village: a peculiar set of double doors.

This architectural redundancy spoke to the Shakers' policy of segregating, as opposed to separating, the sexes. The Shakers were not cloistered: Men and women slept, worshipped, and ate in the same buildings. Special precautions, however, were taken to help Brothers and Sisters avert temptation. As she came through the village, Eunice passed a set of stone stairs, attached to a small platform and seeming to lead to nowhere; this device, called a mounting block, enabled a Sister to climb into a wagon without having to take a Brother's hand. Later, the society would publish a set of rules to prevent unnecessary contact. For example, Sisters were forbidden to sew buttons on Brothers' shirts when the Brothers were still in them. But at the time of Eunice's visit, the rules were simply understood. Each Shaker building was imbued with an invisible yet palpable line that separated the men from the women, and included double sets of everything to make the line clear—stairs, retiring rooms, and more. The separate doors marked the first division.

Eunice entered the dwelling house through a door on the right, while her husband and brother-in-law entered on the left. Inside, she toured an immaculate establishment. Each story of the house served a unique function. On one floor there was a vast dining facility, where tables set for four were lined up in rows. Another story consisted mainly of a large hall that was divided, by day, into offices for the Elders but had folding doors that were drawn back for evening worship. Above were separate sleeping quarters for the Brothers and Sisters, and down below was a kitchen beyond imagination, furnished with all kinds of useful instruments, such as a special low chair for peeling apples and a long row of glimmering pots and pans—a sign of fortune to a woman who had fought over a tin pan with one of her church neighbors.

Although Eunice may not have known it at the time, the Shakers' homes also featured many technological advances. Well ahead of most, the Shakers had running water, which coursed through an elaborate system of aqueducts to their mills, washhouse, stables, and other buildings. They had washing machines to help them with their laundry—a backbreaking chore that commonly involved boiling, beating, and wringing heavy, sodden clothes. And they pioneered many other technologies that are still used now. The Shakers invented the clothespin and metal pen, as well as an early circular saw, which a Shaker Sister fashioned out of a spinning wheel. Before the Shakers, brooms had round heads: It was a Shaker Brother who perceived that a flat surface could better remove dust from corners. Nails were also painstakingly wrought by hand, one by one, until the same Sister who invented the buzz saw realized that they could be cut from sheets, like cookies. Although the Shakers could have profited from their inventions, they rarely patented them, believing that their improvements should benefit all. Likewise, their pursuit of efficiency went hand in hand with their spiritual beliefs: The less time one had to spend on mundane tasks, the more time one had for God.

Eunice could not have been in the dwelling house for long without being introduced to the leaders of the Family, Elder Seth and Eldress Hannah. Elder Seth was a graying man of forty-seven, with a studious air and the kind of face that children know to trust. Eldress Hannah was several years younger and, being a well-trained Shaker, was direct and modest in her manner. In the presence of outsiders, the Shakers were sometimes markedly reserved—cautious to the point of appearing cold, as a matter of self-protection—but not so with Eunice, the wife of a convert. They welcomed her warmly and offered her the very best of their celebrated hospitality.

As an outsider, Eunice was not allowed to eat with the Shakers in their dining hall, but she enjoyed all of the same foods in a guest room where, probably for the first time in years—not since James had gone bankrupt and the servants were let go—she was waited on by another woman. Eunice first received a bowl filled with "milk-warm water" in which to wash her hands. Then dishes appeared before her in sumptuous procession. One visitor from the period recalled enjoying veal stew, boiled beef, pork, potatoes, turnip and squash puree, dried apples, and melon, two kinds of cheese, sweet butter, cider, and several kinds of bread. The abundance was overwhelming.

At night, Eunice was ushered to a spare room, warmed with a powerful little stove and lined with impeccably built drawers. An even row of pegs also dotted the walls, inviting Eunice to air out her belongings. The room was sparse, even austere, in its decor, with little else but a bed and chair, but the sheets were a crisp, pure white, and the blankets thick and warm. As Eunice climbed into bed—under the same roof and across the hall from her husband—she must have wondered at the world she had entered, and about what the next day would bring.

In the morning, Eunice and her brother-in-law returned to the Church Family for public services that were intended to introduce outsiders to Shaker worship. As a lower-ranking Believer and a relative newcomer himself, James was also expected to attend this meeting, but he probably traveled separately or at least remained apart from his guests to enter the meetinghouse with his Brothers and Sisters.

It was an uncommonly cold day. As Eunice drove up the fine, willow-lined avenue leading to the Shakers' elite order, she could see that the great gate that normally separated the Believers from the world was swung open. Rows of sleds already encircled the white church. There were many visitors this morning, and they were something of a mixed blessing to the Shakers. More guests meant more prospective converts, but crowds also inspired a dangerous excitement. With so many thronging the road from Albany, there was no doubt an air of festivity and even frivolity in the air.

The meetinghouse was a remarkable sight, a perfect, creamy white, and was situated at the highest point of the village so that nothing eclipsed it. The building stood three stories high and featured a triple-pointed gambrel roof that served a unique structural purpose, as would become clear when visitors went indoors. The worship hall occupied the first story; the upper floors provided living quarters for the heads of the sect. Visits to the church were a special occasion even to Believers: None of the lower orders had a separate house of worship, and the rank and file came here only on the Sabbath. Legend had it that this sacred edifice had been built in complete devotional silence, Brothers communicating to one another wordlessly, while banging away with their tools.

The church was enclosed with a low fence, and here, once again, Eunice was forced to part from her male company. She entered a separate gate and lined up behind the other female visitors before their assigned door. The crowd was thick, with everyone bundled up and bustling forward to get a first look inside. When Eunice finally stepped across the threshold, she felt a burst of warmth, coming from two small stoves on either side of a great hall. She then gazed upon a wide open space with a shining floor the color of wheat and whitened walls, trimmed blue. A long, high line of pegs traced the walls, and sunlight filtered in through several large windows. There were no pews, no altar, and, miraculously, not a single supporting wall or post to break the flow of the floor. The secret to this architectural marvel lay in hidden supporting trusses beneath the gambrel roof.

Looking down, Eunice saw a floor of choice pine, so pristine that one later visitor compared it to a dining table. Pine spittoons containing fresh sawdust were distributed as defense against the common habit of spitting on the floor (a practice that disgusted the Shakers). Only if she looked carefully could Eunice have detected a faint copper glint coming from lines of nail heads on the floor, forming a barely perceptible pattern whose design would soon become apparent.

Eunice had never set foot in such a church before. In churches such as the one Eunice attended in Bridgeport, various classes and families sat in their own boxes, while deacons (such as Eunice's father) occupied special seats beneath the pulpit. Meanwhile, "tithing men" kept everyone awake and in line with long rods—prodding boys and men with the knobby end of their stick, girls and women with a soft hare's foot on the other. The Shaker interior, in contrast, suggested pure democracy: Eunice sat where she pleased beside the other visiting women on deep brown benches that were built along the right side of the front wall. The visiting men had the same seats on the left, and there were movable benches on the floor for the Shakers.

The Believers themselves, however, were not yet visible, and as the air in the church warmed with the bodies of the spectators and the fire from the stoves, it also became heated with expectation. A local man named Thomas Brown had recently published an exposé in which he had described Shakers whooping like Indians, pecking like chickens, shaking, whirling, and convulsing ecstatically as they felt the spirit of their God move them. To some who came to see the Believers, Shaker worship was a spectator sport, more akin to attending a circus or a freak show than going to church.

Now a bell rang, and sweeping in through their separate doors, in two even lines and without a word, were perhaps a hundred men and women in uniform coats and cloaks. Since everyone dressed alike, individuals were hard to discern. But surely for a moment, at least, Eunice was able to distinguish the man with whom she had spent nearly a decade of her life—by the familiar slope of his shoulders, perhaps, or the way he held his head— before his distinguishing features receded into the crowd.

In a single swift motion, the Shakers removed their dampened outerwear and hung it on pegs before taking their places on opposing sets of benches. As they sat with their hands folded, their eyes downcast, posture erect, the hall became still. All gossiping, bantering, and sizing up came to a halt as the spectators focused on the silent Brothers and Sisters.

During the "age of empire," women's fashion called for slim, high-waisted gowns that made a column of the body and put the bosom on display. White muslin dresses were all the rage, year-round—impractical even when in season but downright dangerous in winter. (It was commonly complained that ladies would rather suffer pneumonia than cover themselves up.) The visiting women who formed a mottled palette against the blank walls of the church—soft pinks, lavender, powder blue, white, gray, and black being the preferred colors of the day—were shivering, no doubt, in their thin muslins and silks or huddling under their cloaks.

Their Shaker counterparts, in contrast, sat comfortably in their serviceable gowns of a uniform, dusky violet hue. Their dresses were singularly baggy. The bodices were draped with loose folds of fabric that came to a point at the waist, and the skirts grew wide at the hips. The Sisters' hair, meanwhile, was tightly bound. Although face-framing curls were in vogue, Shaker women brushed their locks straight back and hid every strand under starched white caps that clung to their skulls. The Sisters' outfits were not considered flattering. Years later, humorist Artemus Ward would compare a Sister's silhouette to a "bean pole stuck into a long meal bag."

The Shaker men, too, were dressed in nearly opposite fashion to the male visitors. The Brothers wore short, wide hats, long vests, and short pants tied with ribbons, at a time when hats were supposed to be tall and narrow, vests short, and pants long. They also sported special hairdos—the Shaker mullet, one might call it—with their hair cropped short in the front and flowing long in the back. The mullet was no more popular then than it is now. As one visitor remarked contemptuously, the Shakers' newly shorn converts "might as well be Shakers as not; for they were fit for no other society, and indeed they were ashamed to appear in any other."

If the Shakers were mortified by all the scrutiny, they showed little sign of it. After their moment of silence was complete, they broke fluidly into song, presenting a tune that sounded almost familiar to their spectators. It was the kind of nameless ditty their visitors might have found themselves humming while they kneaded bread or plowed the fields. The Shakers, however, sang with great solemnity, all in unison, in a single melodic line, with nothing to accompany them, not even a tapping foot. When they paused, one of the senior members, Elder Seth Wells, came forth to introduce their distinctive form of worship: the Shaker dance.

In certain outside circles dancing was regarded as suspect, as a source of carnal pleasure and even as profanity. (In Eunice's former church in Durham, for example, it had been cause for excommunication.) Yet to the Believers, it represented the purest form of devotion, which they called "laboring," since they considered it God's work—a prayer from the body as well as the soul. The Shakers had ample scriptural justification for this practice. The Israelites, for example, danced after they crossed the Red Sea. But the Shakers' central reason for dancing was that it enabled them to devote their fullest selves to God, their minds laboring in unison with their physical bodies in the ultimate communion. The fact that the world used dance as a vehicle for lust, they argued, did not mean that their own sacred motions should be viewed in the same light. Indeed, the Shakers valued dancing in part for the opposite effect: to tire out their bodies and mortify the flesh. In their view, it was the world's people who had perverted movement into a source of shame. The Believers danced only for God.

Elder Seth communicated these views to spectators who were often skeptical, amused, impressed, or even offended in turn. He also presented the Shakers' rules of etiquette, requesting the visitors not to laugh, whisper, or wander about, and above all, asking the men and women not to mingle between the rows or exit by the wrong doors. The Elder had excellent delivery, having once been a schoolmaster. Nevertheless, visitors had a tendency to ignore what was spoken as they nudged each other, fidgeted, or pointed out the prettier Shaker faces, in expectation of the dancing that was to follow.

Everyone leaned in then as a signal was given and, as a later visitor would recount, "the whole assembly rose as one person, with a rustling sound like that of the autumn wind when it shakes down the crisp and sear leaves of the forest." The Shakers cleared the benches from the floor, and the men stripped off their jackets and tied up their sleeves. Soon, the Shakers were lined up in ranks, their feet precisely aligned with the copper-headed tacks that had been a mystery before. The older ones generally stood in the front, toward the audience, while the younger ones occupied the back. Whether this was so the youth might be "saved from the temptation to wandering looks, and their consequence, wandering thoughts," as the writer Catherine Maria Sedgwick speculated, or to shield the younger Believers from the lascivious gaze of onlookers was not communicated to the audience.

Then, while singers provided a lively song, a kind of jig with a staccato rhythm, the Believers began to move gently forward and backward in their rows. They turned in exquisite synchronicity, the men to the right and the women to the left, their bodies never even close to touching but moving together as surely as if they were. All stood straight and tall, stiff from the waist up through the neck, with their arms held close by their sides, but agile in their legs and in their hands, which they pumped lightly up and down. Faster and faster they moved, skipping as they traveled, flying by one another like clouds in a storm. When they came to a momentary rest they did a funny sort of shuffle, stamping back on their heels and bending their knees twice very quickly, a movement that took hours to master. The sound of the stamping carried loudly, for the Sisters wore two-inch heels, which were meant to protect their feet from the cold.

Decades later, Charles Dickens would describe the Shaker dance as a "preposterous sort of trot," and there were others who found the dance movements hilarious—especially the hand motions, which to the Believers signified a "shaking off" of worldly sin. One observer recalled that, with their hands flapping and their elbows tucked in, the Shakers looked like a bunch of penguins. Alexis de Tocqueville, author of *Democracy in America*, thought they resembled "trained dogs who are forced to walk on their hind legs." However, many others who witnessed Shaker worship, particularly in the early years, found it serene, lovely, and even moving.

What were Eunice's thoughts as she watched her husband— a man who had had no control of his bodily urges when she had known him—flapping, flying, and stamping in line with his spiritual companions? As she saw the Sisters, old and young, spinning by on their thick high heels, did she dare to imagine herself teetering among them, her own worn gown traded in for a shapeless dress that was nevertheless well-made and warm? Whatever her feelings were at this moment, Eunice seems not to have been turned off by the Shakers—at least not yet. The Durham Presbyterian Church may have considered dancing the work of the devil, but Eunice had broken from that strict Presbyterian society, and she also came from an open-minded family. Though Eunice may not have relished the idea of joining the Shakers at this point, nothing she had seen so far had closed her mind against the sect.

As for the others in the crowd, anyone expecting a spectacle along the lines of what Thomas Brown had depicted—barking, trembling, flailing, and the like—was surely disappointed. What many did not know was that the Shakers may have first been named for their lack of physical control, but their shaking had since been ritualized. Not that they were never carried away— the Shakers remained ecstatics—but on this particular day, there were no unusual calls from the spirit world, at least none that the Shakers thought worth mentioning in their diaries. Their dance ended as quietly as it began, with the Believers only a bit breathless afterward from the exertion. They sang another song to close the meeting, before filing out the two front doors.

There was much about Shaker life that might have appealed to a woman in Eunice's position. The Shakers were, if not rich, then at least comfortable, especially compared with much of the outside world. With substantial property holdings acquired through donations from their converts and a large, cheap, and devoted labor force, they had the means and the ability (not to mention the religious compulsion) to improve their surroundings in ways that would have been unimaginable to most.

In this postwar period, the material differences between the Shakers and their neighbors were particularly noticeable. Although the Believers faced the same difficulties as everyone else—including the destabilizing effects of the War of 1812, the ravages of a deadly fever, and several years of unseasonably cold weather that ruined their crops—they were able to overcome such challenges much more effectively than many, owing in part to their good planning and strength in numbers. As a result, they were also able to draw large numbers of new converts. From 1810 to 1820, the Watervliet community increased by more than 50 percent, from 126 total members to 193. Some of the others, such as one in Hancock, Massachusetts, grew even more.

The life of a Shaker Sister was blessed in many ways. It might not have been exactly easy, since, practically speaking, women's chores were the same everywhere. Visitors often noted that the Sisters looked pale and tired, in contrast to the robust-looking Brothers, who spent more time outdoors. However, a Sister's life was secure. As a Shaker, Eunice would not have to worry about the future—where her next meal would come from, how to care for her children, or even about growing old alone. If she became sick or unable to work, loving hands would take care of her, as well as her children. She would have to work, to be sure, but there would be others to share the burden; she would not have to toil alone.

Moreover, Shaker women were accorded equal footing with the men in ways that would have been inconceivable anywhere else. Because of the separation between the sexes, the Sisters had their own leaders, who occupied positions of authority parallel to those of the Brothers. Each Family had an Elder and Eldress to supervise spiritual concerns, as well as Deacons and Deaconesses to organize the work. The leaders of each Family, in turn, reported to a higher level of leadership called the Ministry, staffed by equal numbers of men and women. A

Ministry oversaw two neighboring Shaker communities, together called a Bishopric. Each Bishopric was then beholden to
a lead Ministry in New Lebanon, New York, which, in Eunice's
time, was overseen by a single, all-powerful leader—who also
happened to be a woman.

The Shakers told Eunice that she would make an excellent
Believer, flattering her by saying that she could make much of
herself among them. They recognized that a woman like Eunice,
who was educated, well-spoken, and in her prime, could be an
asset. The Shakers also guaranteed care for Eunice's children, a
promise that was surely reassuring to a woman who had struggled
to raise her children alone. Among the Shakers, her children
would be free from want. They would eat nutritious meals,
learn useful skills, and have a secure home among generous,
spiritual souls—which was more than Eunice herself could
promise them. Nevertheless, Eunice left without making a
commitment, and as she rode back to Durham, leaving James
behind, her brother-in-law was skeptical. He warned her, above
all, that she should never let the Shakers take her children. One
week later, however, he died of an unknown cause, leaving behind a wife and seven children of his own—and leaving Eunice
without his valuable counsel.

6

ANOTHER MOTHER

Eunice may have been impressed by the Shakers in Watervliet, but all that changed upon her return home. Perhaps she was never keen on the Shakers in the first place, or she realized that no matter what benefits they offered, she would not fit into their rigidly conformist order. Her experiences with her own church had taught her as much. But another possibility remains, which is that Eunice shut her mind to the sect after reading its so-called Bible, which James brought by during one of his trips home. It was through this book, *Testimony of Christ's Second Appearing,* that Eunice fully came to grips with what Shakerism required: not just adherence to a unique lifestyle or way of worship but faith in the Shakers' providential founder, Ann Lee, whom the Shakers called "Mother."

In fact, Eunice might have identified with Ann Lee had circumstances been otherwise. Like Eunice, Lee overcame a wretched personal life to become a crusader and was ahead of her time in what she demanded from her world. Only partially recounted in *Testimony,* her life story also reveals the suffering and vindication of a mother—albeit a very different kind of mother from Eunice. A complete understanding of Eunice's struggles against Shakerism needs to begin with an account of this remarkable Shaker Mother.

Ann Lee entered the world on a leap-year day in 1736 in the slums of Manchester, England, one of eight children born to a poor blacksmith and his wife. As a child, Lee spent her days running cotton looms and cutting fur and velvet in textile mills. At night, she retired to shabby quarters on a crooked street called Toad Lane, where space was so tight that everyone in the family was privy to everyone else's most intimate business —including lovemaking. From an early age, Ann Lee learned to despise sexual activity—both the spectacle and its results. Again and again she begged her mother to abstain from sleeping with her father, even though her father beat her when he learned of her efforts.

In her own marriage bed, Lee experienced still greater trauma. At twenty-six—the same age as Eunice when she had wed—Lee entered into an arranged marriage with a blacksmith named Abraham Standerin, who, like James, was a man who "loved his beef and his beer, his chimney corner, and seat in village tavern." Standerin joined the Lees in their already overburdened quarters, and there, Lee tragically conceived, carried, and lost one child after another: four, by most counts, eight by others. Only one survived past infancy, and the labors were excruciating. The last child was rumored to have been extracted from her mother's body with forceps, leaving Lee near death.

Ravaged by loss, steeped in misery, and most of all, convinced of her sinfulness, Ann Lee spent days and nights on end sobbing and praying for some kind of redemption. She was deeply isolated in her suffering, for her mother was long dead, and she was afraid to approach her husband, lest she "stir up his affections." At last, she found solace through another kind of family—a religious group known as the "Shaking Quakers," which she had joined some years before.

The Shakers were one of a number of radical sects that cropped up in the aftermath of the English Civil War, railing against the establishment and prophesying the advent of a new day. Such groups were popular in places like Manchester, where the Church of England seemed woefully distant from the struggles of common folk and incapable of providing relief. Led by a pair of married tailors named Jane and James Wardley—called "Mother" and "Father" by their followers—the Shakers were distinguished not so much by an original dogma as by the vigorous exercises that gave them their name. In their quest for an immediate connection to God, they jerked, shook, shivered, danced, sang, screeched, and shouted so violently that their features appeared blurred, so loudly that entire neighborhoods reverberated with the sound of their communing ecstasy. These worshippers met as often as three times daily and considered their day's work done only when they no longer had the strength to move or speak.

It was to the Mother of this group that Ann Lee finally unburdened her marital and maternal woes, her revulsion toward sex and the suffering that it produced. Mother Jane responded by giving Lee permission for the very form of release that she had once urged upon her own mother. Mother Jane said: "James and I lodge together; but we do not touch each other any more than two babes. You may return home and do likewise."

Lee went back to Toad Lane and followed Mother Jane's advice but remained sleepless and tormented. For twelve days and nights, she wept and prayed, begging God for deliverance.

At last, she was gratified with a vision and considered herself reborn. "While I was in this labor," Lee later recalled, "I saw the Lord Jesus in his Kingdom and glory. He revealed to me the depth of man's loss, what it was, and the way of redemption."

In her vision Lee saw Adam and Eve fornicating in the Garden of Eden. Suddenly, she realized where man—and woman— had gone wrong: They had indulged in the sexual act for its own sake, not, as other animals did, at the proper time and season in order to procreate, but purely for their own carnal pleasure. Lee finally understood that the very act that had caused so much grief in her own life was in fact the source of all human suffering. In order to return to an Edenic state of sinlessness, in order to be saved, humanity needed to be cleared of this original sin.

To the other Shakers, it soon became clear that Ann Lee was divinely inspired. Even the Wardleys acknowledged her as their Mother. Now, Lee's ordeals as a mother of one kind gave way to those of another. Under her leadership, the Shakers became deliberately disruptive. They publicly denounced the sins of the flesh; wreaked havoc with sensational, open-air confessions of their deepest sins; and, perhaps most controversially, burst in on others' church services to condemn all other religions and declare theirs the only true path.

As the leader of such activities, Mother Ann was arrested, committed to an insane asylum, and even imprisoned in a dismal Manchester dungeon. It is said that she would have starved had not a disciple managed to nourish her with a thin drip of milk and wine, which he poured into her mouth through a pipe stem inserted into a keyhole. Mobs attacked her repeatedly. One group chased and clubbed her over a distance of two miles, before dragging her by her feet until the skin was torn from her face. Apparently, it was only by divine grace that she escaped branding and stoning. Even her brother is said to have beaten her so forcefully and for so long that he became "out of breath, like one who had been running in a race."

Mother Ann suffered such brutal treatment not just on account of her convictions but also on account of her sex. Like Eunice, she lived in a world where disorderly, outspoken women were unacceptable. The legal system of coverture against which Eunice was to struggle had originated with Mother Ann's contemporary William Blackstone. It was Blackstone who proclaimed that "by marriage, the husband and wife are one person in law" and that "the very being or legal existence of the woman is suspended during the marriage, or at least is incorporated and consolidated into that of the husband." Flouting this orthodoxy, Mother Ann rejected her husband's rule and that of the established church and nation. Here was a woman who boldly pronounced: "I have been in fine valleys with Christ as a lover. I am married to the Lord Jesus Christ. He is my head and my husband, and I have no other!"

With all the trouble she and her people faced, Mother Ann recognized the need for change. In 1774, she led a small group of Shakers aboard a leaking, square-rigged ship bound for America. Her husband came along, too, but left the group when it became clear (at last) that his wife would never have sex with him or bear any children.

In a land that had provided a haven for many fleeing religious persecution, Mother Ann had hoped to find peace, but her trials continued. For years, she lived in poverty, working as a washerwoman in New York City, while her followers lived and worked elsewhere. Then, after leasing a tract of land in a place called Watervliet, she and her group faced the equally daunting task of taming the wilderness into a home. But their worst troubles came when they emerged to share their tidings with the world.

It was now 1780. The War for Independence had begun, and evangelical fervor ran high. Many Americans became convinced that the millennium was near and worshipped with a zeal worthy of the Shakers, dropping to the ground "like men wounded in battle," as one eyewitness recalled, and "screaming so that they might be heard at great distances." Making the rounds at revival meetings, the Shakers succeeded in enlisting valuable recruits—among them a Baptist preacher named Joseph Meacham, whom they would one day call "Father." However, the Believers also encountered powerful opposition, especially because of their female ruler, whom even Meacham questioned. How was it, Meacham demanded, that Mother Ann presumed to speak out on matters of religion, when the apostle Paul had admonished women to be silent?

The Shaker Mother offered a shrewd response. In nature, she stated, "man is the first, and the woman the second in the government of the family." Man was the undisputed leader of his household, but just as "when the man is gone, the right of government belongs to the woman," so too, Mother Ann said, "is the family of Christ." This "absent husband" theory of government, as it has been called, was cannily expressed, for it upheld traditional roles while justifying a woman's recourse to power. It was a line of argument that Eunice would also exploit in years to come.

Meacham was convinced by Mother Ann's explanation, as were many others. Short and stocky, with chestnut hair, intense blue eyes, and a voice that, when stirred, is said to have rung like thunder, Mother Ann possessed a charisma that drew people toward her, even despite themselves. At times she could be fearsome, with her apocalyptic visions and threats of damnation, and she held nothing back, even with children. One summer day, when she was enjoying a piece of watermelon, a youngster came near and gazed at the treat. When Mother Ann asked the child whether she wanted some, the child said no, to which Mother Ann replied, "God hates liars." Yet this Mother also knew how to console lost souls, stroking their faces, weeping with them, and holding them close. She gave her "children" precious victuals and even her own bed, when space was lacking. To those who believed, there was no better Mother.

But not everyone was so accepting. As the Shakers grew in numbers, so did rumors. It was said that the Believers danced naked and drank until they were senseless—that they castrated their men, held "midnight orgies," and buried their "love children." Mother Ann was reputed to be a prostitute, a witch, and even a British spy. Many of the worst accusations came from ex-Shakers. As Daniel Rathbun would taunt his onetime Brethren, "Your Mother . . . was riotous and unruly; she, with many of you, drank hard, sung, and danced all night—strip naked, pushing, hunching, pulling hair, striking, biting, and spitting on each other; this in the most venomous manner, calling it fighting the devil." Asa Pattee further testified of Mother Ann: "I have seen her slap the men—rub her hands on all parts of their bodies—press the men to her bosom—and make them suck a dry breast—All the time she would be humming and making an enchanting noise. We scarcely knew what we did."

Before long, the Shakers began to face persecution, especially as they took their gospel show on the road. Waves of revivalism were now hitting the Northeast, and Mother Ann decided to follow them. She and other Shaker leaders traveled through

New England and New York, staying with whoever would take them in and inviting all to join their worship. The Shakers had their successes, laying the foundations for orders in Connecticut, Massachusetts, and New York, but they also fell under attack. Many Americans of this period and beyond were deeply offended by the Shakers' doctrine of celibacy, which seemed a threat to the social order; by their seemingly treasonous refusal to bear arms; and, most of all, by the audacious woman at their head.

Mother Ann did not help matters with her words of frank rebuke. "I see a vision," she once prophesied, "a large black cloud rising as black as a thunder cloud, and it is occasioned by men sleeping with their wives." To her, the torment of such sinners appeared "like melted lead, poured through them in the same parts where they have taken their carnal pleasure." The Shakers were not the only celibates at this time; other evangelicals also abstained as a show of their faith. However, the majority of God-fearing men and women embraced their sexuality as the fulfillment of a divine order to "go forth and multiply." To them, Mother Ann's prophecy was more than an insult: It was blasphemy.

The Shakers soon encountered staggering violence. In Petersham, Massachusetts, a group of Shakers kneeling in prayer were dragged up—"some by their collars, some by their throats, and some by the hair of their heads"—and driven out of town in a terrible parade. Any who could not keep up during the ten-mile journey, even the sick or elderly, were struck in the face with a whip or cudgel. To provide "a little diversion" along the way, the mob brought out the only English-born Shaker, a man by the name of James Shephard; they ordered him to strip, and then, with sticks, canes, clubs, and horsewhips, beat him until "his back was a gore of blood and the flesh bruised to a jelly."

Mother Ann was singled out for the worst treatment. In Petersham, a torch-wielding mob took the Shaker leader by the feet, dragged her outdoors, threw her into a sleigh "as they would the dead carcass of a beast," and proceeded to commit "acts of inhumanity and indecency," ripping her new dress and tearing out her hair in the process. The mob's goal, as the Shakers noted, was to determine whether their Mother was indeed "a woman or not."

By the time she returned to Watervliet, Mother Ann was physically spent from a lifetime of suffering, and she died a year later, in September 1784, just forty-eight years old. She was sustained, however, by a stunning legacy in the form of a society and religion that would in many ways provide a haven for women fleeing the kinds of ordeals she had suffered. Shakerism gave thousands of women a chance to break from a cycle of childbearing and drudgery. To those who were widowed, abandoned, or just uninterested in being married, it offered an alternative family and a home. Liberated from mundane responsibilities, if not from work, a Shaker Sister could devote herself to a life of the spirit, surrounded by a loving, stable community. It may be one of the greatest of ironies in Eunice Chapman's story that a sect famous for its generosity to women was to become—in Eunice's mind, at least—her greatest oppressor.

If Eunice's disenchantment with the Shakers did not actually begin with her reading of *Testimony*, it surely deepened through her encounter with the book. Over six hundred pages long, the tome was so hefty that Eunice could barely contain it in her two small hands. When she finally cracked open the pages, she was introduced to Mother Ann's life and suffering, her privations in Manchester and America, and her struggles with her soul. This story, in itself, may have been inspirational, but Eunice became increasingly disturbed as she read of the controversial role that the Shaker Mother played in the Shaker religion. The Shakers, as Eunice discovered, considered Ann Lee nothing less than a second Messiah, the female Jesus, or Christ come again. And this, to Eunice, was going too far.

With wide eyes, Eunice read of the Shakers' belief that Jesus of Nazareth—who had inspired her through her worst days—had not quite finished the business that God had set out for humanity's redemption. As the Shakers saw it, the Son of God had done only half the job; its completion required the work of his daughter, Ann Lee. For, just as it had taken two (Adam and Eve) to commit the first sin, so it would take two (Jesus and Mother Ann) to undo the Fall. Jesus was the second Adam, come to heal the world, and Ann Lee was the second Eve, or Christ come again. With her advent, the Shakers proclaimed, a new epoch had begun, one in which true salvation was possible and humanity could live free from sin. All that it took to enter this new millennium was to believe in her example and embrace the Shaker faith.

In fact, Ann Lee herself never claimed to be the second Christ; later Shakers described this role after her death. Moreover, the Shakers did not worship her as their God. The Believers were careful to point out that Ann Lee and Jesus were not deities but that they represented the possibility of light and salvation within everyone. Eunice, however, was typical in overlooking this distinction, as well as other nuances of Shaker theology.

No doubt her haste and animosity clouded her readings. To Eunice, who had been raised as a pious Protestant, the Shakers' boldness in putting their leader on equal footing with Jesus was absolute heresy. It was one thing to experiment with the ways of worship or to see the potential for salvation in everyone, as the Methodists did, and quite another to put the Bible aside for a new set of scriptures, declare that the Old and New Testaments were precursors to a greater Word, or imagine Jesus as a predecessor to a female Messiah. As she read *Testimony*, Eunice was especially shocked by descriptions of Ann Lee bleeding through her skin in her spiritual agony and by the Shakers' direct comparisons between the sufferings of Mother Ann and those of Jesus.

By the time she put down the Shakers' holy book, Eunice was sure of one thing: All the security they promised was not enough to compensate for the fact that, by joining them, she would be abandoning her lifelong faith and betraying her God. The Shakers themselves made this much clear in *Testimony*, when they declared all other churches in league with the Antichrist and theirs the only true path to God.

Eunice may also have had misgivings about the Shakers' intentions toward her children, having been previously warned by James's own brother to keep her children close. But on this count, at least, the "Shaker Bible" was reassuring. The Shakers clearly stated that children were not allowed to join the society unless both their parents agreed, and moreover, that no one was to be coerced in matters of faith. Regarding children, they wrote: "Youth and children, being under age, were not to be received as members . . . except by the request, or free consent, of both their parents, if living; but if they were left by one of their parents to the care of the other, then by the request, or free consent, of that parent." In these short lines, Eunice had written proof that her family could not be forced into the sect.

With her mind made up against the Shakers, Eunice refused to be intimidated, even as James repeatedly abused and humiliated her. He made a habit of forcing the children away from their mother at the dinner table when he came to visit them, saying that they should "not eat with such a sinner." As the youngsters looked on, he would then clear his throat and hurl a wad of spit straight into Eunice's face, saying it was the filthiest place he knew. Eunice, however, would simply wipe herself off and stand her ground. If she had to, she knew she could raise the children on her own.

She knew, too, that the children would do their part, and they were becoming more helpful to her each day. Eight-year-old Susan, who was perhaps most like Eunice—pretty, bright, and capable—already handled most of the household sewing and knitting. And George, as sickly and sensitive as he sometimes was, provided his mother with essential spiritual, as well as practical, support. When Eunice was unwell, he sat by her bed and watched over her. He read from the scriptures each morning and called his sisters to pray with him each night. Even on Sundays, after church, he held his own Bible study for his family. The boy did his best in every way to fill his father's shoes, reassuring Eunice that even if she did not have a husband, she could count on her son in her old age. As for Julia, she may have been too young yet to be of practical help, but she was her mother's admitted favorite.

As Eunice resisted all of James's entreaties to join the Shaker society or to hand over the children, he became increasingly dismayed. He knew that without the Believers near him, he was in danger of becoming the man he had been before. Also, he found Eunice maddening. She would not accept the home he offered or even allow the children to enjoy its benefits, yet she dared to complain that he had failed his family. In James's view it was *she* who had failed in her duties—and on this point, public opinion would have agreed. A man was obliged to support his wife, but a woman was bound to follow her husband's lead. Her home was where he made it, and it was not her place to pick and choose. As Sir Robert Hyde declared in the English case that set the precedent for this reasoning: "If a Woman be of so haughty a Stomach, that she will chuse to Starve, rather than Submit and be reconciled to her Husband; she may take her own Choice: The Law is in no Default, which doth not provide for such a Wife."

James became all the more incensed when Eunice took their troubles to the town. Eunice would dispute this accusation, but James claimed that in the spring of 1814, he came home to learn that his wife had "thrown the children upon the town"; that is, she had declared herself incapable of supporting them. This was an action of last resort, with potentially dire consequences, since a family that became the community's responsibility faced the prospect of being publicly auctioned to the bidder who was willing to maintain them at the least expense to the town. It is little wonder that Eunice had not taken this step before.

At first James was perplexed: Why, after repeatedly rejecting his offers to take care of the children, would she now make them a public burden? Then he learned that by declaring her need, Eunice had forced the town to sell off a piece of property that had recently been left to him. In other words, Eunice had staged the whole ordeal for her own financial gain. Now James had to endure the mortification of being told by a town officer that he would have to do something to take care of his wife and children or they would be run out of town.

Had he not been a Believer, James might have fled again. But he knew he had a duty to fulfill, not just to his family but to his people. Thus he made Eunice a final proposition. He told her that there was a house with a garden that he could rent near the Shakers. She could live near, if not *with,* the society.

What happened next is a matter of contention. James alleged that Eunice accepted his proposal, only to spurn him when he came to tell her that he had made the necessary arrangements. Eunice, meanwhile, claimed that she agreed immediately but that James never intended to keep his promise. This much is sure: In October 1814, Eunice decided to return to Watervliet, leaving her children behind once again.

7

GOD'S CHOSEN

This time, Eunice journeyed to Watervliet alone. It was not easy travel. The Shakers were less than fifty miles away—a distance that could have been covered in a day if one knew the roads, had a fresh team of horses, and was traveling fast. But Eunice was hardly such a traveler. She probably had to make her trip in phases, taking a stagecoach to Albany and then hiring a driver or hitching a ride to Watervliet, all the while fending off suspicious looks. A woman of her social background was expected to travel with an escort, not to seek adventures by herself.

She finally arrived at the West Family on an October afternoon, when almost everyone, including her husband, was out at work. There was much to be done in this peak autumn month: apples to gather and store (two thousand bushels in all, that season), potatoes to dig up, roads and buildings to repair. Able-bodied Brothers such as James were in high demand. Since it was the day before the Sabbath, the Believers were all the busier, sweeping out their shops and baking pies to be eaten cold the next day, when not even cooking was allowed.

With her husband nowhere in sight, Eunice approached the head of the West Family, Seth Wells. He had bad news. There was no separate house for her and her family, as James had promised. Eunice became angry. How, she demanded, could the Shakers justify allowing a man to live with them and work for them while his family suffered? Elder Seth responded that suffering was sometimes necessary before receiving the Gospel. The Shakers believed that no earthly torment could equal the tortures of hell. Therefore it was better to experience some difficulty in the present and be saved than to suffer anguish forever.

Eunice was intent on knowing whether the Shakers might give her anything else. Did James earn wages, then, which she could bring back to her children?

"Nay," the Shaker replied. "We give him only his clothes and board, and if he does not bring his children soon, or make some arrangement, he cannot remain with us."

Elder Seth's parting words should have given Eunice some encouragement. As the Elder made clear, James would *have* to come to a resolution with his family if he wanted to be a Shaker. The society might tolerate her family's suffering, but only so far.

Everything changed, however, when Eunice got to the heart of the village. Here, she witnessed a scene that would haunt her for years. A woman about her own age wailed and wept as she ran from house to house, making a maze of the Shakers' pristine paths. Her words were unintelligible, but she seemed to be calling someone as she went. Eunice watched the woman intently. She was obviously not a Sister, since she did not wear the telltale cloak or cap, yet she seemed not to be a stranger either, since she moved with purpose. The Believers, meanwhile, looked on with surprisingly little feeling. Either they were accustomed to this woman's outbursts, or they knew her to be a lunatic, but in any case, they seemed less interested in determining the source of her anguish than in moving her out of public sight. Then Eunice came to a chilling realization. The woman was crying for her lost child.

Horrified, Eunice asked the Shakers who the woman was and what had happened to her. All they would say was that she had behaved badly and was "very troublesome." Eunice stood up for the other mother at once. Troublesome or not, the woman looked as if she were going to lose her mind. If the Shakers had no respect for a mother's feelings, Eunice said, they should give up the child to protect themselves. Now Eunice showed the savvy that would serve her so well in her own case. Should the Shakers refuse to release the child, she warned, this news would surely circulate, and "do them more hurt than the child could possibly do them good."

When Eunice's first round of threats against the society yielded no results, she tried to reach out to the other mother directly, drawing her aside when she saw the chance. But as soon as the Shakers saw the two outsiders huddled together, they separated them. Fortunately, Eunice had obtained the other woman's name and address, as well as the basics of her story.

Her name was Catherine Bonnel, she was from New Jersey, and her story was alarmingly like Eunice's own. She, too, had been lured to the Shakers by her husband with the false promise of a separate home, but unlike Eunice, she had been unable to leave. She had two young children, and her husband had taken out advertisements against her in the papers, telling businesses not to issue her credit in his name, and effectively stripping her of all means of support.

For months, Catherine and the children had lived unhappily among the Shakers, until her husband decided to take them back to New Jersey. He told her then that he would have nothing more to do with her, that she would have to fend for herself. A year later, Catherine returned to Watervliet with her three-year-old daughter, hoping to persuade her husband to return home. He only said, "You have come, with your old carnal affections; I wish to see none of them about me." Then, as Catherine was getting ready to leave, he grabbed the girl and disappeared. It was at this point that Eunice had first seen Catherine, when she was searching in vain for her lost child.

Determined not to become a victim herself, Eunice went on the offensive against the Shakers. According to James, she demanded financial support for her children, asking for $300 up front—about $3,800 now. She also threatened to have James thrown into jail if they did not comply. For James, Eunice's aggression was too much to bear. He hated the tight, mean look on her face as she attacked him in front of the people he loved. And he felt ashamed that she would speak to him in such an abusive way, especially since he had made every reasonable attempt to take care of his family.

The irony could not have been lost on James that while Eunice blamed the Shakers for his absence, the truth was that if it had not been for them, he never would have gone back home. Thus the very people who had tried to make him a "better man" were being held accountable for troubles that had originated with her. Furthermore, James stood to lose his chance at starting a new life with them.

James knew that he had nothing more to give—not the kind of money that Eunice was looking for, at any rate, since he had lost everything. But if she was truly burdened and unable to provide for the children, as she publicly claimed, he decided he would do her a favor by taking her troubles off her hands.

Early Monday morning, James went to his wife and told her that he was going to work at a neighboring Family. He handed her some clothes to take back to their son and bade her farewell. She should not, he said, expect to see him again. Later, he obtained leave to take out a wagon, along with some provisions, and hurried out of the settlement. He had a long ride ahead.

James can be accused of cowardice for his maneuver, for choosing to return to Durham clandestinely and take his children by stealth rather than being up-front with his wife. After all, he was within his legal rights to move his children as he pleased. Yet he was also being smart. James knew Eunice—that with her stubborn attachment to her children, she would never let them go. The community might take her side, too, for it was one thing to determine that children legally belonged with their father, another thing to allow a man who was known for his unsteadiness to wrench his screaming children from their mother's arms. In this calculation, at least, James would prove to be more right than he knew.

Eunice, too, was ready to leave Watervliet, having discovered, as she put it, "that there was no prospect of having any home near that society, otherwise than by coming under bondage to them." Before starting her journey, however, she wanted a last word with James and asked the assistant Elder of the West Family, Jonathan Hodgson, to find out if James would see her. The Elder soon came back to inform her that her husband had refused, saying that she was not in a "right spirit." This was a polite Shaker way of saying that Eunice was being difficult and antagonistic—or, like Catherine Bonnel, "troublesome."

Eunice hoped to depart at once, but by that evening the Shakers were still unable to provide her with a ride out of the village. Increasingly suspicious, Eunice finally decided to make the journey by foot, even though it was nearly dark. With some luck, she might be back with her children by the following night.

The Shakers obliged her with directions and gave her a parting gift, six yards of fabric, which they said was to make clothes for her children. Tucking the Shaker cloth against her few belongings, Eunice headed in the direction the Shakers pointed out to her, tracing her way past the Shaker graveyard and meetinghouse and entering the woods that led to the city. But somewhere along the way, she became confused—the Shakers had misled her, she was sure—and she soon found herself lost in the darkened forest, with nothing but starlight to guide her out. By the time she emerged, it was long past nightfall. Even the hogs in the street were huddled in sleep as Eunice stumbled through the shuttered city, looking for a place to spend the night.

If one thought could have cheered Eunice, it was that at least she had heeded her dead brother-in-law and left her children behind with her sister. As she bedded down for the night, Eunice could not forget the sight of poor Catherine Bonnel, beseeching the Shakers to give her back her daughter.

8

HOMECOMING

If anyone knew of Eunice's troubles, it was her younger sister Sally. Twenty-year-old Sally Hawley had witnessed the full span of the Chapmans' relationship. She had seen James transformed from an enraptured suitor, eager for her sister's attention, to a husband who was distant at best, heading off to taverns he could not afford and coming home late at night with a glum, mean spirit. She had seen her sister with nothing to feed the children, no clothes or fuel during the worst winter months, when water would freeze indoors if left overnight in a pan. Sally herself had hauled wood to feed their fire and tended to Eunice when she was sick. Sally had also experienced her brother-in-law's rage firsthand. Once, she and her sister had to flee with the children to a separate room in order to escape his violence. Sally personally drew the bolt on the door, fearing for her life.

Now, on this peak autumn day, Sally was in her sister's house once more, with the children gathered near. Before leaving, Eunice had said that she was going to Watervliet to straighten out matters with James. Sally knew that her sister hoped to get support from the Shakers—money, if not a place to live. Eunice had said that she would return after only a few days, so she should arrive anytime now, since half a week had already passed.

So it was with astonishment that Sally saw James at the door, accompanied by his brother Nathaniel. Motioning the children back, Sally turned to face the men.

James announced that he had come for the children. Eunice, he said, had decided to stay with the Shakers and had sent for the youngsters personally. There was not much else to say: They needed to leave at once.

Sally looked hard at her brother-in-law, a Shaker from his hair down to his shoes. Despite his new outfit and righteous demeanor, she would not be fooled. She knew that her sister would never ask James to fetch the children, much less become a Shaker. She also knew what she risked by crossing James. In the past, when her sister's suffering had become unbearable, she had dared to complain to her brother-in-law and experienced his verbal abuse. Nevertheless, she decided to challenge his word.

Sally informed James that if Eunice had joined the Shakers, she would have to hear it from Eunice herself. Her sister had left her in charge, and the children would not go anywhere unless she said otherwise.

James became enraged, and Sally recognized the danger. George was already gone, having taken flight almost as soon as he had seen his father. But Susan and Julia remained near, and they were frightened. Though Sally tried to shield the girls, she knew that she was physically powerless against two grown men. She told the girls to run.

Four-year-old Julia stood no chance, and James grabbed her at once. While the child screamed and reached for her aunt,

James carried her to Nathaniel, who held her steady in the wagon. In the meantime, Susan sprinted for her Aunt Mary's, two miles away. A girl of eight was no match for a man of fifty-one. James seized the older girl, too, and dragged her back to the wagon. Now there was only George.

James scanned the area for any sight of the boy—a small figure running down the road or crouched in the field. He saw nothing. The men would have to look harder for George, taking turns. Left without a guard the little girls were sure to run.

Ten-year-old George was not a natural-born runner. He suffered from chest pains, which worsened when he exerted himself physically, and his eyesight was poor. But he was his mother's son, and what he lacked in size or strength he made up for with cleverness. George had expert knowledge of Durham and its environs, its hidden streams, abandoned sheds, and fields of tall grass. He secreted himself where no one, he was sure, could find him—no one, that is, but a boy like himself. It was a good spot. By dusk, he had not been discovered.

James was becoming desperate. He had lost nearly a day chasing after the children. In the meantime, Eunice was bound to have left Watervliet. For all he knew, she might even be near. He had searched every place he could think of, with Nathaniel's help, trawling the roads, riding out to Eunice's sister's place, and combing much of the surrounding village. He did not know where to go next, and he was starting to lose command of himself. He had begun drinking—although he knew the Shakers would not approve, he felt it was necessary to relieve the pressure. He had enjoyed the familiar taste, the tingle of the spirits as they flowed down his throat, but he was tired. The boy, it would seem, had outwitted his father.

Then James became inspired. A group of boys were playing nearby, and they were about George's age. James had some money in his pocket, more than enough to get him back to Albany. He called the boys to him. If they found George, he would give them his spare change. All they needed to do was to tell George to return to his father, and he would not have to go to the Shakers.

When the boys found George he was worked up with fear. The child had watched his father assault his mother and had suffered abuse himself; once, James had chastised George so roughly out in the street that an older cousin had been compelled to intervene. The moment George had heard his father speak of taking everyone to the Shakers he had taken off for his hiding spot. He did not know how long he had been waiting when the neighborhood boys arrived, only that he was cold, cramped, and tired. He had heard their footsteps, lighter and faster than his father's heavy tread, and his friends were asking him to go back home.

George mistrusted his father, but he was reassured by the boys' promises and their presence. If it came to it, George could put up a fight. It was hard to imagine how his father could take him away with others watching.

As soon as he saw his father again, George realized his mistake. James declared in slurred tones that he was "going to carry him into the ark of safety, and into Christ's Kingdom." George began to cry and begged to be allowed to stay until his mother came home. James replied that they were going out to see her now and if they did not want to stay with the Shakers they could come back at any time. Observing his father's strange garb and the all-too-familiar flush on his cheeks, George refused, but James would not have any backtalk from his son.

By now, a crowd had gathered around the boy and his father. A neighboring judge and a cousin, William Chapman, Esquire— the same cousin who had rescued George from his father once before—tried to reason with James. They wanted him to wait at least until Eunice returned, but they were of little use. These men knew better than anyone else that it was James's legal right to do with his children as he pleased. Before long, George was in the wagon beside his sisters, behind his father and uncle. His uncle probably held the reins, as his father was too drunk to drive.

That night, Nathaniel Chapman took care of the children. The next day, James had recovered somewhat, and he and the youngsters began their journey to Watervliet. In the evening, they pulled in to Albany, where James stopped at a tavern for a final refreshment, leaving the children outside.

We know what happened next from an unidentified local man, who later gave testimony. It was a brisk fall night. The gentleman was rushing along the street—he had some business to attend to—when he saw three children huddled in a wagon, shivering, and poorly dressed for the cold. The children looked so pitiable that he had to stop and ask what they were doing there. They told him that they were waiting for their father, James Chapman, and pointed him toward the alehouse, where candlelight shone warmly through fogged windows.

Though a stranger to the children, the gentleman happened to know James. He entered the tavern and demanded that James bring his children in at once. James complied, and the youngsters were soon warming themselves in the hall. James insisted, however, that the children were not his own, that "they were some poor fatherless and motherless children," whom he was merely delivering to the Shakers. He had "nothing to do with them," he said, beyond his capacity as a messenger.

At the time, the gentleman could do little but shake his head, wonder, and take note. The children looked so lost and forlorn. Why would they have called this man their father? Something was clearly amiss. One of them, he later recalled, had lost its shoes.

As George, Susan, and Julia Chapman approached Watervliet, they were chilled and disoriented. After leaving the tavern where the local gentleman had tried to help them, their father had insisted on finishing their trip that night. They had traveled several long miles out of the city, through a deep forest, which, unbeknownst to them, their mother had crossed not long ago.

When they finally arrived at the Shaker settlement, the village was dark. Now the children climbed out of the wagon, where they were greeted by an odd company of people, the men in oversize hats, the women in baggy gowns. These, they learned, were to be their new "Brothers and Sisters."

Then, to their mortification, the children were separated. The girls remained with their father, but George was taken elsewhere to begin his Shaker life in another house.

Much later, Eunice would learn that George screamed to no end for his mother.

As Eunice came into Durham, there was much to cheer the eye. The trees were luminous with color, October being the prime month for foliage. Ripened apples hung from gnarled boughs, and the streets glittered with the red and gold of fallen leaves. Eunice was cheerful as she thought of the children who were awaiting her at home: her responsible firstborn, George, who tried so hard to be the man of the house; pretty, spirited Susan; and her baby, Julia. But when Eunice arrived in her yard, everything was strangely still. Her children should have been racing around the corner to meet her. Instead, there was only Sally, looking wild.

Her voice shaking, Sally told Eunice what had happened with James. Eunice could barely stand after hearing the story and needed help from her sister to enter her silent home. The house was littered with signs of the children's abduction, a pair of shoes lost in flight, a treasured purse abandoned in haste.

Eunice had suffered trials in the past, but nothing could have prepared her for this moment. As she reflected, "All my troubles which I had thought were insurmountable fled before this, and I said I never knew grief till now." For who knew where James was at this moment? He had said that he was going to Watervliet, but he had lied about everything else. "Oh Lord!" Eunice cried, "Why didst thou not lay them all a lifeless lump of clay! Then I could see and know their end."

In the days following her homecoming, Eunice's house became full again as her community rallied around her. When James had first deserted Eunice, not even her church brethren had had the grace to put aside their own needs and come to her aid. But now that James had left with the children, her neighbors were eager to show their support.

Their change in behavior should not have come as a surprise. In the first case, Eunice had lost only her husband, and for this, she herself may have been to blame. When she lost her children, however—when they were taken screaming from their home, over the protests of her neighbors—it was not just Eunice as an individual who had come under attack, but her family, and even the social order. Regardless of James's legal rights, he had flouted public judgment.

The significance of her community's reversal could not have been lost on Eunice, and the message she received was clear: that no matter how great her suffering, her personal problems would do little to move anyone unless it was understood that public interest was also at stake. Compassion, in other words, required self-interest.

Later, Eunice would become an expert at using this awareness to activate public sympathies, but in this instance, the compassion came too late: Her community in Durham could do little for her when her family was no longer in town. Now Eunice was left to contemplate a new reality, which she had seen in the figure of Catherine Bonnel. The parallels between the two women's situations became ever more apparent when James, following Elias Bonnel's lead, placed an advertisement in a local paper, reading: "I hereby forbid all persons harboring or trusting my wife, EUNICE, on my account, as I am determined to pay no debts of her contracting after the date hereof."

James's action was typical of a man whose wife had deserted him. A woman who left her husband forfeited his support. An advertisement announced this forfeiture, informing her community that she could no longer charge merchandise to her husband's account, take out credit under his name, or enjoy other such privileges. To a modern observer, it might seem that James was out of line in placing such an advertisement, since it would appear that he was the deserter, not Eunice, but in nineteenth-century terms, this matter would not have been so clear. Since it was a wife's duty to follow her husband and live where he lived, it could be argued that by refusing James, Eunice had, in fact, abandoned him.

With James's advertisement in circulation, Eunice had lost her privileges as a wife and all financial leverage against her husband, in addition to her position as a mother. Moreover, with her name in the papers, she was publicly shamed. Eunice had only one recourse. She would have to return to Watervliet and somehow pressure James into returning the children—though with every advantage on his side, it was hard to imagine how.

9

ELDER SETH

Winter was a good time to be a Believer—so good that the Shakers' ranks swelled with "winter Shakers" or "loaf Believers," opportunists who found faith with the first frost, only to lose it when the weather warmed. All fall, the Shakers had picked fruit, repaired roads, fixed buildings, cut wood, and butchered meats to prepare for the coming cold. By winter, their larders were full of cured pork, apples, potatoes, and other sustaining foods, and the Believers were snug in their well-insulated homes. The Shakers continued to be industrious, producing crafts, tools, and clothes, but they also enjoyed sledding and other treats, such as fresh clams for supper.

For George, Susan, and Julia Chapman, there could not have been a better time to enter the society—although they hardly knew so when they first arrived. When George learned that his mother was not waiting for him, he rolled about the floor, screaming. It took more than one Shaker male to restrain him and calm him down. Susan was also rebellious; she resisted efforts by her assigned caretaker to "mother" her, and despite James's cajoling, refused to sign her indenture, a crucial document that gave the Shakers legal authorization to keep children in their society. Eventually, Elder Seth himself had to hold her hand firmly in place while she signed. Julia was more compliant, being just four years old, but she, too, cried piteously for her mother.

The Shakers recognized the depth of the parent-child connection, as a hymn from this period, "Natural and Spiritual Relation," attests:

> *The tenderest feelings that nature can know,*
> *Are found between parents and children to grow;*
> *This inbred affection no rival can find,*
> *Thro' all the soft passions that dwell in mankind;*
> *No ties are so binding, no feelings so near,*
> *No objects so lovely, no treasures so dear;*
> *And here is prefigur'd that heavenly tie,*
> *That tender relation which never can die.*

Of course, the tender ties of family would eventually have to give way to the superior bonds of spirit, but the Shakers were patient, understanding that this displacement required time, particularly for children. As far as the Shakers were concerned, it was evident that the Chapman children had been raised well. The boy, a sensitive creature, knew the scriptures back and forth and already showed a spiritual turn of mind; the older daughter could knit and sew expertly; and even the youngest knew how to say her prayers, which was more than could be said for some children. And thankfully, by late December the children seemed on their way to being settled.

For Seth Youngs Wells, the Elder who had supervisory authority over such matters, this adjustment was a happy turn of events after a highly stressful fall, during which he had been forced to deal with not one but two cases involving unbelieving women: first Elias Bonnel's wife, and then James Chapman's. Not that these kinds of cases were new to the society. Ever since the Shakers had started accepting converts, they had grappled with the problem of what to do with dissenting kin— an inevitable result, some would say, of a society that radically redefined what it means to be a family. However, in some respects these struggles were also a more recent phenomenon. For years after Mother Ann's death, the Believers had closed themselves off from outsiders as they focused on bringing order to their society. Only at the turn of the century had they begun accepting converts again, and then they were primarily concerned with adult converts. Children came along as a byproduct of their parents' faith. But as the Shakers prospered and more people began seeking entrance into their order for reasons beyond faith, issues of membership—especially family matters —became more complex and more troubling.

Elder Seth himself had been a model convert in this regard. He had discovered the Shakers as a single man of thirty and gone on to persuade twenty-four out of the twenty-six members of his extended family—including his nine brothers and sisters—to become Shakers with him. Many of these relatives rose high as Believers. Five Wells siblings became Elders, and a cousin, Benjamin Seth Youngs, became the primary author of *Testimony*. (Elder Seth helped edit a second edition.) For Elder Seth, biological and spiritual family had successfully merged as one.

However, not everyone who came to the Shakers was as unencumbered as Elder Seth: More and more, it seemed, promising proselytes would come with husbands, wives and children. In most cases, these families joined the society together, glad for a place to belong. Yet there were a few, like Eunice Chapman, who wanted nothing to do with the Shakers. The Believers tried their best to reconcile with such relatives, as they did with the Chapmans, as a matter of duty and of precaution. Nevertheless, sometimes an agreement was impossible, and then the society was forced to make difficult decisions about whom to accept and whom to give up.

Officially, the Shakers' policy was straightforward, requiring that prospective members fulfill all outside obligations before joining their society. Actual Shaker practice, however, was complicated by the value that the Shakers placed on bringing in converts. This need itself was a complex matter—hardly as menacing or simple as outsiders often suggested. It was not, as the Shakers' enemies alleged, that the Shakers, desperate for funds, property, and free labor, or "slaves," were intent on increasing their numbers at all costs. Neither was it true that the Shakers targeted children, believing that young minds were easier to indoctrinate. Indeed, the opposite was true in both cases. A large number of uncommitted Believers were a drain on the sect. So, too, were children, who often chose to leave after years had been invested in their care. As Shaker leaders wrote in 1817, "We could have a great many loaf Believers in this distressing time (especially children) if we were willing to take them—doubtless we could have enough to fill all our buildings and consume all our provisions, and by that time they would be willing to go somewhere else."

Yet what the Shakers *did* need were people like Seth Wells and James Chapman, who were in their prime and genuinely inspired by the Shaker religion. It was these mature spiritual seekers, and not mere youngsters, the Shakers knew, who ensured the future of their society. Not surprisingly, when they came upon these promising individuals, the Shakers were loath to give them up. After all, souls were at stake. And so they began making exceptions to their stated policy, admitting certain individuals over the objections of their relations.

Initially, these exceptional cases were probably ad hoc, determined by weighing the worthiness of particular individuals against the likelihood that their relatives would cause trouble. In time, however, a pattern began to emerge, one that would be the focal point of the Chapman controversy. That is, the Shakers almost never took in a woman when her husband stood in opposition, but when it was a wife who dissented, her husband could sometimes still join. This general Shaker tendency can hardly be considered official policy, especially since it was a gradual evolution in practice, rather than an order from above. But the Shakers themselves recognized the trend, well enough to forbid the practice years down the line. As for the children of fractured unions, they usually followed their fathers, as was expected by law.

Practical considerations may explain why a people renowned for their egalitarian attitudes toward gender would allow for such differing treatment. A man could rally a mob or press legal charges, suing the Shakers for "restraining" his family or "alienat[ing] his wife's affections from him." A woman was much less likely to fight back, lacking the rights that empowered her husband. As a matter of safety, it made sense for the Believers to match their practices to the laws of the outside world.

Not everyone in the Shaker community was comfortable with the society's approach to families, especially when children were involved. In 1819, the New Lebanon community would be divided over the Potter children along gender lines. Having sympathy for a "mother's feelings," the Sisters felt that the children belonged with their mother, while the Brothers believed they should remain with their Shaker father, with whom they legally belonged. Elder Seth, however, was shaped by circumstances that made it possible for him to accept such divisions. Indeed, he had been forced to do so nearly from the first.

Seth Youngs Wells had not been intending to convert when he went to visit an uncle who had joined the Shakers in Watervliet. At the time, he was a classically educated principal at Albany's elite Hudson Academy and engaged to be married. But then he came upon a Sister who was speaking in tongues. Wells leaned in to listen with all the enthusiasm of a linguist, becoming even more intrigued as he recognized the Sister's language —possibly Greek or Latin—and understood that she was speaking of him. He called for a translation, whereupon a second Sister offered: "She is talking of that journey you are expecting to take." Wells was stunned, knowing that neither Sister could have known the ancient tongue, much less about his trip. From that moment forth, he was a Believer, and he became living proof that Shaker villages were not merely "places of refuge for the odd, the unlucky, the unhappy, the solitary, the friendless." Despite his status in the outside world, Seth Wells left his fiancée, resigned his post, and joined the Shakers at once.

Wells soon traveled to his hometown on Long Island to share news of the Shakers with his relatives, and it was there, within his own family, that he personally encountered the Shakers' irregular policies, perhaps for the first time. Against the many converts in the extended Wells clan there were two notable holdouts. The first was Elder Seth's father, Thomas Wells, who, following a brief trial in Watervliet, decided to leave the community that now included much of his kin. Meanwhile, Elder Seth's mother, Abigail, wanted nothing more than to become a Shaker, but she was denied admission until after her husband's death. In contrast, Elder Seth's aunt Martha, whose husband embraced Shakerism, was forced into Eunice's dilemma: to join the society in order to be near her children or to give up her family and live alone. In the end, she decided to go her own way, parting from her ten sons and daughters, including a six-month-old infant named Isaac Newton Youngs.

Neither woman had fared well in the years since. Elder Seth's aged mother was miserable in her exile. Martha Youngs was struggling to survive and was alienated from the children she had long ago given up. As a grown man, her youngest, Isaac, would visit her in her shabby quarters (presenting her with a snuffbox, some cash, an orange, and a lemon), but he, like her other children, would have little sympathy for her, feeling that she had abandoned him.

Elder Seth knew of his relatives' difficulties. As a Believer, however, he had been required to come to terms with such instances of unhappiness—even ones close to him—as unfortunate but necessary sacrifices for his religion. This resolution had not always been easy, and Elder Seth was not blindly obsequious, as one failed convert would unfairly assess. The Elder had come into the society at a time when it, as well as he, was vulnerable. The houses were not in order, some of them were occupied by "wicked" souls who violated all that was Shaker, and there was no one to teach him *why* the Believers did as they did; he received only commands that he had to obey. Elder Seth had struggled with these orders and questioned his Elders' judgment, even their authority. But in time, he succeeded in overcoming his doubts. He developed a broad and generous perspective, an understanding that no matter what its particular problems, the Shaker faith was for a larger good. He then rose to the task of writing the religious texts he had wished to read and became the spiritual mentor he had yearned for. By 1814, he was in the position of administering to starry-eyed new Believers, such as he had once been—as well as to fractured households, like those of his parents, the Bonnels, and the Chapmans.

With all that he had personally experienced, Elder Seth was as ready as he would ever be to face these cases, but Eunice Chapman would test him, as she would the Shakers as a whole. Here was a woman who refused to join them or make a clean break, as the Elder's aunt Martha had done. For the Shakers it was a conundrum. If they let James Chapman go, he was sure to become lost, perhaps even suicidal. James had been dangerously depressed, as well as alcoholic, when he had first come to Watervliet. Such individuals often lost their bearings entirely when they left the community. Yet the Shakers could not continue to allow James to remain in their society while his children went hungry and his wife made threats—and neither could they afford to submit to his wife's extortion.

Fortunately, Elder Seth did not have to solve these kinds of problems on his own. In terms of rank, he was what might be considered above "middle management" in the Shaker chain of command. He had charge over his immediate community in the West Family and also played a supervisory role over the South Family, or Gathering Order. The Elder was also gaining a voice in the greater Shaker community, due to his talents as a teacher, writer, and administrator. But ultimately, he was beholden to higher authorities for matters small and large.

Shaker society was rigidly hierarchical. The Elders of the Church Family ranked first in the Watervliet community, and these Elders gave guidance to those, such as Elder Seth, in the lower orders, hearing their confessions and instructing them on matters that might affect the larger community. Above the Church Family was the leadership of the society-wide Ministry, which was led by a single woman named Lucy Wright, or Mother Lucy. Mother Lucy was known as a great delegator, but she was still consulted (directly and through letters) about a wide range of subjects—from permission to travel to another village to larger matters, such as dealings with state legislatures.

Mother Lucy was often in Watervliet—she divided most of her time between there and New Lebanon—and Shaker records show that she was in Watervliet for most of October 1814. Unfortunately, since no one marked the exact date of Eunice's visit, it is unknown whether the two "mothers" overlapped, and thus whether Elder Seth conferred with the head Shakeress, with whom he was known to be close. But if not with her, he probably spoke with Elder Jethro Turner of the Church Family, who had previously counseled him about the Bonnels. Ultimately, the Shakers had decided to admit James and his children as an act of charity. Little else could be done when it was clear that James and his wife would not reconcile. The woman was unreasonable, and the children stood to suffer. Elder Seth had then authorized James Chapman to take a wagon to fetch the children, and when James returned, helped the family make the transition to Shaker life.

Now, some two months later, it seemed that the matter had been put to rest. James's wife had not come after the children, as James had feared, and the children were adjusting. Elder Seth could thus turn his attention more fully to other, more pressing matters—which for him increasingly took the form of paperwork. The Elder's most urgent assignment at this time was to compose a statement for the state legislature, arguing for a military exemption. Pacifism was a cornerstone of Shaker belief, for what could have been more terrifying than the prospect of God-fearing Brethren having to fire muskets at unsaved souls—murdering and shedding blood for the sake of quarrels in the outside world? As a result of their refusal to bear arms, the Shakers had come under attack, first during the Revolution and more recently in the War of 1812. Just the previous summer, Brothers had been drafted and were summoned to a court-martial for failing to report for duty. For years, the Shakers had maintained an uneasy peace with the state by paying fines instead of sending men. But they wished to put an end to this practice as well, believing that by contributing funds, they were financing the very bloodshed that their religion condemned.

In the early years of the sect's history, when relations with outsiders were troubled, the Shakers could not have dreamed of obtaining such an exemption. But the Shakers were now known as good neighbors and faithful taxpayers. Their improved public relations meant that they finally stood a chance for a permanent exemption from military duties and fines. How they pleaded their case would be key. Militia defenses had become an urgent topic for the country at large: From the War of 1812, the states had learned that the federal government was essentially powerless and that it was up to individual states to arm themselves. New York was especially nervous, given the attacks it had suffered during the recent war. It fell to Elder Seth to phrase his society's request in such a way that the Shakers' pacifism would be understood not as a matter of treason but as one of faith.

The Elder was also working on a book about Mother Ann's life, based on eyewitness testimonies. He had not been a witness himself, having joined the society sixteen years after Ann Lee's death. However, he had been deeply moved by stories he had heard, which had revived him during low points in his faith. Elder Seth knew that recording Mother Ann's example was essential, given the rising number of young Believers in the society, and that he could count on her inspiration to help him. This work was all the more critical, since evil rumors about Mother Ann continued to circulate in the world. It was for future Believers, more than anyone else, that Mother Ann's legacy had to be restored.

Thus, as Christmas approached in 1814, Elder Seth was immersed in his literary duties, organizing old Believers' remembrances of their revered first Mother and drafting an impassioned defense of Shaker pacifism with all the tact and grace he could muster. In all likelihood he gave scant thought to the diminutive woman in Durham who had her sights on him and his society—little knowing then how fatefully his present causes would soon become entangled with hers.

10

BOUND

In late December Eunice was finally ready to return to Watervliet. It had taken her this long to consult with her family and find proxies for her brothers, who were unable to make the journey. Elijah Hawley was heading out to homestead in the westernmost part of the state, and Jesse was already in that wild new region, too far away to come to Eunice's aid. Fortunately, her sisters' husbands made dependable substitutes. Peter Penfield, Esquire, and Calvin Spencer promised to talk some sense into James and show the Shakers that Eunice was not alone in her fight.

The party headed out a few days before Christmas, arriving at the West Family very early on the morning of December 22, when it was still dark. As Eunice and her escorts approached the dwelling house, their footprints broke the perfect surface of the newly fallen snow. Eunice had chosen this hour deliberately, hoping to take the Shakers by surprise. She could not forget the sight of Catherine Bonnel staggering from building to building, wailing her lost daughter's name, and she was determined to locate her children before they could be hidden from her. Her strategy worked. On a hunch, Eunice entered the very room where her girls were staying and was reunited with them at once.

The girls cried out when they saw their mother, stunned. Susan wept as she told Eunice that James had forced her to sign a paper, and that she had not known then what it was but later learned that it was an indenture. Legally, Susan now belonged to the Shakers, and Eunice was powerless to protest. Fortunately, Julia remained free, since she was only five—two years short of the age at which the state considered a child capable of giving her consent to a contract. George, however, was probably bound. Susan could not tell her mother for sure, since her brother had been separated from the rest of the family.

As Peter Penfield, a father of nine (soon to be eleven), observed his sister-in-law with her children, he grew mournful, later recalling that the girls "cryed [*sic*] and took on in such a manner that my heart ached for them." When James arrived upon the scene with his Elders, Penfield demanded that the children be returned to their mother, adding that he and Spencer would take care of their expenses. James refused. Eunice then declared that she would "live even in their work-house," if she could just have access to her children, but the Shakers would not agree. The only way she could live with them would be as one of them.

Finally Penfield threatened that if Eunice was not allowed to have her children or to visit them freely he would take matters to the state legislature, where he had connections. James defied him to do so, but the Shakers were not so hasty. In the end, they struck a deal: Although they would not let Eunice live in their village, they gave their word that she could visit regularly with her children, who were to remain in the society at least for the time being.

Penfield and Spencer had hoped that Eunice would return with them to Durham, but she would not go, unable to bear the thought of leaving her children behind. It took the men some effort to find a place for her to board in the nearest outside settlement, the tiny village of Niskeyuna. Then, having done as much as they could for Eunice, and with their own families waiting, they set off for Albany. Penfield, being a lawyer, made sure to give Eunice legal advice before parting: to watch what she said and to bring witnesses on her visits, since the Shakers could use her words against her. In the coming weeks, Eunice would remember his counsel well, even as she found it impossible to heed.

In 1814, Christmas was not what it is today, a time of happy extravagance, with nativities, garlands, and treats. While a few "enthusiastic" souls, such as Methodists, marked the day with joy, most American Christians were too afraid of seeming popish to celebrate with relish. For the Shakers, too, Christmas was a solemn affair. Their observances of the day had begun in Mother Ann's era, when a Sister, rising from her bed of corn husks in what was only a log cabin in Watervliet, began shaking against her will, unable even to tie her shoes on the Savior's birthday. Seeing her, Mother Ann declared that no work should be done on that day and that Christmas should be dedicated to spiritual cleansing and atonement.

The Believers now marked the day by purifying their homes and likewise their souls. They made special confessions to their Elders, danced, and prayed at length. Each Shaker also chose a personal item, such as a piece of clothing, to donate to the poor—an act of giving that also signified a release from the old. The mood about their houses was grave, even gloomy. In the West Family, Elder Seth, Eldress Hannah, and their assistants (all of whom had already made their own confessions before their superiors) bore a heavy responsibility, charged with the reception of their fellow Believers' sins.

Outsiders were never allowed on the premises during these proceedings, and so it is not surprising that when Eunice came to the West Family on Christmas day, she was told that she had to leave. Eunice, however, had no grasp of this context. To her, the Shakers were simply reneging on their promise that she could visit with her children, and she made her feelings known. But here, the Shakers—probably Elder Seth—showed where they had an edge. According to Eunice, it was at this time that she was first warned that her children could be sent to another Shaker community.

Eunice may not have known it at the time, but the Believers had villages throughout the Northeast, as far west as Indiana and as far south as Kentucky—any one of which might have provided a home for her family. Yet she surely realized how hard it would be to track her children once they were sent away.

Eunice ran to James in tears, begging him not to allow the children to be taken away, but he told her to "obey the gift." (In Shaker parlance, a "gift" meant an inspiration, a revelation, or an order from above.) Eunice then went to Eldress Hannah, a woman near her age, "hoping to excite in her some tender feeling for her sex." But Hannah Wells had not become an Eldress for nothing; she tried to coax Eunice into making a confession. Eunice refused and turned at once to leave. Still, it was the Shakers who had the last word. As Eunice drew her cloak around her and headed for the women's door, Elder Seth called for her.

She would do best, he warned, to hold her tongue, for as much as she opposed them now, she might eventually join them.

When Eunice returned to Niskeyuna, weary from the day's trials, she encountered more misfortune. The woman who was boarding her was suffering from an intense fever—a dangerous situation in an age when medicines were primitive, bloodlettings were a common cure for illness, and fevers spread fast. By Christmas evening, Eunice was forced to leave her temporary home.

It was one thing to be a "woman alone" in one's own community, another thing to be homeless in an unknown village, where vagrants were run out of town. Eunice knew she had to find new accommodations quickly if she wanted to avoid being at the Shakers' mercy. Thus she took to the streets and began what would become a veritable career for her in the coming years—telling her story.

As James himself was to attest, Eunice had a gift when it came to self-presentation. Her good looks accomplished much among strangers, who, knowing nothing else about her, were apt to judge her on the basis of her appearance alone. Time and again, Eunice would succeed in persuading people she had just met to give of themselves—to offer her a place in their homes, meals at their table, their time, their trust, and even their political influence—on the basis of nothing more than a stirring first impression.

But beyond appearances, Eunice was also a natural storyteller: She could cite the Bible with ease and had an instinct for creating suspense and eliciting strong emotions—especially fear — in her hearers. In Niskeyuna, she worked up her listeners with a harrowing account of how the Shakers had robbed her of her husband and kidnapped her children. Being the Shakers' nearest neighbors, the villagers grew alarmed. They had good reason to be—not merely for Eunice's sake but because of the possible threat to themselves.

A local family offered to take Eunice in that very night. Soon, Eunice made the most of her misfortune by gathering information about the Shakers and rousing support for a possible confrontation. It appeared that she and Catherine Bonnel were not the first to have troubles with the Shakers on account of their children. Others had been "taken captive," as Eunice liked to put it, and more than once the good people of Niskeyuna had helped rescue them.

In Watervliet, Elder Seth received news of Eunice's misfortune with concern. To be sure, the Shakers' relations with their neighbors had vastly improved since their early years in Watervliet, thanks in great part to the orderliness they had achieved. Nonetheless there were still those who were eager to bring the Shakers down, jealous of the society's success and suspicious of its religion. Among such people, someone like Eunice could find powerful friends.

Three years earlier the Watervliet Shakers had faced their worst crisis to date, which was shrewdly manipulated by a sworn enemy of the Shakers named Jedediah Strong. Strong, a lawyer, had agitated on behalf of a man named Prime Lane (a former friend of the Shakers, if not quite a Believer himself) to sue for the return of his daughters.

The Shakers had felt deeply betrayed by this suit, since for years they had embraced "Old Prime" as an equal, given him a home, and treated him with great charity—all this despite the blackness of his skin, which would have incited prejudice almost anywhere else. At a time when slavery was legal throughout the nation, including New York, the Shakers invited blacks (as well as Irish immigrants and others who faced discrimination) into their villages as equal members, believing that all beings were equal in the eyes of God. Officially, the Shakers did not yet require their adherents to free their slaves (some Believers remained slave owners and were opposed to manumission); however, they began to do so in 1819.

Prime Lane was a free man, but he had benefited from the Shakers' generosity. They gave him land and livestock; fresh meat, butter, fruit, and other nourishment; plus valuable lessons in spinning and weaving for his girls. Yet in spite of these gifts, Lane turned away from the Believers for reasons that went unexplained and insisted that his daughters join him. When they vowed to remain, he dealt the Shakers a terrible blow. With Strong behind him, Lane claimed that at least one of his daughters belonged to him as a slave and he sued the Shakers for illegally keeping his property.

During the bitter proceedings that followed, the Shakers suffered three separate mob attacks. In the first attack, one of the daughters, Betty, was dragged from the South Family dwelling and up to the gates before she broke free. Later, the girls hid, and the Brothers were able to block their enemies. These attacks ultimately came to naught—the sisters remained Believers, and the Shakers won their case in court—but the society suffered a tremendous shock.

The Shakers' anxiety at this time was compounded by a second, equally threatening case, which also involved an angry, litigious father. Matthew M'Dowle had bound his sons, Hugh and John, ages six and eight, at the request of their dying mother, who had been a Believer. But when the boys returned home to pay their final respects to their mother, their father had a change of heart. He and his family wrested the youngsters away from their Shaker caretaker, even while the boys cried and reached for the old man. Then the father took his children into hiding.

With the law on their side and with the help of hired constables, the Shakers eventually recovered Hugh and John, only to be sued by their father. The Shakers won the case after the boys said that they preferred to remain with the Believers; but before they were able to leave the courtroom, "the Irish," as a Shaker scribe called the crowd, "rose in a riotous manner to take the boys by force." The Shakers finally brought the children back to their village at great cost. As they traveled with court-appointed guards, they could not help looking over their shoulders, fearing retaliation, and they had to marvel at the nearly $350 (roughly $6,000 today) that they had spent on this case alone.

Eunice Chapman's situation differed from Lane's and M'Dowle's in critical ways that should have provided some reassurance for Elder Seth and his people. As a married woman, she lacked the legal rights that even Lane, a free black man living in a time of slavery, possessed. But Eunice also had her advantages. Unlike the fathers, she had never had any kind of voluntary or legal association with the Shakers, and so she could better claim to be their victim. She could also plead for assistance as an unprotected woman. In a sense, her vulnerability threatened to become her source of strength.

Moreover, although the Watervliet Shakers had not had any serious confrontations with women like Eunice, Believers in other states had, as Elder Seth and the others well knew. Five years before, the society had faced one of the most terrifying assaults in recent history, inspired by the case of Polly Smith, a Kentucky woman whose husband had taken their children to live

with the Shakers in Ohio. In August 1810, a mob had converged
on the Shakers at Turtle Creek to rescue Smith's children, as
well as others believed to be held hostage by the society. Some
two thousand spectators swarmed the grounds, wielding crude
weapons, such as studded sticks, stones, hatchets, knives, and
clubs. Later, a voluntary corps of five hundred more militiamen
took the village by storm. As in the Lane and M'Dowle cases,
the Shakers triumphed after the children in question insisted
that they preferred Shaker living and wished to remain where
they were. Still, the Believers were long haunted by that "scene
of horror."

Motivated by cases like Polly Smith's, the Ohio legislature
passed an act by which any married man who left his wife to
join a celibate sect—i.e., the Shakers—stood to lose his property and children. The act prevented such a man from deeding
his property away from his family, allowed him to lose custody,
and criminalized the Shakers by issuing a fine of $500 ($8,500
now) on anyone found "with intent" of persuading married individuals to forsake their vows for a celibate society. In 1812,
the Kentucky legislature went even further. Its law allowed
men and women to sue for divorce when their spouses had
joined the Shakers, and it enabled wives of Shakers to claim
property and custody rights. This law also allowed for writs of
habeas corpus to be used when a wife or child was suspected of
being hidden by the sect. As for Polly Smith, she eventually
obtained a divorce and custody of her youngest child.

As of yet, Eunice had not threatened the Shakers with any
kind of far-reaching action. Nevertheless, once the Shakers
learned that she had lost her housing and was spreading ill will
toward their society, they knew that they could not take any
chances. It was finally agreed that Elder Jethro Turner from the

Church Family would go to Eunice directly and invite her into their society on a trial basis.

Being inveterate idealists, the Believers must have hoped that their renewed act of charity would soften the woman. In the best-case scenario, they might even convert her. After all, if past experience gave the Shakers reason to fear, it also gave them reason to hope. Eunice Chapman might go the way of women like Catherine Bonnel and Polly Smith, but she might just as well take the path of another formerly resistant woman— none other than their own Mother Lucy.

11

MOTHER LUCY

Lucy Wright was the kind of woman who had no practical reason for joining the Shakers. Critics could understand why women like Ann Lee or Eunice Chapman might find refuge in Shakerism. As one visitor to the Shakers remarked, the society seemed ideal for "single females without friends and protectors, orphan children without relations, pilgrims in the world struck with melancholy by the way . . . ," and "all those who in one way or the other seem left out of the game or the battle of life. . . ."

By such standards, Lucy Wright presented an enigma. Even the Shakers observed that she was a "naturally handsome" woman. She stood taller than average, with strong, shapely shoulders, a fine figure, and dark hair that showed only a hint of gray. Her face was "open and serene," her black eyes were at once "clear and penetrating" and "mild and placid," and her smile was transfixing. Outsiders marveled that a woman like her—one who had been born with every advantage—would sacrifice everything to become a Believer.

The fact that the Shakers had managed to enlist a woman of this caliber would have made the prospect of converting someone like Eunice seem easy by comparison, all the more so because Mother Lucy herself had once been resistant to their efforts. The story of her conversion provides a model for what the Shakers may have hoped to achieve with Eunice. Lucy Wright may never have had any children to give up, but in the eyes of the world, she had much, much more.

She was born on February 5, 1760, in Pittsfield, Massachusetts, just a mile and half northeast of where the Shakers would later build a settlement. Her parents were well-to-do and well regarded, and with her lively nature and good looks, young Lucy was a popular girl who enjoyed a childhood that could not have been more different from that of the Shakers' first Mother. Whereas Lee was illiterate, Wright learned to write and read beautifully, much at her own initiative. And whereas Lee spent her earliest years preparing looms and cutting fabrics for other people's clothes, Wright entertained girlhood fantasies about owning a sky blue dress and eventually had one made of silk, which she set off with fine jewels.

In her marriage, too, Lucy Wright was much more fortunate than Ann Lee or, for that matter, Eunice Chapman. At nineteen, she married a successful merchant nine years her senior, the talented Elizur Goodrich, who came from one of the most established families in the region. By all accounts, the two were deeply in love. Elizur was said to have been so overwhelmed by his wife's grace and beauty that he "could not bear to spoil her with the flesh"—although other sources report that he declared himself incapable of restraining his sexual feelings prior to joining the Shakers.

Just months after they were married, however, the newly-weds' lives took a dramatic turn when an intense religious revival swept through the region, a movement known as the "New Light Stir." Throngs of worshippers prayed day and night in fields and around campfires, feverish with the presence of the Lord. Of the two, Elizur was especially excited by all the talk of a kingdom come, but he was equally dismayed once the spiritual fires died down and there was no sign of lasting change. It was a perfect time for him to meet the Shakers.

The Shakers often swooped in on disconsolate spiritual seekers, offering themselves up to hungry souls eager to rebound from their broken faith. In nearby Harvard, Massachusetts, for instance, Ann Lee and her company had stumbled upon an odd square house, where a mystic named Shadrack Ireland had established a communal home. Ireland had preached perfectibility and celibacy—while he himself (being already perfect) enjoyed multiple sex partners. Ireland had died ten months earlier, but his followers had yet to dispose of his remains, believing that he would rise again. Ann Lee took the dazed devotees firmly in hand and informed them that their leader had been close, but not exactly right, in his prophecies. She told them that she knew the right way, and many (including Ireland's first lover) followed, eager to believe again.

Elizur Goodrich was likewise convinced. Mother Ann promised the kind of total spiritual transformation that he had been yearning for, and not long after meeting the Shakers, he knelt to confess his sins, ready to give up all that he owned and loved —including his bride. Lucy was another story. She was not any less religious than Elizur. She, too, was a longtime spiritual seeker, and had recently recovered from a near-death experience that had left her convinced of her depravity. While in the throes of a fever, she suddenly envisioned a bright, pure man, who led her to a house that was so spectacularly clean that she felt a deep sense of sinfulness and impurity. (Later she would recognize these people as the Shakers.) But as eager as she was to be saved, Lucy was never impetuous or emotional. Rather, as one Shaker described, she tended to follow "natural instincts of cool, calculating discretion" and was understandably skeptical of this strange new religion, about which she knew so little and which demanded so much.

Elizur himself had doubts that Lucy could be overcome. In the tense days following his conversion, he brought his concerns to Mother Ann, worrying that his wife came from too proud a family to connect herself to a humble people like the Shakers. Mother Ann preached patience. "We must save Lucy, if we can," she is said to have remarked as she watched Lucy pass by, "for if we save her, it will be equal to saving a nation." Mother Ann herself wisely refrained from trying to draw Lucy in too early or in such a way that she would feel cornered and become rebellious. Instead, she waited for the perfect moment to come forward— a moment in which the young woman would not so much be chased and caught as fall into her Mother's waiting arms.

The moment came after a nearly continuous series of frenzied worship services, from morning until night, during which "visible operations" were actively at work among the Shakers. As Lucy tried to hide in the farthest corners of the worship space, men and women fell, shook, and spun around her, some in apparent ecstasy, their eyes closed and their palms thrust upward, others seeming to spar with demons. Still others would drop to the floor on their hands and knees and bark like dogs, speak in unknown tongues, or lie silent. It was undoubtedly overwhelming for a young woman of nineteen who had just been married to witness such spectacles, particularly when her husband played such an active role. One inspired Elder broke from his trance to thrust a finger in her direction and cry, "God knows what is there, and so do his servants!" Lucy was terrified, not knowing herself what lay beyond and feeling as if she had somehow been seen through.

Later that evening, after being singled out again, Lucy sank down, feeling lost. She bowed her head in her lap, unable to move. It was then that Ann Lee took action. The Shaker Mother lowered herself before the beleaguered girl, resting her great weight on her knees, and gently wept before starting to sing in low, sweet tones. As the Shakers pressed around, Mother Ann assured Lucy that there *was* a way of God for her, if she would only make a confession and embrace the Shaker way. Lucy submitted. Now it was her turn to fall to her knees as she unburdened every sin, every vanity, and all the worries of her world to the blue-eyed woman who made her recognize the true "value and importance of a Mother."

Naturally, there was some period of adjustment for Elizur Goodrich and his bride. It was rumored that extreme methods were required to "wean" them from each other, that Elizur was repeatedly bound at Lucy's feet and humiliated in her presence in order for him to become repulsive in her eyes. Yet their so-called "partial affections" were overcome in time, and Mother Ann's observation that gaining Lucy would be equal to gaining a nation would prove true. Lucy Wright, as she was now called, rose to the top of Shaker society, eventually becoming the third leader to succeed Ann Lee.

This rise in itself was a triumph. Even though the society's most powerful leader to date was a woman, there was opposition to female leadership, especially from male Believers—at least one of whom left the community declaring that "wimmin [*sic*] are fools and that men that are willin [*sic*] to have a woman to rule over them are fools also." The two leaders who succeeded Mother Ann, Joseph Meacham and James Whittaker, were both Fathers. But Joseph Meacham saw tremendous potential in Lucy Wright and insisted on appointing her as his co-parent in the Ministry. When he died in 1796, Mother Lucy resolved not to replace him, becoming, in effect, a "single mother" for her society.

Under her subsequent guidance the Shakers achieved much of what they are known for today. When Mother Lucy's rule began, the Shakers were a somber, introverted group of worshippers, scattered here and there through New England in primitive communities, ill at ease with a hostile world. Mother Lucy organized them and thrust them outward, sending emissaries to chase new religious fires that roared across the frontiers of the South and West. Through her initiative, the Shakers built seven settlements in Ohio, Indiana, and Kentucky, and became a "national communal society of Believers." They also wrote a detailed statement of their beliefs for the first time, introducing Mother Ann as Christ in his Second Coming. By the second decade of the nineteenth century, the Shakers were stronger than ever before, with a record number of members, a unique theology, and gleaming utopian villages that were fast becoming the envy of the world.

With such a Mother as an example, the Shakers had every reason to believe that great things could come even from those who seemed the most resistant to their faith. Thirty-five years before, Mother Lucy had been a young bride, barely out of her teens, holding fast to her one true love. She was now a veteran

Believer who had successfully channeled her preferential feelings into a "fountainhead of love" for an entire society, a model
Mother who had led her people to greater material and spiritual wealth. It made sense for the society to give someone like
Eunice Chapman another chance: For who knew how far she
might rise or what she might accomplish if she were shown the
proper way? But first she would need some lessons in humility.

12

BELIEVER

Eunice was coming unhinged. This became clear when Elder Jethro Turner and two Eldresses came to her lodgings in Niskeyuna, bearing gifts. They brought a secondhand Shaker gown and a pair of stockings, which they hoped she would wear as a member of their society. At the sight of the somber, middle-aged threesome, Eunice fell apart. These people, she knew, had the power to determine her relationship with her family. As she clutched their presents and expressed her thanks, Eunice began to cry. She was going "crazy," she said, without her children.

The Shakers were unmoved. While Eunice wept, they admonished her in terms that made her burn with shame. They deplored her fallen nature and her indulgence in the sins of the flesh, the proof of which lay in the fact that she had borne children.

To Eunice, the Shakers' elaboration of these "delicate" issues, which were not discussed in polite society, was scandalous, and when writing about their conversation, she would excuse herself from recalling their words on the grounds of modesty. Other accounts, however, indicate how colorful the Shakers' expressions could be. In his address to an errant Believer, Father James Whittaker described the women living in the man's house as "idle hatchers of Cockatrice eggs and breeders of Lust and abominable filthiness." To his own relatives, Whittaker declared: "I hate your fleshly lives and your fleshly generation as I hate the smoke of the bottomless pit." The Shakers' message to Eunice might be summarized by a hymn called "Carnal Professors."

> *Ye carnal professors, whose works are unclean,*
> *In all your deception you're openly seen;*
> *And now, to deal plainly, the truth we declare,*
> *With all your profession, you're naked and bare;*
> *Your cloak is too short, tho' you swell in your pride*
> *Your works of uncleanness you never can hide.*

Against the world's vile habits, the Elder and Eldresses affirmed their own cleanliness. They then urged Eunice to renounce her fleshly life and worldly affections, confess her sins, and unite with them.

For a mother who saw her bearing of children as a source of pride and a blessing from God, the Shakers' exhortations to the contrary—that she was sinful for having committed the act that brought them into the world—only set her more firmly against their religion. However, she could not refuse the Shakers a second time, when they sent James and a young Brother to bring her back to Watervliet. As Eunice herself later explained, "If I had refused to go, the Shakers would have said my husband had provided a home for me, and I would not go to it." In the eyes of the public, she would have appeared not as a woman wronged but as a willful and disobedient wife. In legal terms, this was a crucial point. If it was believed that James had deserted Eunice, she had grounds to sue for his support; if, on the other hand, it was perceived that Eunice had left James, she was no longer entitled to anything. Thus Eunice had little choice but to follow her husband to the Shakers, with the sole consolation that she would once again be with her children.

Eunice left behind her trunk, since her worldly possessions were unnecessary among the Shakers. Attired in her new gown, and with the Shakers' warm woolen stockings pulled snugly over her legs, she rode behind James and his Brother toward Watervliet. To her surprise, they drove past the West Family, where she knew James and the girls resided. She would not see her daughters; neither, she discovered, would she be joining her son. The carriage stopped at the South Family, where Eunice was aghast to discover that she would face her trials alone.

At the South Family dwelling house, the heads of the order, Elder Calvin Wells and Eldress Fanny Waterman, told Eunice where she stood. She would be allowed a two-week trial in the society to see whether she wanted to join. If at any time she wished to confess her sins as a first step in embracing the faith, she should go to Eldress Fanny—a woman just a year older than Eunice, who had become a Shaker the same year that Eunice had borne her first child. Likewise, if she wanted to see her children, the Eldress would make the necessary arrangements at her discretion. Although no less clear in their goals, the leaders of the South Family spoke more gently than those from the Church Family. They told Eunice that her willingness to confess her sins and join their religion would be cause for celebration.

Later, Eunice was shown to the room she would share with three other Sisters. It was spare and neat, furnished with no more than the Shakers needed to pass a night. There were beds, tidily made, and set on wheels so that they could be moved about for easy cleaning. There were a number of tall commodes, and Eunice was given a drawer for her clothes. A woodstove, a small mirror, a desk, a lamp, and a few lightweight chairs were the only other articles of furniture. Not a single picture or adornment cheered the eye—not even a stray flower or pattern on the blankets—and there was little in the room to indicate anything about the women who inhabited it. The only books in the room were the Bible and *Testimony*.

That night, Eunice lay beside another warm body perhaps for the first time in months: the body of a grown woman, long and unyielding, so unlike the small, tender limbs of her young girls.

At half past five the next morning, when the dwelling house was still dark, a conch was sounded, summoning all Believers to rise and pray. Brothers and Sisters slipped out from beneath their warm, heavy blankets to kneel beside their beds, suddenly alert in the cold. Eunice knelt, too, and then dressed before following her roommates in their chores. The Sisters swiftly pulled back the covers to air the beds, rolled the frames aside to sweep, emptied the chamber pots, and dusted the furniture. Then they crossed the hall to the Brothers' rooms and did the same (the men having left for their own chores), picking up the dirty linen and darning what had been left for them.

Now the conch was blown again to announce breakfast. The Sisters lined up in the slowly brightening hall, the wood floors gleaming beneath their high heels, the white of the walls aglow in the slight light of the morning. Here, as the women quietly gathered, Eunice had the chance to see a group that was more varied than might be expected. Although they were called "young Believers," on account of their spiritual age, the Sisters, about twenty in all, ranged from teenagers to older matrons such as Hannah Train, a mother of seven, whom Eunice was to shadow for much of the next two weeks. There was at least one black woman in the group, the daughter of "Old Prime," Betty Lane, who had clung to the sides of the dwelling house when a mob had tried to carry her out.

The Sisters stood in single file and Eldress Fanny led them in silence to the dining quarters below. In this hall were rows of wooden tables, each set for four, the men's to one side, the women's to the other. At a sign from an Elder, the Brothers and Sisters knelt to offer wordless thanks for their meal, and all simultaneously dug into communal bowls of steaming food. The Shakers ate a hearty breakfast, consisting of such filling fare as potatoes with codfish and gravy or hot mince pies, plus steaming loaves of bread with butter and applesauce.

Eating was a serious affair. All communication—chatter, laughter, and even winking—was forbidden. When they were finished, the Believers each used a piece of bread like a sponge and sopped off their plates—or "Shakered their plates"— swallowing the juicy remainders. After fifteen minutes, a signal was given, and everyone knelt together again before quietly dispersing for work, any dallying being against the rules.

For most of the remaining day, Eunice was busily employed alongside Sister Hannah and the other Shaker women. The women worked in teams, rotating through chores such as cooking, cleaning, and laundering. Because this was ordinary domestic work, Eunice was able to take up her tasks with relative ease. There was seasonal work, too; when Eunice arrived, the Sisters had just finished putting up pork and applesauce, and in the coming months, they would spend much of their time spinning yarn, braiding rugs, and sewing clothes.

At some point during the day, however, Eunice enjoyed a break from the routine when her daughters paid her a surprise visit. Eunice was thrilled to see her girls and took this initial visit as a positive sign that the Shakers might be more accommodating than she had originally supposed. She was quickly proved wrong.

As Eunice had already begun to see, the life of a Shaker was not about doing as one pleased but about falling in line. From the moment they woke, the Believers followed a regimen; even in the evenings they had scheduled activities, usually worship services. But the schedule was only the beginning. The Shakers were beholden to countless other regulations that governed nearly every aspect of their existence and underscored the fact that, in their world, personal will was subverted to community needs. In 1815, these rules were not yet written down, since Mother Lucy feared that a book of laws could lead to a dangerous rigidity in the society. However, the society's "Millennial Laws," which were published in 1821 after Mother Lucy's death, document the kinds of orders that Eunice was sure to have encountered.

Among the Believers, Eunice could no longer wander about as she pleased. She had to inform others where she was going at all times and travel with another Sister. Privacy was practically nonexistent: In prayer, at work, even in bed or in the privy, she would have watchful company. And, if she wished to leave the Family grounds, even to go to another Family, she needed special permission, which was not often granted.

What is more, the Shakers' contact with the outside world was limited. Not only were Believers prevented from traveling beyond the community at will, but they could send and receive letters only with permission, and all correspondence was monitored. Reading was similarly controlled. While copies of *Testimony* and the Bible were readily available, other materials were scarce—although Elder Seth managed to maintain a cache of Greek, Latin, and French books, which he gave up only much later. As a rule, the Shakers valued the spirit over the letter and considered free access to books hazardous to the soul.

There were also constant demands for confession. Even after they had recited their entire life's sins, Believers were expected to "open their minds" on a regular basis. During these sessions, they were responsible for revealing not just their own wrongs but any they had witnessed. Violations varied greatly. Some sins were obvious, such as seeking a "private union" with a member of the opposite sex or indulging in sexual self-gratification. Yet Believers were also forbidden to read a newspaper on the Sabbath or to eat bread on the same day that it was baked. No matter what the transgression, Shakers were supposed to accept their Elders' judgment without question. They were not allowed to talk back to their superiors, refuse assignments, or otherwise challenge decisions that had been made for them.

Not surprisingly, rules regarding relations between the sexes were among the most rigid. Men and women were not supposed to pass one another on the stairs, visit one another, or work together without permission. Even horses and mares were prevented from roaming together in the same pastures, lest they begin copulating in public sight. Some allowances, however, were made for the Brothers and Sisters to mingle. Mother Ann had observed that if men and women were entirely cut off from one another, their temptation would be even greater. Thus, one night a week the Shakers had "Union Meetings," where men and women met in assigned groups to enjoy light snacks and chat. They sat across from each other in rows—close enough, as Eunice noted, that Brothers and Sisters could light each other's pipes— being careful not to fixate on any one member of the opposite sex, for if they did, they were sure to be reassigned.

Eunice never complained about the Shakers' requisite celibacy, but clearly this intimate injunction was a trial for many. As a young man, Elder Seth's cousin, Isaac Newton Youngs, confided in his diary: "I may take up my cross against the flesh, but I am either willingly or unwillingly harassed with all the dirty thoughts that could be invented." Brother Isaac tried his best to conquer his urges by continually opening his mind to his Elders, praying fervently, and throwing himself into his work. He crafted clocks, fashioned pens, tailored clothes, fixed roofs, drew maps, kept school, penned songs, and choreographed dances with a zeal that benefited his society. Yet despite his best precautions, he would sometimes wake up in a wet bed. At other times, he would consciously gratify himself, although he was usually repentant the next day. Only with age did Youngs finally overcome the "snare of Satan" that so "beguiled his soul."

But it was not just sexual relations that were off-limits: Any kind of intimate relationship that threatened to take precedence over the community was similarly restricted, whether between family members or same-sex friends. Although Believers enjoyed deep friendships and close ties to one another, the community intervened when any relationships became exclusive. Friends were assigned to separate work stations. Brothers and Sisters suspected of harboring special affections were kept out of each other's sight. And occasionally, when relations became too intense, Believers were moved into different communities.

To critics, such orders often appeared cruel and arbitrary, but there was a logic to the Shakers' demands. Obedience was an exercise in humbling the spirit—a requisite for all Believers, and even more so for those in charge. In fact, the most promising Shakers were often singled out for humiliation, so they would not feel that they were better than anyone else. One later apostate would never forget the sight of a white-haired Elder on his knees, with tears streaming down his wrinkled cheeks, doing penance for a minor transgression. In effect, the Shaker leadership was composed of those who had best proved their ability to consider the society's needs above their own.

For those who embraced Shakerism, spiritual pleasures, fellowship with other Believers, and material comforts were among the many rewards that made the Shaker life worth living. Eunice, however, found no joy in her Shaker existence. She was a headstrong woman, with clear ideas about how she wanted to live, and, as her conflict with her church reveals, an unwillingness to bow down to authority. These traits doomed her relations with the Shakers from the start. But ultimately, it was her inability to see her children as she pleased—or even to know when she would see them next—that made Shaker life wholly unbearable for her.

Following her initial visit with her daughters, Eunice tried repeatedly to arrange for a second meeting, only to be put off. Every time she mentioned her children, Eldress Fanny asked for a confession, making it clear that visits with her family were not a right but a privilege. Meanwhile, the Eldress and others in the Family employed all possible strategies to convert Eunice, alternating between the extremes of love and torture, as Eunice recalled, in a process that she found excruciating.

At one moment, the Shakers would be kind, telling her that she showed great promise. Eldress Fanny even confided her own conversion story, relating how she and her brother had embraced the Believers together and renounced their mother, who refused to believe. But in another instant the Sisters would all crowd around Eunice, painting torturous pictures of the hell she would face as one who had spurned salvation for the ways of the world. As Eunice sat trembling, with the Sisters' excited faces moving into and out of her range of vision, she could only imagine how much harder it would be for her children to stand up to the Shakers and their religious demands.

In a calmer interlude Eunice tried to appeal to Hannah Train, hoping that a fellow mother might have more sympathy than the spinster Eldress and that Hannah might intervene on Eunice's behalf. However, Hannah simply repeated the Eldress's command, adding that if Eunice did not confess soon, she might not see her children at all.

No more than two days elapsed between Eunice's first and second visits with her daughters, but she became exhausted by the suspense. Seeing the girls did little to revive her. This time Eunice went to visit the West Family, and her daughters were suddenly restrained, tense and unexpressive before their caretakers. Eunice tried to pull the girls into another room, but a Sister rose to say that Eunice could not be with the children alone or move them without permission. With no other option, Eunice and the girls sat stiffly apart, while the Shakers observed them.

By now, Eunice was horrified by what had become of her family. She had caught a glimpse of James carrying steaming pails of swill to the Shakers' swine—a chore that he would never have deigned to do at home. Her children were plainly as homesick as she was, though they dared not express it. She therefore decided that she would try to appeal personally to her husband, even if it meant making concessions, not to mention breaking the Shakers' rules.

She had her chance when James and another Shaker accompanied her back to the South Family later that day. As the other Brother walked ahead, Eunice slowed her pace even more to make her case. Could James not see that it was his duty to return to Durham with his family? She promised that he could practice his religion and even teach their children Shaker ways, if only she could raise the children herself. James, however, categorically refused, declaring that he had no interest in living with Eunice again.

That evening, while the Shakers were in their members-only meeting, Eunice was deeply agitated. On other nights, she would wander outside during these evening services, enjoying drafts of fresh air, bitter with the nighttime cold. Tonight, however, she paced the floors, alive to the sounds of worship coming out from behind closed doors: nimble shuffles across smooth wood, a stamp here and there, the voices of the Brothers and Sisters raised in song. She felt, in all ways, profoundly alone.

But then Eunice realized that she was not, in fact, by herself. Seated in a nearby waiting room was a well-dressed gentleman, also by himself. Seeing her, the stranger invited Eunice to join him. Without a doubt, Eunice knew that the Shakers would never have approved. Nonetheless, she promptly agreed.

Soon she learned that he was a distant relative of Elder Seth (the brother of his aunt Molly) but no friend to the Shakers.

With a sympathetic listener beside her, Eunice began to speak freely, as she had not spoken in days. She told of how the Shakers had deceived her, conned her husband, stolen her children, and broken every promise they had ever made to her and her family. She did not stop when the Believers, their meeting over, began filing past the door. Before long there was an audience, and Eunice's new friend and his Shaker brother-in-law, Benjamin Youngs, were engaged in heated argument, the outsider denouncing the Shakers as "hypocrites," the Shaker defending their gospel.

Hannah Train rushed in at once and pulled Eunice away, warning that she would surely face retribution. At some other time, Eunice might have flinched, but at the end of this very long day, she remained unperturbed, vindicated by a stranger's understanding. She replied that she "had not said anything but the truth" and that if the Shakers were "ashamed of the truth, they must do better."

After that night, Eunice became increasingly rebellious, in what was probably a conscious attempt to be thrown out of Shaker society. As Eunice had learned with her own church, rebellion carried risks, and her strategy could backfire if the Shakers managed to convince their neighbors that she was guilty of disorderly conduct. The Shakers could also retaliate by withholding or moving her children. However, through expulsion Eunice could gain the grounds to claim abandonment by her husband. And the alternative was simply to wait and face the same awful choice she had faced before—join the Shakers, or leave and allow James to claim that she had deserted *him*.

Alert to the dangers, Eunice began to assert herself incre-
mentally. First, at the Shakers' Union Meeting—a high point
in the week for many, since it was a rare occasion for men and
women to socialize—Eunice wandered away from her assigned
company and, to the Shakers' astonishment, sat herself down
uninvited among a group that was more to her liking. Two days
later, Eunice's insubordination took a more serious turn during
a visit to the West Family. Eunice had been anticipating her
first overnight stay with her girls and was dismayed to learn
that her visit would be cut short. The Shakers were in great
excitement—inspired communications that had been received
in the Church Family were now coming their way—and they
were anxious for her to leave. Eunice, however, defied all of
their commands, until the Shakers were finally forced to close
their doors and proceed in spite of her.

Eunice's misbehavior continued in the aftermath of the
meeting, when James called on her in the South Family. James
was in a good mood, flushed from the previous day's religious
exercises, and was thus unusually kind to Eunice. Encouraged,
Eunice tried to engage her onetime husband, speaking so
warmly to him that the Sisters became outraged and accused
her of trying to seduce him.

Matters only intensified the following week, as the Shakers
continued to refuse Eunice's requests to visit her son. It had been
months since she had seen George, and when Eldress Fanny
denied her yet again, Eunice went to Niskeyuna without asking leave, perhaps to share her troubles. When she returned, the
Shakers were at worship, and the entire building was shaking.
Eunice peeked into the meetingroom to see the Brothers and
Sisters frantically "spitting [on] their hands," as she later wrote
—"stamping, jumping, and whirling about," crying, "hiss, hiss,

hiss!" "hate the devil, hate the devil, hate the devil!" and "chain the devil, chain the devil, chain the devil!"

Afterward, Hannah Train explained that they had been exorcising the evil spirits that Eunice had unwittingly brought into their home by going abroad without proper leave. The spirits, Hannah said, were palpable: They crept around like caterpillars and crawled everywhere, even into people's mouths. She then offered to clear those spirits from Eunice, too, and this time, Eunice went along, holding still as Hannah and other Sisters circled around her, praying feverishly for her release. Unfortunately, her compliance did not have its intended effect. When Eunice asked if she was now clean, Hannah replied, "Yea," but when she further inquired whether she was clean enough to see her boy, the Sister responded that only a full confession would purify her sufficiently for that.

The Shakers had good reason for denying Eunice access to her son, well beyond providing an incentive for better behavior. George was in the Church Family, where even covenanted Believers could not go freely. But all Eunice knew was that she had not seen her son for more than two months. And as the days passed, she became increasingly fearful that the Shakers would not let her see him at all.

Toward the two-week mark in her stay, Eunice finally called for James to demand an explanation. Much to her surprise, he said that she had finally obtained clearance to visit George and offered to take her to the boy himself. They soon set off, joined by others, including Hannah Train. It was this Sister, whom Eunice had once sought as a confidante, who gave her the most painful reminder of her place in the world. As Eunice would remember, Hannah called out, "You must not walk by his side— you must follow after him; that is your place."

Ignoring orders, Eunice hastened ahead, and when the others could not hear, she beseeched James once more to bring his family home. Looking "very wild," James responded even more passionately than before. He cast her off with a strong Shaker "Nay" and told her that they now belonged with the "people of God." Besides, he added, he had found a peace here that was unknowable in the world. Then, although Eunice tried to hold on to him, begging him for his hand as they approached snowdrifts in the road, James turned swiftly back to the West Family, leaving her to finish her journey with the other Shakers and enter the Church Family without him.

Of the three children, George had the most difficult time adjusting to his new life. Unlike the girls, he had been alone all this time, and when he first arrived, he threw such terrible fits that "a strong man could not hold him," as one Sister confided to Eunice.

Months later, however, George was growing accustomed to the predictable rhythms and even the comforts of Shaker living, such as the rich meals that he could not have enjoyed at home. He learned to assist the Shaker men in the fields or in their shops, and at a time when many youngsters did not receive a formal education, had separate time for lessons. For now, study sessions were held in the evenings, but a Shaker day school was set to open that very month. All in all, it is extremely unlikely that George was overworked or mistreated in any way. The Shakers' gentleness with youngsters is well-documented, and being pacifists, they rarely used physical force.

Eunice, however, assumed the worst when she saw her son. George was seated in a workshop, among piles of hide, with long, thin strips of leather flying out of his hands. He was braiding whip thongs—work that chafed the skin, if one was not used to it—and Eunice could see that her child's hands were flecked with blood.

Convinced that George was being abused, Eunice became even more recalcitrant, thus reversing the Shakers' hopes that a meeting with her son would help tame her. Rather than show gratitude for the reunion and a greater openness toward their faith, she began to attack their religion, pointedly challenging a Shaker Elder, possibly Jethro Turner, on matters of scripture. She condemned the Shakers' separation of husbands and wives as a sin, quoting from the Bible: "What therefore God hath joined together let no man put asunder." And in the end, she proved so dogged that the Elder under attack had to leave the room, and the Church Family gave up on her.

Years later, Eunice would flinch as she remembered her last moments with George. It was all she could do to keep from breaking down. But just as she had done years before, when she had been left to raise the children on her own, she held herself in check, knowing that any display of emotion would only increase her child's suffering. As she left George in the Shakers' care, Eunice could only hope that if he was of an age at which he could comprehend their denouncements of her, he was also grown enough to resist their dogma until she saw him again.

At the West Family, where Eunice decided to stop on her way back to the South Family, her disruptive streak continued. The Shakers were in their Union Meetings when she arrived, and she wandered down the hall to spy on her husband, who was talking obliviously with his assigned partner, or, as Eunice considered her, his "spiritual wife." That night she begged for permission to share a bed with her older daughter, causing the girl to burst into tears when the Shakers refused. The next day Eunice challenged a second senior Shaker over matters of scripture—scandalously, in the presence of vulnerable "young Believers." She also spoke privately with young Shaker women about her woes, prompting at least one of them to confide that she thought it "wrong" of the Shakers to "take children from their mother."

The Shakers and Eunice were now at an impasse, but for several days the Shakers took no action. They were busy preparing for the arrival of Mother Lucy, who was coming to stay for the month. On January 11, Mother Lucy and her helpers finally rode into Watervliet. The next evening, exactly two weeks and a day after her ordeal had begun, the Shakers asked Eunice for a decision.

The Elder of the South Family, Calvin Wells, called her forth, accompanied by James, but he spoke for more than just himself. His brother, Elder Seth, made the calls for both the West and the South Families and was sure to have consulted his own superiors at the Church Family—including, perhaps, Mother Lucy.

Elder Calvin was blunt. "Eunice," he asked, "do you want any of our faith?"

Eunice's immediate response was "No," to which the Elder replied that she could stay no longer. But then Eunice offered a compromise: She would be willing to live with the Shakers, if that was what her husband wanted, and she would follow most of their ways—all, that is, but one. She was a Christian woman, and she would insist upon maintaining her own faith.

This was a brilliant move on Eunice's part. Now, she could claim publicly that she had not been defiant or unruly, as the Shakers were sure to argue. She had been perfectly willing to acknowledge her husband's authority; she had just wanted to put God first, as was only proper.

For the Shakers, of course, such an arrangement would be impossible, especially considering all the trouble that Eunice had already caused. Elder Calvin firmly informed Eunice that she could not live with the Believers unless she became a Believer herself. Then James stepped forward to inform his wife that she must get ready to leave at once.

Eunice had won the moment, but the possibility of being separated from her children forever precipitated a spiritual crisis. As she later imagined, it was as if she were Abraham, forced to choose between his beloved son Isaac and his Almighty Lord. Should she renounce her Christian faith, or leave her "captive babes," who were dearer to her than anything else in the world?

Like Abraham, she went with God, believing that somehow her children would be redeemed. However, she did not go easily. She begged James for mercy, calling attention to the wind and rain that were gusting outside and imploring him not to leave her on her own. Then she became belligerent. She declared that she would not go and that James had to support her. She further decried his failures as a husband and, turning to the Sisters who had gathered at the scene, told of how James had tried to crawl into her bed at night, well after becoming a Shaker.

This was more than the chaste Believers could take. By Eunice's account, Hannah Train pulled her by the arm and dragged her down the stairs to the front door of the dwelling. Other Sisters rushed around with a coat, hat, and pair of stockings, which they tied to her struggling form as best as they could. Together, the Shaker women managed to take Eunice outdoors and to hoist her into the back of an open wagon, where James was waiting. Then they looked on as the wagon pulled away, and "the most abusive and refractory of any woman that ever came among us" left their community for good.

In the open wagon, behind her husband and his companion, Eunice was in such a state that she did not even think to adjust her garments. Rain-soaked, with her stockings dripping and tied to her sleeves, Eunice beseeched James to let her say goodbye to her children or to take her back to Niskeyuna, where she had left her trunk—and where she no doubt meant to advertise her troubles. But James drove on past the West Family and the church, away from Niskeyuna, and along a route she had never seen.

As they traveled through a dark stretch of woods, Eunice began to panic, not knowing where they were headed and fearing what her husband and his Shaker friend planned to do with her. She was all the more agitated by James's lighthearted behavior, his laughter with his friend, since her experience had shown that his joy was often a prelude to disaster. But somehow, through these back roads, they ended up in Albany, on busy South Pearl Street, where James pulled up in front of an inn. He told Eunice to get out and gave her an ultimatum. She was not to come looking for him or the children for at least three months, or he would move the children to where she would never see them again. He then turned the wagon around and headed for home.

Eunice was left alone on a strange street. Carriages passed by, splashing mud and rainwater. She had no money and no way to return home. A group of young women who happened to be gathered nearby gazed in her direction and exclaimed that a "crazy woman" had come—rousing the attention of the innkeeper's wife, who rushed outdoors to see what was the matter.

By her own admission, Eunice was crazed indeed. Not only was she dressed like a lunatic, but she was nearly mad with grief. However, Eunice Chapman was nothing if not resilient. As she gazed up at the house full of strangers, the inn warmly lit against the long winter night, she was convinced of one thing: She would do whatever was necessary to bring her children home. If she had to bring down the Shakers in the process, she gladly would.

13

VENGEANCE

Soon after her arrival in Albany, Eunice learned that James had again advertised against her in the papers, warning businesses not to extend credit to her in his name. Once again, however, Eunice managed to survive by way of her personal charisma. Despite her initially crazed appearance, she won the sympathies of Mrs. Andrew Cooper, the proprietress of the inn where she had been left. Before long, the two became friends, and Eunice had an invitation to stay with the family. From Cooper's Tavern, Eunice was also able to send word out to her relatives, and about two weeks after her arrival, her sister Catey's husband, Peter Penfield, joined her in the capital city.

Penfield acted quickly, contacting an old friend from Delaware County, Asahel Paine, who was in Albany as a member of the New York State legislature. The forty-five-year-old assemblyman, a Connecticut native and doctor, filled many roles in the town of Delhi, among them county clerk, and he had at least one son, who was several years older than George. After hearing Eunice's story, Paine agreed to accompany Eunice and Penfield back to

Watervliet. Penfield was confident that with Paine along, Eunice would be able to bargain for the release of her girls, at the very least.

It was early February, when the Chapmans should have been celebrating Eunice and James's eleventh anniversary and young George's tenth birthday. Instead, Eunice was once more on the road to Shaker country, with Penfield and Paine. At the West Family, they asked to speak with Elder Seth. The Shakers were obviously not happy to see them and brusquely remarked that the Elder had left for New Lebanon. Nevertheless, perhaps motivated by Penfield's presence, they arranged for Eunice and James to meet.

After a hard look at her prospects, Eunice was willing to negotiate. Even though she was deeply attached to George, she knew that she had little chance of claiming him, for a son had special value as an heir and a laborer, and as a provider for his parents in their old age. So she placed her bets on her daughters, who were of less practical value. She would take just one of the girls, if she could not have them both.

The girls themselves were sure to have clung to their mother and begged their father to let them go. James, however, was furious that Eunice had defied his orders to stay away and that she had disturbed the children, just when they were becoming settled. He vowed that he would "as soon commit suicide" as give up either one of his daughters, and nothing the men proposed—not even Paine's threat to go to the legislature—would persuade him to compromise.

Paine and Penfield decided to make one more attempt to negotiate directly with the Shakers. On Sunday, February 5, the two gentlemen and Eunice drove back to Watervliet. This time, the men went straight to the church, where the Elders had gone for services, while Eunice walked on for another mile to the West Family to see her girls. As they went their separate ways, the visitors were unaware that the day they had chosen to call on the Shakers was of particular importance to the society— that the Believers had special cause to gather about their own beloved Mother.

February 5 was Lucy Wright's birthday—her fifty-fifth, in 1815. To honor her, the Shakers of Watervliet gathered in the meeting-house. They began by singing a special hymn for the occasion, sending their voices up through the highest floors of the building, where later that night, their Mother would take her meal and retire. Mother Lucy sat serenely before them, with a smile like no other. As an aged Elder would rapturously re-call, "No coquetry or ostentation was ever manifest in any of her words or ways. Yet her countenance ever wore a pleasant smile, and when she smiled from effect, it was the most pleas-ant and beautiful smile I ever beheld on mortal face."

Lucy Wright had come far since her first years in the soci-ety. From a bewildered bride who was loath to leave her hus-band, she had become a disciplined leader who was known for moderation and her vigilance against "particular affections." This is not to say that she was without spirit: She once told the Shakers somewhat testily that they clapped as if they had cushions between their hands and made them do it right. She was also a perfectionist, rebuking her charges for slumping and fidgeting, for example, or using slang such as "em" for "them." She even set up a school to correct such unseemly slips of speech. But she became suspicious when anything was taken to extremes.

There was the matter of Shaker "labor" or dance, for example. Whereas the first Shakers had thrashed about hysterically, to the terror of onlookers, turn-of-the-century Believers had gone to the opposite extreme. Their pace had slowed to such a degree that they barely seemed to drag themselves across the floor while intoning curious, wordless tunes, called "solemn songs," which struck some as the sound of angels but others as terrible droning. Mother Lucy lightened their steps and let them sing with words.

In her view, even the quest for excellence could become excessive. She lectured one group of Sisters, for instance, about taking too many pains to cook "extraordinary" foods. In labor, as in everything, the Shaker Mother believed, it was best to avoid any undue attachment, any inordinate zeal.

Mother Lucy looked out now on an audience whose experiences as Shakers were vastly different from her own. Most of these Believers had never known their original Mother. They had never wept for their sins in her thick, strong arms—neither had they seen her overtaken by mobs, her face distorted from beatings, her ribs broken beneath her blood-soaked gown. What is more, they had never experienced Watervliet as anything but a model community. In short, many of these men and women had never known pain, want, or persecution as Believers.

This lack of experience was a liability, as Mother Lucy knew. When she felt distress, she had only to recall Mother Ann's sufferings to appreciate her own good fortune. Shakers now missed the force of this example and risked becoming lax—especially those who had joined the sect for material reasons, rather than spiritual ones. As she faced her spiritual children, Mother Lucy knew that she needed to rouse them with a renewed sense of urgency and a productive zeal that, in her own experience, depended less on sudden revelation than on hard work.

And so she told her listeners that she understood their struggles—that she herself had struggled, too, especially after Mother Ann's death. But in time, she assured them, she had learned that it was not Mother Ann's physical presence that mattered, so much as the spirit of her faith. She herself managed to find even greater joys as a Believer than ever before, and she promised that this was possible for each one of them. Obedience, however, was the operative word, as was vigilance. "The people of God," she said, "ought to labour for a spirit of discernment, for they are beset on every side by the devices of Satan. I think you need eyes before and behind, in order to see them, and shun them."

In warning against such dangers, the Shaker Mother had no way of knowing how close her society's public enemies actually were, or that a woman whom they would consider in league with the devil was just down the road.

While the Shakers were in their meeting, Eunice slipped into the West Family dwelling and saw her daughters. With the Elders out of the house, the girls sat close by their mother and freely complained that they were miserable and wanted to go home. Eunice comforted them as best she could, knowing that their uncle and his friend were at the church, fighting for their release. But if Paine and Penfield had had success, James, at least, seemed unaware of it when he returned to his Family. He ordered Eunice to leave.

Now that she had friends nearby, however, Eunice was emboldened to issue threats of her own. According to James, she said she could have him thrown into prison; that she had powerful allies in Albany, including members of the legislature; and that she would have an act passed that would not only take the children away from him but also force him to support her wherever *she* wanted to be. Most chilling of all, Eunice announced that she was "able to command any assistance" she wanted and warned: "If you don't take care . . . you'll soon have your buildings burnt about your ears. Your village will be laid in ashes."

Eunice's threats represented all of the Shakers' worst fears. The legal attacks were bad enough, considering their current efforts to lobby the legislature for a military exemption. But mob violence was a real and much more immediate danger. Arson was especially serious in these times—the equivalent of a bomb threat—because people were so ill-equipped to put out fires. Even with a village full of highly organized Believers lining up with buckets of water, there was a good chance that the entire cluster of close-set buildings would be lost.

Nevertheless, the Shaker Elders, who had arrived by this time, wrested Susan and Julia from Eunice and hustled them to a private room. Eunice ran after them and banged on the door until a Sister emerged. Glimpsing her younger daughter just inside, Eunice rushed to take the child into her arms. But Eldress Hannah pulled Julia away and, with help from two other Sisters, forced Eunice out of the room, closing the door in her face. "That," Eunice later wrote, "is the last sight I had of my dear babe."

Penfield and Paine arrived to find Eunice distraught. Unfortunately, they had had no better luck at the Church Family. The Shaker authorities were unwilling to negotiate for the children's release, asserting that the conflict between the Chapmans was a private affair between husband and wife, a matter in which they had no say.

Eunice's party left Watervliet in defeat but planning a counter-attack. Dr. Paine assured Eunice that he would take the case to the House of Assembly, where he would request state assistance in retrieving the children. Surely when the Shakers saw this they would alter their course.

Two days later, February 7, Paine briefly presented Eunice's grievances to the legislature. By the next day, Eunice's brother Elijah had finally arrived from Ridgefield. It was decided that he would ride to the Shakers and inform them where matters stood. If the Believers agreed to cooperate, there would be no need to take the case any further, but if they refused, their problems would be made public, and then it would be up to the authorities to determine whether the Chapmans' quarrel was truly a private affair.

As far as the Shakers were concerned, Eunice had already gone far enough, and her antagonism could not have come at a worse time. Elder Seth had finally finished writing a statement requesting a military exemption from the state. Hundreds of pamphlets were being printed for distribution. With the legislature soon to deliberate on their appeal, the Shakers knew that they could not afford any bad publicity, official or not.

But the Shakers had a last resort for dealing with women like Eunice, as they had indicated to her before—one that was effective even in states like Kentucky, which had passed an anti-Shaker law, as the case of Sally Boler demonstrates.

Like Polly Smith, Catherine Bonnel, and now Eunice Chapman, Sally Boler challenged a husband who had left for the Shakers with her child. In court, Boler's people conducted a dirty war, introducing testimony from one witness who claimed that Elder John Rankin "threw unwanted babies into the fire."

Whether Sally Boler might ultimately have won the rights that her state had placed within her reach would never be known, for when the Elders in Kentucky communicated their distress to New Lebanon, the mother community decided to give them support. Before a verdict was reached, Sally Boler's husband transferred his property over to the Shakers and fled north with his boy. Father and child then took shelter in New Lebanon, where the highest-ranking members of the society resided— among them, Mother Lucy—and were sure to have welcomed them.

Sally Boler would continue to attack the Shakers in Kentucky, serving them with as many as nine writs of habeas corpus in an effort to get back her son, but Daniel Boler remained among the Believers and grew up to become one of the central leaders of the society. Throughout, Shakers themselves rested easy and even gloated over their success. "Barking up the wrong tree," one Elder would say, as the mother's lawyers pressed on. "The child whose life Herod seeks had been gone a whole year since."

14

A CONSECRATION
UNTO GOD

Although not the firstborn, Elijah was the most dependable son in the Hawley family. When Eunice's father was
sent to jail, Elijah bailed him out and gave him a place to live.
When their sister Sally seemed destined for spinsterhood, he
provided for her, as well. So it was little surprise when Elijah
again left his young family behind in a wilderness and made the
long trek to Albany to help Eunice.

In Elijah, Eunice may have sensed her best chance at negotiation. A postmaster in Schoharie and then in Ridgeway, Elijah
was a respected member of his community. He was also a
Mason, alongside influential New Yorkers such as DeWitt
Clinton, mayor of New York City and soon to be governor. More
poignantly, Elijah knew what it meant to lose a child. Around
the time Eunice's children had disappeared from Durham,
Elijah's four-year-old son, William Edgar, had died unexpectedly. Elijah had chiseled the boy's name on the gravestone himself while an older son looked on.

On February 8, Elijah made the journey, prepared to announce that Assemblyman Paine had introduced Eunice's complaint to the legislature. But when Elijah asked to see James, the Shakers bluntly informed him that the father and his children had left the village. The Shakers would give no clues as to when or how James had departed, where he intended to go, or how long he was planning to stay away. As far as they knew, James was gone for good. All that remained of him was a letter.

In Albany, Eunice opened the letter, which was dated February 6, 1815, two days before Elijah had left for Watervliet. She read, in an all-too familiar hand, James's declaration that their marriage was over, that he had "consecrated [himself] unto God," and that he had thus consecrated his children as well. God, he said, had commanded him to bring his children "out from the wicked world of mankind" and among "his chosen and peculiar people."

James went on to recite his grievances against his wife. He claimed that she had tricked him into marrying him, laying her "snares," and rousing him up into the same delirious state as "the young man spoken of by Solomon, where he says the way to her house was the way to hell. . . ." Then, once they were safely wed, she proceeded to torment him with her outrageous temper, quarreled shamefully with her neighbors, and finally ruined his estate. He had endured all this, but her actions against the Shakers crossed the line. He wrote to Eunice:

> You have persecuted [the Shakers] with satannic [*sic*] rage—and for what? Because they have taken my children in charity, without fee or reward, and children which you said you could not maintain without charity. This charity is furnished by the people of God—and what is your

return? Why the most bitter persecution and slanderous reports—the most vile and impudent language while in their dwellings; and in fine, you have done every thing to provoke God and his people that has been in your power.

For this ungodly carriage, you are shut out from the society of God's people, and this you have brought on yourself by your own baseness and ingratitude. Indeed you have forfeited all right and title to me as a husband and friend, and likewise to the feelings of the people of God. When you was here last you threatened to burn them out. For the above causes you are spewed out of the mouths of God's people; and for these causes you have compelled me to move myself and children to that part of Christ's kingdom where we can find rest to our souls; and it is wholly on account of your baseness.

If you had conducted yourself like a rational creature, you might have had the privilege of visiting your children as often as necessary, but now you are not permitted of God, whose children they are. I shall live with the children probably till they are of age, if I live so long; and then they will possess their own agency—then they may act their own judgment.

You will not see my face 'tant [?] likely in this life, nor the faces of the children of which you are the natural mother, and you yourself are the only cause.

Yours,

James Chapman

By the time Eunice put down James's letter, she was sure that regardless of what the Shakers claimed, her husband and children were still in their society. James had said so himself: He had gone to "that part of Christ's kingdom where we can find rest to our souls." To an avowed Believer, "Christ's kingdom" could mean only a place within the Shaker world. Moreover, Eunice's own experiences had shown her that nothing could be done without a "gift" from the Elders, that no one could travel anywhere without permission from higher authorities. To her, it was obvious that the Shakers were complicit in James's departure.

But to have a belief was one thing, and to prove it was another. As long as the Believers insisted that they knew nothing, Eunice was not likely to discover which of the many Shaker villages across the country had become her children's home. All she had to go on, as winter turned to spring in 1815, was her intuition, confirmed by James's letter, that her family was somewhere in Shakerdom.

Eunice's instincts were exactly right. The Shakers' own documents reveal that George, Susan, and Julia Chapman were still in Watervliet the day their uncle asked to see them. It was only later the same evening that James took the children, for the second time in four months, and began the long journey toward their new home.

By George Chapman's recollection, the night was brutally cold. He and his sisters had no idea where they were headed when they were pulled out of their dwellings and smuggled into a sleigh. They saw their father and another Shaker in the driver's seat, conferring with Elder Seth and his assistant, Joseph Hodgson. There were also two Shaker women—probably the children's Eldresses, Hannah Wells and Patty Carter—who were sure to have furnished the sleigh with provisions for the days of travel ahead. George managed to steal a glance at the directions Elder

Seth had written and handed to his father, and learned that their destination was Enfield, New Hampshire, the site of another Shaker community.

For years, the Shakers would maintain that James had left with the children completely on his own, just as they had told Elijah Hawley. George's recollections and the Shakers' own writings, however, show that the Shakers lied. In a Church Family journal, kept by Freegift Wells (another one of Elder Seth's siblings), it is written in a tidy, slanted script: "James Chapman, on account of his troubles with Eunice and wife, took his three children and started for Enfield. . . ." Jethro Turner's diary reads: "James Chapman, with his three little children start for North Enfield." Manuscripts from the Enfield Shakers document the other end of the trip. The Shaker Museum in Canterbury, New Hampshire, holds an enormous leather-bound history and record book kept by Elder Henry Blinn in which the children's arrival is recorded for all to see.

Who made the decision to send the Chapmans to Enfield? Shaker diaries do not give names, but they do provide some important clues, particularly when read against George Chapman's testimony. From George, we know that Elder Seth and Joseph Hodgson were involved in the move. But the fact that at least two high-ranking Shakers in the Church Family also knew about the journey—and cared enough to make note of it in their journals, which they kept for the benefit of the entire community—shows that the leaders of the West Family could not have acted alone. Indeed, with so many people in the know, the highest authorities must have been involved.

Who were these authorities? The Shaker journals point to none other than Mother Lucy. Lucy Wright had come to Watervliet to spend her birthday, and she remained there until February 11. Of course, there is no paper trail to implicate the Shaker leader directly in anything involving the Chapmans. The Shakers were understandably protective toward their Mother, and although a stunning collection of their papers survives, many were also destroyed, some at the Believers' own hands. (Here and there, tantalizing pieces can be found—letters, for instance, that have been blacked out or torn.)

Existing documents, however, show that Mother Lucy was consulted about all kinds of issues, many much smaller than what the Shakers faced with Eunice. Although Mother Lucy was known to delegate tasks, she gave advice on everything from the mundane (how to eat certain kinds of bread) to the religious (how to present Mother Ann to the world) and the political (how best to approach the state for a military exemption). It is apparent that she was a leader who had an eye on everything. Mother Lucy may not have been in the habit of attending public worship sessions held at the church, but from her private quarters on the upper story of the meetinghouse, she had a hidden view (a peephole, some would call it) into all that went on below. She was sure to have known what was happening with Eunice. Eunice had made herself not just a private nuisance but a public threat, and a decision of this magnitude—one that potentially involved the well-being of the society—would not have been made without the Shaker Mother's input, especially not if she happened to be in Watervliet.

In the years to come, Eunice would hold Lucy Wright personally responsible and would call upon Mother Lucy to release her family, with a powerful note of warning. "Remember that a woman can be as mighty to pull you down," Eunice wrote, "as a woman was to build you up." Yet Mother Lucy's position may have been more ambivalent than Eunice supposed. The Shaker Mother recognized that nothing good came from admitting children of non-Believers. Such children never remained in the society for long and often caused trouble. One later Shaker leader recalled that Mother Lucy often warned that taking in these children would "run down the society." Even so, plans to move the Chapmans to Enfield had evidently been set in motion well before the Shaker Mother came to Watervliet in early 1815. James Chapman signed the Articles of Agreement (a preliminary covenant) in Enfield in the spring of 1814, months before the children even left Durham. And now, as the executive authority of her society, Mother Lucy was forced to make an excruciating decision on how to proceed.

On the surface, Mother Lucy's final call might seem callous, if not cruel, but it is also possible to see this as the only feasible choice. There were only three real options to begin with. First, the Shakers could simply return the children to their mother and demand that James concede. However, there was no guarantee that their troubles with Eunice would end there. By yielding to Eunice, moreover, the Shakers would be turning their back on James, a troubled individual who had vowed that he would rather die than relinquish his children. To give up on him now would be to lose a soul forever—not to mention the souls of his children.

A second option was to maintain James and the children where they were, but clearly this was not in the society's best interest. Not only had Eunice already begun taking legal action, but she had also raised the possibility of mob violence and arson, which the Shakers could not risk on any account.

A final possibility remained, and that was to allow James to remove himself and his children to another Shaker community. This move would be legal, given James's rights as a father, and in a sense it offered the Believers a perfect compromise, allowing them to stand behind James while moving the source of his conflict with Eunice off their immediate premises. It would also keep Eunice distracted and reduce her chances of success in court. For how could a woman petition the state for the return of her children—and how was anyone supposed to help her—if she could not say for sure where the children were?

Ultimately, the decision to move the Chapman family was founded on a wager. Despite a few bad incidents, mainly in Kentucky and Ohio, experience had shown them that a woman like Eunice stood little chance of success, and even less in New York State, where the family laws were famously stringent. Unbeknownst to them, all this was soon to change. In the late winter and early spring of 1815, Catherine Bonnel—the mother whom Eunice had seen in Watervliet—was conspiring to bring a mob to the village. Another mother, a woman named Catherine Kingsbury, was conferring with lawyers to sue for her indentured children. And Eunice was building her case in Albany—meeting with lawmakers, gathering research, and sharing her story with anyone she could—well aware that her chances of winning were slim, at best, but also knowing that she had already lost the worst.

PART II
TRIAL

"Be what you seem to be;
and seem to be what you really are."
—Father James Whittaker

1
CAPITAL CITY

The highest point in Albany was occupied by a lone female figure, carved in wood. Nearly two hundred feet above the Hudson River, atop the dome of the state capitol, was an eleven-foot-tall statue of Themis, the goddess of justice, armed with her scales and sword. She commanded a spectacular view. Beyond the tidy public square where she held court, the whole of State Street rolled out before her, wide and steep. Here, on the city's main street, Yankee grocers swept out their brand-new store fronts, aged Dutchmen in their "sharp cocked hats" puffed on their pipes as they walked toward the wharves, free blacks went to market, and Irish journeymen headed to work-shops for their daily labor.

Previously, two large churches—one Dutch, one Episcopal—as well as the old city fort had blocked this well-traveled road, but they had been moved to create parking spaces for the hun-dreds of wagons and other vehicles that passed through the city each day. Now State Street ran straight down to the Hudson, where sloops and steamers nodded past one another at all hours of the day and night, bringing teas from the Orient, fancy wares from England, merchants from Manhattan, and news from everywhere in between.

Albany was down on its luck when Eunice first made it her home. At the end of the recent war, the English had deluged the markets with their cheaper wares, devastating local producers. The city jails, which had once imprisoned Ann Lee, were now crammed with debtors who appealed piteously for what "broken meats and vegetables" their neighbors could spare. An alms house was called for, and lawmakers had to consider putting a permanent end to imprisonment for debt.

But the city had too much going for it to be down for long. Albany ranked among the most populous and prosperous cities in the nation. With a resident population of ten thousand, Albany was a small fraction of the size of Philadelphia, Boston, or New York, but a steady influx of visitors continually replenished its numbers, especially in the late winter and spring when the legislature convened. Physically, too, the city was positioned for a comeback. Situated 150 miles north of New York City, halfway to the west, this onetime frontier trading post was a commercial hub with premier placement on the water. The second ship ever to travel from America to the Far East had been launched from the city's shores in 1795, returning two years later with a bellyful of Chinese cargo. More recently, Robert Fulton ran the first steamboat along the Hudson between Albany and New York; ships taking this course alone numbered in the hundreds. Within the next decade, traffic would become even heavier as the Erie Canal became a vibrant pathway between the Hudson River and the Great Lakes, making Albany, more than ever, a "gateway to the West."

A generation earlier, Albany had been considered a Dutch province, its burgeoning cityscape defined by the distinctive rooftops favored in the Netherlands—steeply pitched with slants shaped like staircases and long, overhanging gutters. By 1815, however, the offending gutters had long been sawed off (people complained that they collected too much mud), and new streets abounded with rows of stately Federal homes, built by transplanted New Englanders like the Chapmans and Hawleys. Yankee speculators had become the richest folk in town, the Presbyterian Church rivaled the Dutch for spiritual influence, and increasingly, men with names like Williams or Oakley were running for office—although the Van Vechtens, Van Burens, and the like continued to wield a powerful influence.

Just about anything could be had in the shops and warehouses of this newly minted Yankee town—cigars from Spain, indigo from Bengal, wine from Portugal, and gilt jewelry from Morocco. The Provision Store on the corner of Hudson and Dock streets stocked pork, lard, smoked beef, cheese, butter, codfish, white beans, cider, and other staples, while others carried such treats as lemons, oranges, tamarinds, raisins, and fresh almonds. Down on South Market Street, near the water, Allen's Lucky Lottery Office dangled the possibility of sudden fortunes. A "Patriotic soldier who had lost his leg in service of his country" won twenty-five thousand dollars there. All forms of entertainment could also be found, despite ongoing protests against the impropriety of theater. Albanians flocked to see *The Magpie or Maid; Or, Which Is the Thief?*, hear an "Infant Columbian Singer" in concert, and take in panoramas, animal shows, and legerdemains. All in all, Albany had the feeling of a "new town," as the eminent New England clergyman, Timothy Dwight expressed with approval. The people of Albany, he said, were "intelligent and refined," and "few towns in this country appear so advantageously to the eye. . . ."

Of course, some improvements were left to be desired. Hogs, which continued to outnumber humans, still enjoyed free rein in the city, gorging on waste as they had done since the years of Dutch dominion and doing so until cholera became a concern at midcentury. The spirit of speculation that was becoming prevalent in cities across America was here, too, creating greater and more visible disparities in wealth. For every grand mansion boasting ornamental pillars, finely wrought railings, marble edging, and other luxuries, there were shabby shacks, shops, and backstreet boardinghouses. As of yet, the architecture was intermixed, "good" streets alternating with "bad" ones; but in growing numbers, those who could afford it were retreating to the western and southern edges of the city, leaving poorer residents to occupy the noisy, congested areas downtown and by the water.

Eunice was among those who lived at the city's core. Cooper's Tavern, her temporary home, sat on one of the busiest streets in Albany: South Pearl, which ran parallel to the Hudson along the edge of "Gallows Hill." Her crowded block represented the many faces of the city, with the "Widow Bedford's" school on one side, a theater and baker a few houses down, a Presbyterian church across the corner, and groceries and a police office nearby. But what was most convenient about Eunice's location was that it placed her near State Street, halfway up capitol hill. She would have to walk only two blocks north, past two churches, a burial ground, and a coach house, before arriving at the intersection of Albany's most tumultuous thoroughfare. From there, she could see the capitol dome and upon it, the goddess Themis, wielding her scales and sword.

* * *

Designed by Albany's premier architect, Philip Hooker, the capitol was not much to look at, candidly speaking—a "gloomy pile of stones," as one witness recalled. The brown freestone building had strong classical pretensions, and from a distance it seemed to loom large, but that grandness was illusory. The building was a mere two stories high, although the strategic placement of the dome, forty-foot columns, and oversize windows made it seem taller. Its materials were also not what they seemed. The pilasters and window trimmings may have been genuine marble, but the columns, portico, and pediment were formed of brick or wood and merely sheathed in "marble veneers." Funds were lacking, and architectural "deception" was the only available solution.

Inside, the capitol housed not just the legislature but a jumble of other political tenants, including the supreme court and mayor. Fortunately there was sufficient space for the house and senate to have their own lobbies, although some abstemious citizens were dubious of what went on inside them. The capitol, it was noted, was "most judiciously stocked with refreshments of every kind, including strong beer and cider," which surely helped make the legislative sessions as heated as they often were.

Drunk or not, New York's lawmakers had much to argue about in these formative years of their state's history. In 1815, they were to grapple hard with some of the defining issues of their times, including the future of slavery in their state and the funding of internal improvements, the shining example of which was the Erie Canal. A technological hallmark of its age, "America's first superhighway" was an achievement to which Eunice had some claim, for it was her brother, Jesse Hawley, who had first proposed the canal's overland route. Yet there were more mundane concerns to be dealt with as well, such as the incorporation of banks, payment of government officials, and most tedious of all, as far as politicians were concerned, turnpike legislation. "I wish the devil had all turnpike bills!" one frustrated legislator scribbled to his neighbor.

One of the reasons why legislators were so often overwhelmed was that the country's legal system was still quite new. Too often, existing laws failed to provide a solution to a given problem, and the legislature was called on to determine how to proceed. This was precisely the situation in which Eunice found herself in early 1815.

The fact that Eunice even turned to the law was remarkable for her times. It would not have occurred to most Americans of this era to go to the law as she did: Family disputes—no matter how painful—were supposed to be managed at home. Legal justice was an extreme last resort, usually reserved for problems that threatened more than a single family. Eunice's earlier actions had conformed to these expectations. She had tried to negotiate with her husband privately, urged him to rejoin his family, and even suggested that they divide the children. But when James fled with their brood, he crossed a crucial line. Not only did he abandon his station as a husband, but he made it impossible for Eunice to perform her defining roles as a wife and mother. At the same time, he left her trapped in her wifely role, for as long as they were married, she remained bound to him regardless of his presence, and civilly dead in the eyes of the law. In effect, fixing her status with the law was the only recourse Eunice had.

The problem was that there was nothing in the laws that spoke directly to Eunice's needs. The laws of New York were silent on the subject of child custody. Fathers' rights were so much assumed that mothers had no designated means to challenge their authority. Even after her husband died, a woman had no guarantees; a man could appoint his lover, parent, or anyone else to be his children's guardian after his death. Technically, it was possible for the state chancellor to use his discretionary powers to rescind a father's rights, but it was highly unlikely that he would.

Divorce would seem to lie more within Eunice's reach, assuming that Eunice was accurate in claiming that James had committed adultery, which provided the sole grounds for ending a marriage in New York. According to Eunice, James had actually volunteered at one point to publicly confess his adulterous behavior so that they might be divorced (an offer he evidently rescinded). Even with a divorce, however, Eunice would lack the power to obtain custody over her children. And, in fact, if she had a divorce without any provisions regarding custody, she would be in worse shape, since she would have lost her leverage against James, lacking status as his wife.

As it was, a divorce was far from guaranteed. Then, as now, marriage was not simply an agreement between two people to be made or broken at will. It was considered a religious, as well as a civil, contract that provided the basis for social stability and thus needed to be protected at all costs. At the same time, individual marriages were safeguarded as private: Only when public standards came under threat did the possibility of divorce even begin to enter the picture. In this context, divorce was perceived not as "a right," as one historian has explained, but as a "remedy for a wrong," and divorce proceedings were handled like criminal trials. One spouse charged the other with a crime (with adultery, say), and punishment was by divorce. The "criminal" lost the civil right to marry again, while the "victim" was free to do whatever he or she pleased. (All bets were off, however, if the prosecuting party was also found to have cheated or otherwise sinned. Then, it was said, the two parties deserved each other.)

What constituted a "crime" varied from state to state, and across much of the country the definitions were broadening. The years between the Revolution and the Civil War constituted what one historian has called a "formative period in the history of American divorce." The Revolution had been popularly imagined as a kind of divorce between England, the oppressive groom, and America, the innocent bride. In the years that followed, the idea of marital tyranny seemed incongruous with the new nation's democratic principles. Marriage was seen increasingly as a contract requiring consent, as opposed to mere submission. As a result, nearly every state of the union, including New York, broke with the English tradition of forbidding "full divorce," which is to say that these states granted divorces permitting at least one party to remarry. Most states went further, expanding the grounds to include not only the biblically sanctioned cause of adultery, but other causes such as abandonment, cruelty, incest, and bigamy. In response to these changes, the national divorce rate was dramatically on the rise.

But New York stayed "pure," as it was said with pride. Here adultery remained the sole criterion for ending a marriage. This purity was part of a larger conservative trend. Although the Federalist Party of Alexander Hamilton was dying everywhere, old-style Federalists who feared rule by the rabble (or who favored aristocracy, as Republicans alleged) still held sway in Albany, as well as in the courts. All recent efforts to relax the divorce laws had been quickly quashed. In 1813, a group of lawmakers had lobbied to add excessive cruelty, among other causes, to the grounds for divorce. Yet in the end, the state opted to make these grounds for an entirely new category of divorce, known as "divorces from bed and board." These "partial divorces," as they were also called, allowed couples to live apart but guaranteed little more, especially to women. A "partially divorced" woman remained bound to the terms of coverture and could not remarry. The bottom line was that in New York, a woman whose husband fled west or went off to sea and was missing for years—even a man who discovered on his wedding night that his bride was of "doubtful sex"—lacked the legal means to be fully divorced.

As for Eunice, given James's philandering, did she not already have proper grounds for seeking a full divorce? Indeed, this was a question that lawmakers would frequently ask over the years. The simple answer is yes, but the problem was that she had no guarantees. Evidence of wrongdoing was insufficient. What has been called a "guilty mind" was required, and in the Chapmans' case, this would be difficult to prove. Regardless of James's prior offenses, Eunice would be hard-pressed to present her husband as an incorrigible adulterer in need of punishment, when he had joined a celibate sect. It could be argued that, in this case, the criminal had chosen the means to punish himself and therefore no legal remedy was necessary. Whether Eunice was happy was beside the point.

Yet there was another possibility—another long shot—that was open to Eunice at this time, one that a brave soul might consider. Rather than go to the chancery, or court of equity, which was the normal venue for divorces, Eunice could petition the legislature for a personal "act of relief" that would grant her

an exception to the existing laws. In other states, such proce-
dures were popular. Legislative divorces were becoming scandalously common, particularly in western territories such as
Indiana, where vigilante justice was normative and legal pro-
scriptions were few. But once again New York stood alone: Not
a single legislative divorce had been granted in the history of
this state.

Still, New York was hardly impervious to the social changes
that were sweeping the nation, and here Eunice had reason to
hope. Westward migration, the broadening markets, religious
revivalism, and a heightened sense of individualism in the post-
Revolution era were all helping to transform the model of the
republican family. Men were still seen as the heads of their
households, but women and children were becoming recognized as individuals with separate rights and needs. Moreover,
mothers were becoming increasingly valued in the popular culture as guardians of young souls, instillers of virtue.

The law was responding to these changing views. Although
Eunice could hardly have known it, America was entering a
period of transformation in custody law. In 1813, a Pennsylvania court ruled that two girls should remain with their mother,
reasoning that their "tender years" warranted her special care.
Soon to follow suit, the New York supreme court would issue a
judgment against a father's rights, ruling in favor of maternal
grandparents after a mother's death. Paternal rights would remain presumptive for years, but the importance of a mother and
the "best interest of a child" would begin to carry weight in
custody disputes.

There were also more practical reasons for Eunice to go to
the legislature. To make her case anywhere else, she would

need "money and lawyers," which she knew the Shakers had in abundance. Moreover, a decision in a court of law would be final. If the judges sided with James and declared him not guilty of the charges Eunice brought against him, she would have to accept their ruling for good—not so in the legislature, where there was no such thing as double jeopardy.

A legislative course had its own challenges. In order to become law, a bill had to pass through both houses of the legislature, and then obtain further approval from the Council of Revision, an elite tribunal that had veto power over all laws passed by the state. A bill like Eunice's could easily stall or falter, making it through one house but not the other, or failing to pass muster with the notoriously conservative council. Yet at any point, Eunice could begin again. All that she needed to open her case—and keep it going indefinitely—was a willing sponsor, and she already had one in Asahel Paine, who had accompanied her to the Shakers before and had proved himself a supportive friend of the family.

The bill that Paine and his associates presented to the assembly in March was appropriately cautious. It did not propose to expand the grounds for divorce or suggest any other radical changes to the existing laws. And it did not grant Eunice an instant divorce or custody rights by direct legislative authority, which would have been a first in the state. Rather, the proposed act simply enabled the chancery (the court where divorce cases were normally reviewed) a onetime opportunity to hear Eunice's case, based on the grounds stated in her complaint, namely, that James had abandoned her and kept her from her children. The chancery could then award Eunice a divorce and custody rights as it saw fit. Significantly, the act refrained from determining what kind of divorce Eunice deserved, full or partial. Neither did it lay any blame on the Shakers. All it did was to enlarge the scope of the chancellor's authority in this single case.

Such a bill had passed before, on behalf of Elizabeth Ross, whose scurrilous spouse had beaten her, wrongly accused her of committing incest, left her to die when she was giving birth, and finally deserted her and her baby. But as Ross's case shows, a bill of this kind—one that merely authorized the chancery to grant a special divorce—carried risks. Although the legislature allowed Ross to apply for a divorce on special grounds, the judge who heard her case denied her plea, and she was forced to apply again for legislative relief. Still, Ross ultimately succeeded, and her model was far less risky than the alternative—to apply for rights that had never been granted.

The precedent was not enough. In early April, the house voted down Eunice's bill, 44 to 33. However, lawmakers did not give up on Eunice entirely. The assembly proceeded to investigate the larger issue of child custody, and on April 17, both houses of the legislature united to pass the first custody law of New York State, which was in turn approved by the Council of Revision. The "Act Concerning the Custody of Children" enabled women who were divorced or merely separated to apply for custody of their children. It also allowed them to use writs of habeas corpus to have their children brought before the supreme court in order to initiate custody hearings.

The passage of this act was a legal triumph, and it should have helped Eunice achieve her ultimate goal. Whether or not she was able to obtain a full divorce, she now had the legal means to seek custody over her children, as well as a way to demand that they be brought before the courts. Yet a fundamental problem remained. In order to take advantage of this law, Eunice had to know where her children were being held. To obtain this information, she had to return to the site of the children's disappearance and plead with the people who she believed had the answer: the Shaker Elders.

In May, Eunice journeyed back to Watervliet, where she begged for a "privilege" to speak with the leadership, but she was shut out. No matter her tears or even her offer to confess her sins, the Believers would not allow her near their leaders. Ultimately, they showed that they understood her predicament all too well. According to Eunice, when she insisted that she had a "lawful right to demand a maintenance from her husband," the lower-level Sisters whom she confronted aptly observed, "You must find him first."

Hoping to do just that, Eunice proceeded to ride out to every Shaker village she could, the closest ones being in New Lebanon, New York; Hancock and Tyringham, Massachusetts; and Enfield, Connecticut. Each destination required hours of travel and a handsome fare for a terrible ride. Thrown together with strangers of all classes in a coach, Eunice rode over cobblestones and dirt roads, which were clogged with dust, animals, and country traffic. If she was lucky and sat by a window, she had some air; otherwise she was trapped, her bottom sore from the bumping, her gown soaked from the enclosed summer heat. At night she stayed at taverns of varying quality, sharing rooms and even beds with people she did not know. At every destination she met the same blank response: The Shakers would tell her nothing. The best intelligence she had indicated that her family remained in Watervliet. With no further leads, Eunice was forced to return to Albany.

By now Eunice had discovered, as other Shaker wives had before, that her existing legal rights would do her little good. She could make a case for claiming her children, and yet she remained paralyzed by her lack of information and the Shakers' refusal to cooperate. It was clear that she would have to take a stronger stand against the Believers if she was going to see her children again.

2

EVIL REPORTS

Over the next year, Eunice settled into a new life in Albany, supporting herself by teaching. Her choice of occupation is not surprising, given that teaching was one of few "respectable" wage-earning options for a woman of her class. She might have considered starting up a business making fancy goods, such as hats, but teaching required little investment or overhead. All she needed was a basic education and a willingness to be with children. Though her earnings were scant, Eunice knew how to live within her means. Every day, as she helped small hands scratch out letters over slates and taught youngsters their sums, she had renewed motivation to put everything she had toward her ongoing hunt for her children.

So far, she was without success. Now and then, Eunice would hear alarming rumors that James was dead, but she could find nothing to substantiate this claim. It was as if her family had altogether vanished. No letters arrived to tell her that her children were safe or even alive, and there was no further word of James in Durham.

Nevertheless, there was progress on other fronts. Since her arrival, Eunice had tapped into a veritable network, in and around Albany, of people antagonistic to the Shakers—people like Derrick Veeder, a onetime Shaker Deacon who was struggling to recover property and daughters in Watervliet, and the embittered relatives of a young Sister named Susannah Shepard in New Lebanon. Everyone with a gripe against the society seemed to know everyone else, and all these people pooled their resources as they planned their various attacks. They passed on news of happenings in different Shaker communities, kept each other abreast of the latest legal cases, and gave each other crucial moral support.

Among these new confederates Eunice found another kind of home, a place where others understood her grief. And through these friends she became acquainted with a whole new world of writings about the sect: works like Valentine Rathbun's *Some Brief Hints of a Religious Scheme, Taught and Propagated by a Number of EUROPEANS, Living in a Place Called Nisqueunia, in the State of NEW-YORK* and Thomas Brown's *An Account of the People Called Shakers*. Perhaps more than any other source, these critical first-hand accounts educated Eunice about strategies for dealing with the Shakers and helped shape her future course.

Such writings preyed upon the fears of an American public that was already predisposed to be suspicious of the sect. The Shakers' odd appearance, unusual sexual practices, social isolation, and peculiar forms of worship—not to mention their female leader—all made them vulnerable to others' mistrust and hostility. Americans prized "candor" and reviled exclusive, secretive orders, as the concurrent and growing movement against the Masons attests. Anti-Catholic sentiment also ran high, and to many, these strange people with their rigid hierarchy and demands for confession smacked of popery. Even the Shakers' prosperity, which had earned them respectability, could count against them. To some, the Shakers simply seemed too rich, too cultish to have made their money through honest means.

The men who wrote against the Shakers—until Eunice came along, there were no women—enflamed these anxieties. The more extreme accounts portrayed the Shakers as Tories or foreigners who had promiscuous sex and ran a system of "wage slavery" in which Elders got fat off the backs of rank-and-file drones, but even the more moderate accounts claimed that the Shakers deprived their citizens of key liberties—above all, the right to think for themselves and worship as they pleased. All of the critics insisted that the Shakers were far more ambitious and insidious than they seemed. As the ex-Shaker Valentine Rathbun colorfully wrote: "The leaders of this dreadful catastrophe, like the bowels of Aetna, are ever vomiting up their sulphur; like wildfire it flies, and catches at a distance, and spreads like a plague."

For a mother with children living in Shaker society, such books could not have made for happy reading. Even Thomas Brown's famously "objective" account, which president Benjamin Silliman of Yale College would admire for its apparent evenhandedness and Thomas Jefferson had in his library, included shocking allegations. Brown suggested, for instance, that the Shakers once practiced self-mortification and that some of their men had been castrated. Every time Eunice came across such charges, she must have recoiled, wondering if her children were being subjected to these tortures as well. Yet for a rising anti-Shaker like Eunice, these polemics were also inspirational.

The more she heard and read of broken Shaker families—of women like herself ravaged with loss, crazed, and homeless—the more Eunice began to see her personal journey as part of a larger mission and to see herself in a new role. All this time, she had believed that God had a plan for her, even if she did not know what it was. Now she realized that God had put her through these trials for a reason—to speak out not just for herself but also on behalf of the countless other anguished wives and mothers who had permanently lost everything they had to the society and become, as she said, "wandering idiots."

In her mind, her quest was not just biblical, it was epic: She was Abraham put to the test, Rachel weeping for her children, but even more, a heroine of sorts—even a kind of savior—who was needed to free society from the Shaker curse. She viewed herself as an "instrument" in God's hand. This convergence of the religious and sentimental in Eunice's imagining of her quest would prove to be pivotal, not only helping to convince others of her righteousness but buoying Eunice herself with singular confidence. Knowing that she was part of a preordained narrative, with God as its author, Eunice could be sure that somehow she would succeed.

One year after her children had disappeared, however, she had a way to go. Eunice recommenced her legal case against the Shakers in early 1816, a season of brutal cold and flooding. One day in January, merely by walking from the dwelling to the sawmill, Elder Seth suffered frostbite on his face. That month, sudden thaws caused dangerous floods between Albany and nearby Troy. By one report, a sloop full of wheat was carried away and sank dramatically within view of the capital city. Undeterred by the elements, Eunice resumed her regular walks up State Street to the capitol, her poor winter garb drawn closely about her small frame.

Sensing that her luck had run out in the assembly, Eunice turned now to the senate, where she found a new champion in her local senator, Moses Cantine of Catskill. The towering, forty-one-year-old Republican lawyer was known for the "purity" of both his public and private views and for being so giving and open that it was impossible to dislike him. What the senator lacked in terms of natural ability he was known to make up for with ardor. After hearing Eunice's story, Cantine agreed to sponsor a new petition for her relief, a divorce bill that, with luck, would amount to something more.

Eunice's new ally would be one of a series of legislative sponsors in the years to come, most of them lasting no more than a season. Much of this turnover was inevitable. Assemblymen held one-year terms, and while senators' terms were longer, elections rotated by region, so that the senate changed annually, as well. But there were other cases (for example, Asahel Paine, Penfield's friend) where lawmakers who remained in office dropped out for unexplained reasons. Their motives, while undocumented, are perhaps not surprising given Eunice's history of conflict.

Luckily, these cases were offset by still others, such as the one-term assemblyman Michael Freligh, a physician and father from Niskeyuna, who continued to help Eunice long after leaving office. These men joined a core group of largely unnamed supporters without whom Eunice surely would not have gotten as far as she did. This anonymous crew of friends, anti-Shakers, and politicians gave Eunice free counsel, spread her message, distributed materials, and even did behind-the-scenes dirty work. Freligh, for instance, was said to have ghostwritten petitions lambasting the Shakers.

Yet even with legislative sponsors and other supporters, Eunice did much of her work alone. Her stamina was formidable. Following the opening of the legislature, she personally met with nearly every member—126 assemblymen and 32 senators—to promote her cause. These interviews were nerve-racking for Eunice, since she was well aware that women were supposed to shun the public eye. Her task was made all the more difficult because most lawmakers did not have separate offices. Instead, they met in the taverns or public houses where they lodged—ambiguous spaces, where the line between public and private interaction became blurred, and decent women were not expected to wander alone. Being determined, however, to appeal directly to every member of the legislature, Eunice set foot in such spaces when necessary, opening herself up to charges of brazenness, or worse.

Fortunately, Eunice's hearers seemed to forgive her for her transgressions—at least for now—so movingly did she speak of how she and "other poor distressed women" had been "robbed of their husbands and children, and all their property, and left friendless and forlorn, to the mercy of the world." What if it was true that the Shakers were not the harmonious folk they seemed, but cultists, fanatics, secretly bent on robbing society of its young, of destroying the social order? If there was even a possibility of truth, the state was required to investigate.

But beyond sharing her own story, Eunice attacked the Shakers on a second, more subversive front as the legislature reconvened in the early months of 1816. Well aware that the Shakers were bringing their own case for a military exemption to the capital, Eunice conspired with her anti-Shaker associates to launch a public smear campaign against the sect. She and her friends, including the brother of a Shaker Sister and an angry apostate, circulated scandalous tales of Shaker abuses, telling lawmakers and anyone else who cared to listen that the Shakers harmed youngsters, denied children a proper education, and rejected the Bible. They also dredged up old rumors of how the early Shakers would strip and dance naked. (In one eyewitness account, which Eunice may have cited, an apostate recalled seeing a young Shaker order his father to strip before a large crowd of men and women. The son then screamed abuses before hanging his father upside down by his feet.) The Believers were rattled by these accusations—and their results. In early March, Elder Jethro Turner mourned that the "evil reports" Eunice had spread had inspired much prejudice in the house and ultimately stalled the Shakers' case before the legislature.

The Shakers were forced to respond. For them, too, it had been a tumultuous year, with escalating crises involving the families of converts. Catherine Bonnel had stormed through Watervliet with her pistol-wielding brothers and seized her daughter Caroline. In New Lebanon, the enraged relatives of Sister Susannah Shepard led two mob attacks, threatening to tear down the Shakers' gates if the young woman did not come forward. Then there was the case of Catherine Kingsbury, an "artful young widow" who had nearly managed to win her children through the courts, even though she had signed a paper giving them up. The woman's lawyers had swayed justice with vicious incriminations, making much of how the Shakers parted parents and children and leading one judge to conclude: "That faith which teaches children to treat their parents as strangers —which alienates their affections from those that gave them birth and makes it criminal to love them cannot be entitled to the highest veneration or respect."

In addition to such family matters, conflicts over the state militia laws had come to a head over the past year, causing even greater turmoil in the Shaker community. The previous fall, two men, one of them a constable, had gone to Watervliet pretending that they needed axes. Once within the village, they seized a young Brother named Justice Harwood, hauled him to their carriage, and jailed him for failing to report for duty or pay military fines. Justice was eventually released when his fine was paid by a non-Shaker friend, but one week later, the Shakers were harassed again. While a group of Believers was traveling back from the Kingsbury trial, mourning their defeat, a second constable seized their wagon as payment for militia fines owed for other Brethren. The Shakers were stranded and forced to pay a hefty sum for a ride home. The next day, the constable returned their wagon and one of the horses, but he sold the other and pocketed part of the proceeds.

Determined to protect themselves against further persecution, the Shakers had spent much of the year lobbying hard for a permanent release from military obligations, courting legislators, circulating thousands of pages of written materials, and spending countless hours meeting with the governor, the attorney general, and other state officials. Now they were closer than ever to reaching their goal. They were not about to lose their chance on account of Eunice.

The society's biggest guns came in from New Lebanon, and a rotating team of Brothers began traveling into Albany on nearly a daily basis to meet with legislators and attend sessions. Day after day, the normally reclusive Believers also played host to lawmakers in Watervliet, treating their guests to village tours and exquisite Shaker feasts. Even Lucy Wright, who normally shunned worldly affairs, got involved, despite the personal cost. The Shaker Mother was in considerable pain at this time, her left arm so lame that she could not comb her own hair. Still, she came out to offer special prayers for the Brothers headed to the legislature.

The Believers worked diligently to counteract Eunice's charges. They presented lawmakers with handwriting samples from children to prove that their youngsters were schooled. They dispensed reading materials about their religion. And, at every opportunity, they presented their own side of the story, exposing Eunice as a disorderly woman, a troublemaker, and a shrew.

To Eunice, the Shakers' attack on her character was more than an embarrassment. This was an era when men killed one another over matters of reputation. Dueling was still a legal, if controversial, practice, and not many years ago, a bloodbath had taken place on State Street after a group of Republican statesmen publicly questioned the honor of an illustrious Federalist general. For a woman, even more so than a man, maintaining a good name was a matter of survival. In Eunice's own words, a woman's "only dependence for existence" was her reputation, and she was appalled at the Shakers efforts to "maul and mangle" hers—"like so many *hounds*." In order to clear her name, she had her father and brother-in-law, Peter Penfield, both justices of the peace, gather depositions from people who could attest to her virtue as a wife, woman, and mother. These witnesses included one young woman and three men from Durham and several of Eunice's relatives, including Penfield.

Toward the end of March, witnesses for both Eunice and the Shakers were called forward to testify before the senate committee headed by Moses Cantine. By now, both sides were at risk of losing more than custody of the Chapman children. A woman's honor and a society's security were also on the line.

3

CIVILLY DEAD

Seth Youngs Wells was no stranger to Albany. Almost two decades earlier—in another lifetime, it seemed —he had been a young schoolmaster in the city. In those days, he had ambled about the city in his teacher's frock, cutting a markedly different figure from the one he presented now as he entered the capitol in his homespun Shaker mantle, his shoulder-length locks bobbing behind him. If the Shaker Elder struck an odd appearance in the city, Albany, too, must have seemed changed to him, its buildings and inhabitants looking garish and dirty next to those of his simple Shaker home.

The prospect of attending the senate hearing must have been troubling to Elder Seth, given that he was sure to be interrogated about the circumstances of James Chapman's departure from his society. The Elder could not, in all honesty, deny knowledge of this event, since he had personally given James directions and a wagon to Enfield. However, he could not very well reveal everything he knew—not without giving the lie to the Shakers' appearance of sanctity and straightforwardness.

Elder Seth was thus in the awkward position of having to present a kind of fiction, whereas his people stood for the truth.

But Elder Seth was a veteran Believer, one who had overcome far greater challenges than what he faced now. He had been a Shaker in Watervliet when there was scarcely enough to eat, inadequate living space, and not even a nearby source of water. In those early days, he had been required to labor hard to "overcome the flesh, and crucify a carnal nature," all the while receiving little spiritual guidance from his Elders or support from his peers, many of whom were corrupt souls merely posing as converts. At his worst, the Elder had come close to despair. As he wrote: "I did not then think that one person in a hundred, under my circumstances, could have endured his trials, and still maintain his faith and station." Yet he had persevered and never once considered leaving his people. Throughout, he was sustained by his conviction in what the Believers stood for and by his ability to see past surface imperfections to the good he knew was at the society's core. A similar kind of conviction would carry him through on this day. Whatever he had to say and however he had to say it, he would do so knowing that he acted in the service of God.

Again, the Elder was fortunate that he did not have to face the trials alone. He traveled to Albany with his assistant, thirty-six-year-old Joseph Hodgson, who was well equipped to deal with various people of the world. A native of England, Hodgson had traveled to the West Indies, outfitted in a fine merchant ship provided by his wealthy father, and lived for a time in Spanish captivity before meeting the Shakers in Watervliet. Despite fortune and a family waiting for him overseas, Hodgson had quickly given everything up to become a Believer and, being well-educated and entrepreneurial, presented a good public face for his society. Along with Elder Seth, Hodgson had been present on the winter night when James Chapman had begun his journey to Enfield, New Hampshire. Still, as both men knew, it was Elder Seth who was principally on trial.

The two Shakers climbed the dark stone steps of the state capitol, passing under the statue of Themis and crossing a grand, open hall paved with fine Italian marble, before entering the senate chamber for their interview. The room was stuffy, poorly ventilated even by the standards of the time, and oppressively decorated, with a ridiculous ornamental eagle hanging overhead, and useless classical flourishes everywhere. But worst of all, in the middle of that airless, gloomy space were some of the very last people the Shakers would have wanted to see. There was Eunice herself—no longer clad in a modest Shaker gown but wearing the close-fitting style of her times—appearing all injured and tearful, while gazing contemptuously at them. And beside her was an ugly crew of what the Believers often called "backsliders," "bad apples," "heaven-daring rebels," or "troublesome, unsound, rotten-hearted hypocrites": ex-Shakers.

To the Shakers, such apostates were the lowliest of all souls, since they had knowingly turned their backs on salvation. The Believers told dark tales about what happened to such people, a large number of whom seemed to suffer from mysterious ailments, sudden reversals of fortune, and "extraordinary" or "untimely deaths." One Selah Abbot Jr., who agitated an anti-Shaker mob in New Lebanon, was said to have died "in an awful manner, with his eyes wide open." His friends were unable to shut them, so the poor man was sent to his grave with his eyes ghoulishly turned toward the heavens. Another man who joined an anti-Shaker mob rotted away at the limbs and shook uncontrollably. As a result, he was unable to perform sexually and became celibate despite himself.

From the beginning, these former Believers had caused some of the worst public damage against the sect through the outrageous tales they told about their experiences in the society. They whispered of Brothers and Sisters frolicking naked and coupling in private corners, of Elders hanging children from trees or torturing converts—lies that insulted true Believers like Elder Seth, who had fought so hard to mortify their carnal appetites. Looking at the regrettably familiar group of men and women assembled before them—formerly their Brothers and Sisters, now their enemies—the Shakers could only guess what kinds of falsehoods they would hear today.

The Shakers had little time to reflect, however, for they were soon called forth to testify as the first witnesses before the senate committee. With Elder Seth taking the lead, the two men tried their best to put forth their version of what happened between Eunice and their society. The Elder insisted that James had made every reasonable attempt to take care of his wife and children, even renting a house for them near the society, but that Eunice had rejected everything. If anyone were to blame for the family's collapse, he argued, it was the woman herself. Certainly, the Shakers should not be held responsible: Without their intervention, Eunice would have lost James long ago.

The Shakers may have gained some ground as they spoke of the Chapmans' marital problems, but they lost their footing as the discussion shifted to the circumstances under which the children came into their society. The committee began by asking if the children had been indentured. To this, Elder Seth gave a firm "Nay." There was soon the sound of shuffling, as

Peter Penfield's deposition and other papers were produced, showing that the children had been indentured to the sect. The Elder was now in the discomforting position of admitting that, in fact, "the children were bound."

"To whom was the eldest daughter bound?" the committee next asked. With greater prudence, Elder Seth answered, "I cannot say." This time, Eunice herself could not hold back, and she exclaimed, "Can that be possible?" She told the room that Susan had explicitly said that Elder Seth had held her hand to sign the paper. The Elder simply replied, "The child was mistaken."

If the Shaker had hoped that the lawmakers would check Eunice for interrupting, he quickly learned his mistake. Rather than dismiss her, the senators continued to ask, "Was not that child capable of knowing and relating such a circumstance?" After some pressure, Elder Seth was forced to give the name of the person to whom she had been bound. (It does not remain on record.)

Now the committee insisted that the Shakers reveal James's and the children's present location. "Where is Mr. Chapman and where are the children? How did Mr. Chapman and the children go away? Did he take wagon and horses or a sleigh?" they asked in rapid succession. In each instance, Elder Seth protested his ignorance with a simple "I cannot say." "How could Mr. Chapman take the children and go from your house without your knowing it?" was their final, incredulous response. The Shaker persisted, "I cannot say."

Here another one of the Shakers' enemies intervened. Calling himself a former Deacon in their society, Derrick Veeder—a man both Believers knew all too well—cut in to say that "it was impossible for any of the Shakers to take horses and car-

riage, and go off without the Elders' knowledge." Veeder added
that the Shakers' earlier claim that James had rented a house
for Eunice was also a lie. For the third time the senators pressed
Elder Seth, and he was at last forced to admit that "he did not
know for a certainty" that James had rented a house.

The matter of housing was a crucial point and a pivotal con-
cession. If James had indeed offered Eunice a home of her own
and Eunice had rejected it, then she was essentially to blame
for the dissolution of their marriage. A wife was entitled to support from her husband, a home and other necessities, but not
under whatever terms she pleased. If, on the other hand, the
offer of a house was merely a ruse, then the case could be made
that James had failed in his husbandly duties and that the Shakers, as his accomplices, were also at fault.

As the interrogation drew to a close, Elder Seth tried to make
a final case for his people, focusing not on their actions but on
Eunice's bad character. But the mood in the senate chamber
had become overwhelmingly hostile toward the Shakers, and
the leaders of the committee silenced the Elder, warning that
he would only damage his cause more by going on any further
about Mrs. Chapman, who had numerous depositions attesting
to her virtues as a woman, wife, and mother.

Thus chastened, the Believers were forced to watch in silence as, one after another, Eunice's witnesses recited their
complaints against the Shaker world. Derrick Veeder was especially trying. The man made a great show of being a Believer,
addressing the Shakers in the room with "thee" and "thou" and
calling them Brothers. Veeder had indeed been a Shaker Deacon, but he had lost his faith and his position roughly around
the time that Eunice first lost her children. The two upstarts had
something in common. Veeder's five daughters, like Eunice's

children, remained in the society, although in Veeder's case, it was the girls themselves who refused to leave.

Veeder testified that he had been a Shaker for sixteen years (roughly as long as Elder Seth had been) and that he had left the sect two years earlier. He said that he had been in Watervliet when James Chapman first entered the society and that he held the Shakers accountable for Eunice's suffering. According to Veeder, James had spoken highly of his wife and had left her only because he considered it "his duty to forsake all for Christ's sake," as the Shakers believed. Veeder also said that he had personally offended the Elders when he had complained about James being allowed to remain in the society when his family was helpless in the world. Veeder concluded that Eunice's charges against the Shakers were all true and that Thomas Brown's book—which Eunice wanted the committee to consider as evidence—told the truth as well.

Hearing Thomas Brown's name, Elder Seth leaped up from his chair and faced Derrick Veeder, Jonathan Hodgson springing up beside him. Brown's account of his experiences as a Shaker proselyte had caused more damage to the Shakers than any previous work. The book was not as lurid or dramatic as others, but that was precisely why it was so powerful. Presenting himself as a candid and impartial former Believer, even a kind of historian, Brown was able to give credibility to what was basically a polemic against Shakerism. Both Elder Seth and his companion appeared in the book, and Seth, in particular, came off badly. He and Brown had been novitiates together, and in Brown's eyes, Brother Seth had been the perfect young Believer, utterly blind and willing to ignore his own judgments in obedience to the Shaker faith—"whether it be right or not."

Elder Seth knew that Brown was neither as sincere nor as

balanced as he pretended to be. Like Eunice, Brown had had numerous fallings-out in his hometown, a testament to his combative and unstable character. And while Brown continued to bill himself as a former Shaker convert, who had demonstrated strong leadership potential in the society, the Shakers took issue with this presentation. To them, Thomas Brown was nothing more than a small-time salesman, petty preacher, and occasional visitor, who had shown a bad habit of picking fights on matters of doctrine with anyone who would engage him.

Elder Seth tried to state his objections to the committee, even standing up to be heard, but whereas Eunice and Veeder had been allowed to intervene, the Shaker was silenced. Veeder had the last word, protesting piously, "Brother Seth, you need not contend against Thomas's book, for he has wrote as much for thee, as he has against thee. I have personal knowledge of the most part of it; and I being so well acquainted with Thomas, know him to be so candid, that he will not misrepresent anything."

Even more destructive witnesses were called forth to testify. One woman from Niskeyuna swore that during the previous spring, Eldress Fanny Waterman had told her that the Chapman children were still in Watervliet. Another man from Albany reported that he saw James abandon his wife in the city streets and that he had personally gone with Eunice's brothers-in-law to the Shaker village and learned that her children had been bound to the society.

But worst of all was Catherine Geddis, who had lived with the Shakers for ten years, since the age of ten. Geddis claimed that the Shakers treated even sick children cruelly and that the leaders of the society gorged themselves on "the most sumptuous food, when the youth had to accept the most ordinary." She also said that young people were forbidden the use of pen and paper (she herself could not even write her name) and that they were not allowed to read the Bible as they pleased. As a former schoolmaster, Elder Seth must have found this testimony especially hard to bear. It was true that the Shakers favored a limited education, believing that too much learning hindered the mind, sense, and spirit, but there was no doubt that they taught their children basic and necessary skills. The Shakers had hoped to put such allegations to rest by sending children's writing samples to the legislature, yet, incredibly, the committee allowed these charges to be heard again.

Geddis further testified that she had personally witnessed one of the most damning incidents reported by Thomas Brown. Three girls in Watervliet had reportedly enjoyed watching two flies copulate on a windowsill. As punishment for "gratifying their carnal inclinations," they were allegedly forced to strip naked and whip one another. They did so until one of the girls screamed "murder!"—at which point they were told to stop and wash themselves in a nearby brook. They followed orders under the steady gaze of two Shaker men, one of them an Elder, the other a mere Brother.

Geddis's final blow was to draw strong parallels between herself and the Chapman children. Geddis claimed that her mother, like Eunice, had tried to visit her in the society, but the Elders had forced her to push her mother away and tell her not to come "with her carnal and old natural affections." Eventually, Geddis's father obtained a writ of habeas corpus to force the Shakers to present her before a court, but then the Shakers, she claimed, sneaked her away to another village under the cover of night. During the journey, she "had to ride over hills, rocks, and logs, and swim her horse across a deep creek . . . and then ride ten miles in her wet and frozen clothes, which caused her a fit of sickness." Meanwhile, the Shakers told her father she had "drowned herself." One could only wonder if the Chapman children had suffered a similar fate.

By the time Geddis was finally dismissed and the hearing was over, the other witnesses and even the senators were glaring at the Shakers, scornful of every word Elder Seth had uttered. Even so, the Shakers knew they had an edge, for, regardless of what anyone suspected, what action could their enemies take against them without proof that the children remained with them—without knowing precisely where the children were?

Moreover, while Eunice had her supporters, the Shakers boasted even better connections beyond the senate chamber. Although they had their enemies, the Shakers also had many friends in and around Albany on account of their excellent industries, good works, sharp business skills, and virtuous piety —not to mention their willingness to pay high taxes. Among their allies were men in the highest levels of state government. For example, the lawyer the Shakers hired to win their most difficult legal cases was the former state attorney general Abraham Van Vechten. Even more important, they had the sympathies of the present attorney general, Martin Van Buren—one of the most influential men in New York and a future American president.

Van Buren, a neat, fastidious gentleman whose home in Kinderhook, New York, was twenty miles away from the New Lebanon Shakers, was a longtime admirer of the Shakers' peaceful, efficient communities. He considered the Shakers his friends and neighbors and helped them whenever he could as a representative of Columbia County. He was particularly useful now, since he happened to be related to Senator Cantine by marriage: The two men's wives were sisters.

Van Buren had already persuaded his brother-in-law to put off Eunice's case as long as possible, so that it would not interfere with his own efforts to push the Shakers' military exemption through the legislature. His calculation proved perfect. The very day that Elder Seth faced his hostile tribunal, the Shakers learned that the assembly had finally approved their military exemption. Two days later, the senate followed suit, and Freegift Wells exulted that, despite "much opposition from the prejudiced part of the legislature, occasioned by the slanderous tongue of Eunice Chapman," the bill was to become law.

The Shakers' celebration was short-lived, however. A month after interviewing the Elders, the senate committee finally completed its report, and its findings were scandalous.

Early in the evening of April 12, as the sun sank behind the capitol dome and servants moved through the senate lighting candles, Moses Cantine rose to deliver his committee's finding on Eunice Chapman's request for relief. The session had started at five o'clock in the evening, and the senators had already endured multiple readings of bills passed, plus a tedious statement of appropriations—all at an hour when most Albanians were washing up for their evening meal. However, the senator from Ulster County would hold them off even longer with an unusually detailed report.

For nearly two months, the committee had examined witnesses, studied depositions, and combed through piles of evidence, including advertisements James Chapman had placed against his wife and a letter he had sent her after fleeing with their children. They had determined, unequivocally, that Mrs.

Chapman had been wronged—not just by her husband but by the Shakers.

It was true, the committee acknowledged, that many rumors about the Shakers were unfounded; yet their fundamental tenets were unmistakable. They considered marriage "unlawful and immoral" and had no respect for the legal, moral, and religious bonds and duties of the outside world, a world they considered sick and sinful. "It would be a waste of time," Senator Cantine concluded on behalf of his committee, to give a detailed proof of how damaging such ideals could be to families, especially to wives and children. That much would be obvious to anyone with sense. It was equally obvious that the law needed to step in. The problem the committee had wrestled with was determining *how*.

They had feared, first of all, that if they granted a divorce in this particular case, they would be opening a door for unscrupulous persons to obtain easy "Shaker divorces": All anyone would have to do to end a marriage would be to join the Shakers for a short time. But even more than that, the committee worried about the question of religious freedom. It was the state's responsibility to interfere with a religion if it became a public hazard; yet it would be better to err on the side of tolerating too much, the committee believed, than to threaten the principle of religious liberty, "the brightest gem in the political institutions of the state."

But at last, Senator Cantine announced, the committee had come upon a solution that they believed would protect women like Eunice Chapman, prevent "Shaker divorces," and support the Shakers' freedom of religious expression, all at once. Dissolve the Chapman marriage, he proposed, and further declare anyone who, like James Chapman, left his family to join the Shakers civilly dead—allow the law, in short, to treat such people as if they were actually dead, incapable of owning or inheriting anything. This deprivation of civil standing, he reasoned, should provide ample deterrence against mere seekers of divorce, while providing a legal affirmation of what the Shakers already stated as their beliefs. After all, the Believers themselves declared that they were not of this world and that they rejected private property and all family ties.

The proposed law, the senator observed, was "not without analogy" in the existing laws. In New York, convicted criminals faced the same fate, a civil death, while their spouses became instantly divorced. And, in the committee's view, there was "no difference in the sufficiency of the cause of divorce," whether a man was permanently separated from his wife "by the strong arm of the law" or by "religious delusion."

But there was yet another parallel, which the committee did not acknowledge, and indeed, of which they may not even have been consciously aware: Married women, too, were bereft of their civil identity. What Eunice achieved, then, or could hope to achieve from the senate's report, was an exquisite reversal of roles. If the legislature passed what the committee prescribed, it would be James and the Shakers who would be dead to the world, while Eunice herself would be civilly reborn.

In the end, the senate committee's proposed resolution read as follows:

RESOLVED . . . that it would be expedient and proper to pass a law, declaring Eunice Chapman divorced from her marriage contract with her husband; and also declaring that all persons having families and who shall hereafter attach themselves to the society called Shakers, shall be considered as civilly dead: That their estates shall be disposed of as though they were really dead; and rendering them forever thereafter incapable of taking any estate, real or personal, by inheritance.

The Shakers were appalled by the committee's report. Spiritually, they may have considered themselves "not of this world," but without a certain amount of support from the world they rejected, the society could not hope to survive. Were the senate committee's proposal to become law, the Shakers could lose hold of all their hard-earned property, since people with Shaker relatives might demand the return of their real estate and other belongings or even a share of what the Shakers owned in common. Also, the insults to their religion could not have been worse. The proposed law made Believers no better than criminals, nonentities in the eyes of the world.

Fortunately for the Shakers, no further action would be taken anytime soon. By the time Cantine presented his committee's findings, the legislative session was soon to end. There would not be time to pass a bill in the senate, let alone both houses of legislature. All that Cantine could do for Eunice was to order copies of his committee's report to be distributed throughout the legislature—as a set of recommendations, nothing more. The Chapman case would be put off until the legislature convened next, which was not for many months.

For Eunice the postponement was no doubt agonizing. Well over a year had passed since she had seen her children, and she would have to wait nearly a year more to have any hope of claiming them. And while the senate committee had made some excellent proposals, who knew if their resolution would be picked up when the legislature met again? Yet in other ways the break between legislative sessions was to her advantage. Watching Elder Seth stammer and bristle at the mere sound of Thomas Brown's name during the senate hearings, Eunice had witnessed the power of the written word. Shortly after the legislature closed for the season, she made it clear to the Shakers that she meant to harness this power herself. The Shakers received a "very threatening epistle" from Eunice, demanding that the Believers give her back her children and swearing that if they did not, she would write "a great heap of dreadful bad things" about the society and send her writing throughout New York, to other states, and even to Congress.

At the time, the Shakers did not bother to answer her. Later, however, when there were rumblings about Eunice's writing, they began to worry. James and his presiding Elder, John Lyon, came up together from Enfield to speak with leaders in New York. It was decided that James would remain in New Hampshire with the children but that he would be on call. With a woman as "crafty" as Eunice, as Elder Seth said, one never knew what might come next.

4

TORTURED IN THE WHIRLWIND OF AFFLICTION AND WOE

The late spring and summer of 1816 were freakish times for the skittish or superstitious. In April and May, dark spots were visible on the sun—about "the size of a musket ball," by one Shaker's estimate. Wild winds raged about the Northeast, promising rain but yielding nothing. By June, the weather had become positively bizarre. The hills around Albany and all the rooftops were white with so much snow that any reasonable person might have thought it was January. When Shaker Sisters put their handkerchiefs out to dry in the summer sun, the light cloths froze within minutes. Everyone wore mittens, and when the Brothers went out to work on the highways in June, they wore their greatcoats and wrapped fabric around their ears.

These ecological oddities (attributed much later to volcanic activity on the other side of the world) were accompanied by other uncanny events. Early in the summer, two Brothers came upon a corpse in a nearby marsh, the body of a madwoman who had strayed from her home. Then, toward the end of summer, a visitor who had come by with his four daughters met a brutal death when his horse threw him to the ground and—within full view of his girls—pulled his wagon wheel smoothly over his neck. For a people who believed in signs and premonitions, such events could not have boded well.

All this time, Eunice was surviving on her own in Albany. By now she had found new quarters on Albany's Market Street, a long, bustling avenue that ran parallel to the Hudson, stretching out toward Watervliet in the north and abutting the ferry docks in the south. At the heart of this street was a vast covered market. On warm afternoons, after the butchers had left for the day, those who could afford to would drag their chairs out to where the meats had been and, ignoring the lingering smell of blood, would smoke, gossip, and scheme—politics being foremost on everyone's agenda. The Shakers were another common sight in this area of town, reminding Eunice daily of her children's ongoing existence as Believers.

Eunice lived on the homelier lower end of the street, at 610 South Market, in the house of a man named Thomas Lynch. As a single woman, she did not lack for company in this corner of Albany. Four widows lived a block or so away, one working as a hatmaker and the others, like Eunice, boarding with families. A pair of male hairdressers lived next door to Eunice, and there were grocers all around. Two houses down was also the steamboat office, which doubled as the captain's home. The neighborhood was a poor one, as the nearness of the docks and the concentration of widows attest, but in a way it was familiar; from her doorstep, Eunice could smell the river and hear the sound of moored boats slapping against the docks, all of which recalled her girlhood in Bridgeport.

Eunice spent much of her time in these intervening months teaching, probably in the same room where she ate and slept. As she worked with pupils about George, Susan, or Julia's age, she could not help reflecting on how her own children were doing and whether they had forgotten everything that they had learned with her. George had been an especially avid student of religion and history. He had read through the entire Bible before he was ten and seemed to retain every story. Once, Eunice had overheard George telling his friends about Cyrus, the Persian king, and she had flushed with pride. She secretly believed that there was something extraordinary about her son and was prone to weeping whenever she thought of him.

Eunice became equally emotional when she imagined her daughters. She missed Susan's lively chatter and dreamed of holding Julia, her "long-lost babe," in her arms. Eunice was painfully aware that, being so young, Julia was the most likely to adapt to Shaker life—and thus the most likely to forget her. Nearly six years old, Julia had already spent a third of her life as a Believer. Who knew if she even remembered her home?

However, Eunice refused to be paralyzed by such thoughts. Never one to languish, she spent every spare moment channeling her distress into her writing. As the sights and sounds of the city receded in the dark, and her hard-earned candle dripped down, Eunice would hunker down with pen in hand and struggle to recall the smallest details of her dealings with Shaker society, from the timing of her visits, to the Shakers' harsh words. At times she could not see clearly for crying and would have to stop to blot her page, but she always pressed on, working her anguish into her narrative and describing her falling tears in the hope that one day, a distant reader might share in her feelings.

For Eunice to choose to write at this time was a bold and uncommon move. Decades later, after the advent of the penny press, it was popular for individuals, women included, to turn out personal exposés that would promote their battles in court. In the early nineteenth century, however, such works were still rare. Printing was expensive, all the more so for self-published authors like Eunice, who had to secure enough subscriptions to cover costs or foot the bill themselves.

Then there was the personal cost of publishing. "Respectable" people were not supposed to flaunt their woes, in public or on paper—although of course there would always be a market for memoirs, especially scandalous ones. The *Albany Gazette* advertised the thrilling tale of Miss Lucy Brewer, who crossdressed her way into becoming a sailor aboard a United States frigate, and the story of Robert Adams, who was shipwrecked in Africa and enslaved by desert Arabs.

First-person accounts invariably began with disclaimers in which the authors insisted that their friends had pressed them to tell their stories. For a man to publish his personal affairs was considered distasteful; for a woman to do so was unthinkable. But Eunice was remarkably prescient in perceiving how effective literature could be as a legal tool. She also recognized that writing was her one chance to make her case before a public that was likely to be hostile if she spoke out in any other way. If she dared to address a crowd, she would surely be shunned or ridiculed. Through print, Eunice could speak without being seen. Far from all scrutiny, she could create an acceptable public persona, improving her image until she appeared on paper exactly as she wished.

Her resultant work—a sixty-page publication entitled *An Account of the Conduct of the People Called Shakers*, which the Shakers dismissed as a pamphlet and Eunice called her "book"—was so compelling that it was commonly speculated that a ghostwriter was involved. Skeptics found it hard to believe that a country teacher like Eunice could have produced such a sophisticated work by herself. (Little is known of Eunice's schooling, but given that her brothers had a modest education, attending village schools and studying at home, she is sure to have had no better.) Eunice, however, insisted that her words were her own, and it is not hard to believe her, for the genius of her *Account* lies not in its literary might or originality, but in its author's characteristic resourcefulness—in this case, her ability to seize upon the few literary conventions available to her, and make them speak for her.

When looking for literary models, Eunice had little help from the anti-Shaker writers who came before her. As men, these writers were freer to recount scandalous tales without appearing dissolute. They could also promote themselves as rational observers, a move that was off-limits to Eunice, since women were popularly believed to be governed by passion. Fortunately, she had more effective examples in the writings of other women. Female authors were still few, but they were growing in numbers, publishing poems and stories in newspapers, and books such as conduct manuals for young women. Women had also helped pioneer one genre that was particularly useful to Eunice: narratives of Indian captivity. These terrifying, often lurid first-person accounts—in which native "savages" are portrayed scalping, kidnapping, and otherwise tormenting white men, women, and children—were immensely popular, and they featured a built-in motivation for writing. Witnesses to the events were duty-bound to tell their story in order to warn others and save them from a similar fate.

Eunice deftly adopts the captive's plea in the opening lines of her book, where she informs her readers that she speaks for many other women, not just herself. She also addresses her vulnerability as a woman, imploring her audience:

> If the reader should observe anything in the following statement, not becoming that meekness which ought to characterize my sex, I wish that reader to consider, it is written by a persecuted woman, who has been hurled from a state of wealth and happiness, and now enduring indigence and grief! One who has been tortured in the whirlwind of affliction and woe! Very aggravating and calamitous!

She then proceeds to spin a sensational narrative perfectly calibrated to electrify an early nineteenth-century audience. James comes off as a philandering, drunken failure who refuses to provide for his family, while Eunice appears as the aggrieved wife who faithfully endures his cruelties. The two are stock characters from a melodrama: the ruinous rake and the pure, suffering victim. But even more than James, it is the Shakers— especially the Sisters—whom Eunice depicts as the true villains of her story, and shrewdly so. With this focus, Eunice underscores the idea that the Shakers were a public menace whose injustices demanded public intervention and, ultimately, a larger solution. She also turns the Shakers' reputation on its head, suggesting that the very people who appeared to be honest, decent, and peaceful were actually wolves in sheep's clothing.

Again and again, Eunice compares the Shakers to Indian captors, while she calls her children captives. She also denounces Shaker "slavery" in a similarly savvy manner. Narratives of American slavery had yet to reach their peak (Frederick Douglass published his famous *Narrative* in 1845), but northern newspapers regularly deplored slavery's ills—above all, the separation of husbands and wives, and mothers and children. Eunice's references were particularly well-timed given that New York was poised to abolish slavery for good. Like Indians and slave drivers, Eunice claims, the Shakers were despots of the worst kind. She tells how the Shaker Sisters would literally hold her lips together to prevent her from speaking, strike her, and taunt her by saying that she would burn in hell. She also portrays the Shakers as strange, insensible, and even dirty in their worship, jumping around and screaming such nonsense as "Jub, jub, jub" and "Lobble, lobble, lobble," while kicking up clouds of dust—a far cry from their famous cleanliness and order.

Eunice's account suggests that even Shaker celibacy was a hoax. Eunice tells of the Shakers having "spiritual husbands and wives" who would sit together in "Union Meetings" before proceeding to withdraw "to different apartments," presumably in pairs. Interestingly, Eunice is coy about what the spiritual spouses actually did, writing: "I learned by them that they have their union dances, but could not ascertain what they were. I believe that none except those whom they consider as faithful believers are permitted to join in the union dance." This admission of ignorance was another smart move. Eunice knew all too well the risks of being any more specific in her accusations: She could be perceived as indelicate, tainted by indecency. By being vague, she was able to remain "pure" while encouraging her readers to imagine the worst.

This is a powerful strategy that she uses throughout her book. Eunice repeatedly describes actions that might be interpreted as innocent but instead appear depraved. For instance, she recalls Sisters fixing their caps before the mirror and jumping up at the sound of a male voice—actions which they may well have taken, since their caps signified their purity and the nearness of men was a cause for alertness, but which, in Eunice's rendering, suggested vanity and interest in the opposite sex. Perhaps the strangest example of all is Eunice's recollection of an embrace from a Shaker Sister. The moment occurs halfway into her stay, after she has begged Eldress Fanny to see her son. Dejected by the Eldress's refusal and fearful that the Shakers intend to send her away, Eunice breaks down in tears. Then, she writes:

> As I sat weeping, with my head borne down with grief, Fanny walked up, and took hold of me, and bid me rise. She lifted me out of the chair, and told me to "look in her face." Hannah said, "Eunice? Sister Fanny has got a gift for you, and you must look her in the face." I replied, I cannot—here I must acknowledge, that, through fear of enchantment, I durst not look up! She pressed me to her breast and kissed me, and bid me kiss her. I told her I could not. After she had, alternately, flattered and tortured me as long as she pleased, I retired to give vent to my grief!

It is possible that such a "kissing gift" took place: Mother Lucy once issued a similar gift to two Shaker men. Yet in Eunice's telling, what was probably intended as a mutual pledge of love and loyalty becomes twisted into something sinister. Nineteenth-century readers, who were accustomed to same-sex displays of affection, may not have read the Eldress's move as a sexual advance, but they would surely have seen her behavior as inconsistent with the Shakers' ban on intimacy. And they would have suspected the Eldress of mesmerism—a kind of hypnosis that was a popular subject of fear and fascination in this age.

Above and beyond such scare tactics, however, literary sentimentalism is the most persuasive narrative strategy Eunice exploits in her book. Read today, her writing is likely to sound overwrought. Eunice makes abundant use of exclamation points and capital letters and sometimes even stops her story to say that she cannot see straight for crying. In one such passage she writes: "But here I must drop my pen—and vent my grief in tears!! Ye wise men who sit at the helm of government WEEP! Oh, WEEP for such unfortunate mothers!" But among early American readers this maudlin style played to great effect, as demonstrated by the enduring popularity of Susanna Rowson's novel *Charlotte Temple*—America's first best seller, as it has been called, and a showcase of the sentimental style.

Charlotte Temple, a "tale of truth," is a seduction drama, featuring the unfortunate Charlotte, who is plucked from her parents' home in England, seduced by a rakish villain, and cast off in America, pregnant and crazed. What made the book so compelling is what one literary critic has called Rowson's ability to reach "off the page," her skill at inviting and even requiring the reader to participate in the action of the story. As she tells of Charlotte's suffering, the narrator of the tale coaches her readers' reactions. She interrupts the plot to badger her audience to cry or feel pain on Charlotte's behalf and suggests that they are as bad as the villain if they do not. Rowson's readers obliged: Well through the nineteenth century, girls visited Charlotte's supposed grave in droves, bearing bouquets, poems, and locks of their own hair, and watering the heroine's headstone with their tears. Not until the appearance of Harriet Beecher Stowe's *Uncle Tom's Cabin* in 1852 would there be another such literary phenomenon in America.

By employing the familiar sentimental style, Eunice was able to tap into the appeal of stories such as *Charlotte Temple* and invite readers to identify with her as a heroine—one who is all the more sympathetic as a Christian persona, in contrast to a fallen woman like Charlotte. At the same time, Eunice managed to take the strategies of literary sentimentalism one step further, well before Stowe did with such resounding success. The typical sentimental tale is told from a point of completion. The heroine has fallen and died, and the story has come to a close. When Eunice addresses her reader and interrupts her narrative, in contrast, she makes it clear that her story is still running in the present—the reader can play a part in determining its resolution. In other words, after rousing her readers with an appalling picture of Shakerism, and presenting herself as a sympathetic heroine, Eunice assures her readers that a happy ending is still possible, if only they will help her. Then she shows them what they must do.

Eunice includes in her book a full transcript of the senate committee's report, with its recommendation of a civil death for the Shakers, and a divorce for herself. She specifically addresses her need for a divorce, explaining that only this remedy will free her from her husband and from potential abuse by the Shakers—and give her any hope of recovering her children before they become wholly "enslave[d]."

This last observation indicates the highest stakes in her cause. Eunice could already anticipate the major arguments against the senate committee proposals: Such measures would violate the Shakers' religious rights, be an abuse of legislative power, and compromise the institution of marriage. Eunice turns these arguments around, suggesting that the Shakers are the true violators of religious liberty, and a threat to the American family, above all to women and children. Her indignation is severe. "Do not women and children make up a part of the community," she demands, "and if the Shakers are permitted to continue their present course of destroying families, where is there a woman or child whose peace and safety is not in danger?" Eunice goes so far as to admonish missionaries and other do-gooders for deploying their energies abroad, when there are so many souls to be saved at home and Christians such as herself are under siege.

This is the heart of Eunice's call to action. The Shakers, Eunice asserts, have their sights on nothing short of world domination. Bringing children into their sect is just one step. The Elders believe that "the whole world must yet come under [their] power, and all who refuse, must be swept away in their sins, by the several judgments which are making their ravage in the world." Even the Shakers' military exemption, Eunice cannily suggests, is part of this plan. According to Eunice, the Shakers object to what she calls a "Military Tax" not so much because they are morally opposed to war, but because they want more money to expand their society. In making this point, Eunice was sure to touch a nerve. Military defense was a critical preoccupation in the wake of the War of 1812, especially in New York, which was hit hard by the conflict. It was no small matter for the state to have excused the Shakers from military service and fees in 1816. If what Eunice said was true, the Believers would be nothing short of traitors.

Lest her readers fail to fully appreciate how blasphemous and wrong-minded the Shaker religion is, Eunice closes her book with three pages full of quotations from the Shakers' own *Testimony*, featuring Mother Ann Lee. She deliberately picks passages to suggest Mother Ann's brazen impropriety. As Eunice tells it, the Shakers considered Mother Ann on par with God and believed that she actually "sat with God and assisted him in the creation of the world."

The Shakers, Eunice concludes, are a dangerous society founded by a dangerous woman who claimed more for herself than anyone, let alone anyone of her sex, had a right to. Seen in this context, the senate committee's proposals become the perfect antidote. An act to make the Shakers civilly dead would ultimately not inhibit religious expression but protect religious and civil liberties; it would not radicalize women's roles but defend the traditional order. As the proponent of such a step, Eunice herself becomes a representative heroine, standing for the plight of countless others: a woman writing and fighting, with great reluctance, not to gain unprecedented rights, but to return to the home where she properly belongs.

In January 1817, Eunice took her finished pages up the noisy length of Market Street—past the marketplace and the stage offices and the fancy hotels—to State Street, where the printing shop of Churchill and Abbey stood five doors down from the Episcopal church. There, she laid her scrawled text directly in the hands of Mr. Dorephus Abbey, printer of temperance tracts, ballads, Indian addresses, city directories, and even a Shaker pamphlet. (The Shakers had previously hired Abbey to print copies of their statement concerning their military exemption.)

In an age before steam power and other mechanization, printing was muscle work, requiring so much force that the journeymen who took turns inking and pressing each page became permanently unbalanced in their musculature, leaving the right foot and shoulder much larger than the left. But with the opening of the legislature as their deadline (and no doubt urged on by their anxious client), Abbey and his assistants worked quickly to transform the rough pages of Eunice's craggy penmanship into stacks of slim, freshly printed volumes.

The Shakers may have been accurate in calling these sixty-page publications "pamphlets." If Eunice had funds to spare, she might have had nice covers made from paper or leather. As it was, her writing was printed onto second-rate material, the kind of rough paper used for newspapers, made of poor-quality rags. The pages were then quickly "stab-stewn" or stitched down the middle, without a separate cover and special binding. In addition to her personal story, her publication included depositions supporting her character and vilifying James's—testimonies which Eunice's brother-in-law and father had begun gathering in Durham the year before.

With copies of her newly printed publication in hand, Eunice began making her distributions through the city and beyond, beginning with her advance subscribers. Well before she had taken her text to press, Eunice had solicited subscriptions to help finance the printing of her book. Who exactly these subscribers were remains unknown. Eunice notes only that they included "a number of respectable ladies" around Albany. However, it is not hard to see that there was an excellent market for her story. With all the social change and dislocation occurring in and around the capital city, the widening gulf between the rich and the poor, and a dramatic increase in the cultural diversity of the populace, there was mounting concern—particularly among the culturally dominant Yankees—about both the physical and the moral health of the city's inhabitants. In recent years, a "Ladies Society for the Relief of Distressed Women and Children" had been formed, as well as the "Albany Society for the Suppression of Vice and Immorality." Churchgoing women were especially anxious to alleviate suffering. Amid such a population, Eunice's story was likely to have received a sympathetic hearing, and through organizations like the "Ladies Society" and the Presbyterian Church—as well as anti-Shakers, who surely subscribed to get their own copies of her book—Eunice may have found an efficient means of publicity and distribution.

Eunice took her books, then, to the kind ladies of Albany, her friends, and her anti-Shaker associates. She sent more through the mail to contacts in other cities. Still other copies went to stores such as Mr. Steele's Bookstore, on South Market Street, and Mr. Hutton's and others on State. Precisely how much they sold for is unknown, although a later edition would fetch thirty-seven and a half cents a copy—more than *The Female Marine*, which cost twenty-five cents, but less than the sixty-two and a half cents commanded by one "Mrs. Taylor," author of *Maternal Solicitude* and *Practical Hints to Young Females*. The most important copies of Eunice's books, however—over a hundred in all—brought in no revenue: These were the copies she set aside to take to the capitol.

5

INFAMOUS SLANDER

On January 14, 1817, Albany was all astir as the capitol opened its doors for its fortieth legislative session. Boardinghouses were full once more, and taverns ran an even brisker trade, as legislators descended upon the city to discuss New York's most pressing matters of business, including the fate of slavery and the viability of the Erie Canal. Less time than usual had passed since the statesmen had last met, because a special fall session had been held on account of the presidential elections. President Madison was now on his way out, to be replaced by James Monroe (who, incidentally, would visit the Enfield Shakers on his tour of New Hampshire the following year). New York's Federalist candidate, Rufus King, had lost the election by a landslide, failing even to win his home state, but with Governor Daniel Tompkins headed for the vice presidency, New Yorkers were to have one of their own in the White House nonetheless.

With all the change and so many urgent tasks, lawmakers had all but forgotten about Eunice as they reassembled in the

windswept capital. The senate committee's recommendations
to provide relief for Eunice and a civil death to the Shakers had
been news nine months ago. Then they reached their seats.
Laid upon each desk was a slender volume, bearing the name
Eunice Chapman in delicate italics, beneath the word *Shakers* in
a thick bold script.

As lawmakers scanned the contents of her booklet, Eunice's
prospects in the legislature were transformed. Her heady com-
bination of emotional appeal, polemic, and spiritual fervor struck
a perfect chord with an audience that was particularly susceptible when it came to matters of religion. Officially, the state
was supposed to interfere with a religion only when it posed a
public threat, and many lawmakers spoke grandly about the importance of religious liberties. Yet, in reality the line dividing
faith and politics was often unclear. Chaplains opened every
session with a prayer, and legislators frequently cited scripture in their arguments. Eunice's appeal touched on both instincts of the ambivalent lawmakers. After reading her book,
some saw the need to defend her right to free religious expression, while others saw the urgency of protecting the Christian
faith from the encroachment of a bizarre and heretical sect. In
both cases, the Shakers' rights were all but forgotten.

Then there was Eunice's sentimental draw. Some lawmakers were so moved by her tale of suffering that they insisted on
giving her money. Others pledged to take up her cause and pass
an act on her behalf—vows that some would later regret. Eunice's
writing exerted a similar force beyond the legislature. In Albany, her female subscribers reached deep into their purses
and contributed whatever they could, so that Eunice was able
to recover the cost of her initial printing.

Perhaps the most telling sign of Eunice's success was the hostility that the Shakers encountered in Albany. Brothers could barely show their faces in public, owing to all the abuse. Even young children screamed insults as they passed by. As Elder Seth recalled in a letter to a Shaker in the western territories, "the common people swallowed" the book with greed "and soon began to disgorge its bitter contents." The Shakers seemed to have lost all their allies overnight. Their most reliable friends in the legislature and the city at large seemed "struck dumb," as the Elder grimly reported, by a work that was "artfully calculated to produce . . . all these effects."

Adding to all of this hostility was rising popular resentment against the Shakers. The wintry climate of the summer before had been followed by debilitating cycles of drought and cold that destroyed the harvest. Then there was a sudden onslaught of pestilent worms, which were so troublesome in Watervliet that the Shakers had to stand guard with lanterns over their gardens throughout the night. The result of these poor growing conditions was a "season of scarcity," exacerbated by the unprecedented cold. Not far from the Watervliet Shakers, a woman and her children were found starved, and a stage driver froze to death in nearby Troy. In New York City, the papers reported, soup houses were serving more than eight hundred people at a time.

The Shakers struggled as much as anyone, but they fared better than most. Anticipating the troubles ahead, Deacons in Watervliet had wisely invested in a large supply of grain, wheat, and rye, well before panic in the world raised the prices to extremes. They had also reduced their livestock to save feed, and generally cut expenses. To those who did not know better the Shakers looked suspiciously rosy and well fed, and wild rumors began to spread. One, for example, asserted that "the Shakers had predicted a seven years' famine and were buying up all the grain in the country."

Eunice's book made the Shakers' already strained public lives intolerable. Brothers traveling to Albany to sell their wares at market, just a few blocks from where Eunice lived, were routinely harassed as they had not been in years—perhaps not since Mother Ann's days. Only when the Shakers got their hands on their own copy of Eunice's publication did they finally understand why.

Sometime in the early winter of 1817, a copy of Eunice's book arrived in Watervliet—possibly sent by the author herself, as a warning to the society. It probably came through the trustees' office, but as soon as it was recognized, it was rushed to the Ministry chambers upstairs in the meetinghouse. There, among the heads of the society—Elders, Deacons, and, most important, Mother Lucy—Eunice's writing received as strong a response as it had in Albany. It was "infamous slander," Elder Seth cried, no more worthy of regard than "the whistling of the wind."

For twenty-four hours, the Shakers were overcome. They danced hard all night, their arms stretched toward the heavens, and prayed for deliverance. Mother Lucy herself took the lead, despite the physical strain. At last, surely weakened by the exertion but energized by the call, the Shaker Mother received a gift from above. "No weapon formed against Zion shall ever prosper," she pronounced in her fine low voice.

These words, once spoken by Father Joseph Meacham, Mother Lucy's former co-parent in faith, stilled the feverish crowd. At once, a clean feeling seemed to sweep through the

Believers and purge them of all bad sentiment. Mother Lucy then received another gift urging them to be "so watchful, so careful and so prayerful as not to give offense to anyone, nor to take offense from any one, whether Believer or unbeliever." This, too, lifted the Shakers' spirits.

In the days that followed, the Shakers resolved to take action against "that filthy daughter of old Mistress Babylon" and her "nasty little pamphlet," which by now had "circulated among the great folks and little folks, and wicked folks and silly folks in Albany and all round about the country." The situation in Albany had gotten out of hand. Not only were Brothers being attacked, but there was talk of passing an anti-Shaker act, and there was discussion of repealing the Shakers' military exemption. The Believers were reluctant to address Eunice directly, for they considered any contact with the woman akin to "dipping [their] hands into dirty, stinking water, which instead of cleansing them, would only defile them the more." However, they also knew that their silence would be seen as a tacit admission of guilt. The problem had become a public matter, and they could not risk suffering a civil death. A response was in order.

The leadership began by issuing an internal proclamation, society-wide, concerning the treatment of unbelieving women such as Eunice. Mother Lucy and the Ministry sent out an order "never more to receive a married man into our society whose wife did not believe; nor a married woman whose husband did not believe." Though unknown to Eunice, this proclamation represented one of her greatest triumphs to date. Through all her agitation, she had forced the Believers to reexamine the double set of rules they held for men and women and, ultimately, to alter their policy for good. Although previously, as the Shakers observed, it was their practice not to accept women with objecting husbands, their official decision to deny men with unbelieving wives was a first.

Having begun to put their own affairs in order, the Shakers launched a counterattack in "the world." Calvin Green, a leading Shaker spokesperson, missionary, and theologian, who had arrived among the Shakers in the belly of his unmarried mother nearly forty years before, was called in from New Lebanon to assist in the operations. He and Elder Seth were charged with writing a public statement against Eunice, while James Chapman was called in from Enfield to compose a statement of his own.

Such writing did not come naturally to the Believers, who were suspicious of the written word. Faith for them was a living, changing thing, and a matter of inspiration, to which print, fixed and indelible, was fundamentally opposed. Mother Lucy was especially reluctant to commit matters to writing. She had authorized the sect's first published theology, as well as Ann Lee's biography, but with great caution, lest the society's words be misinterpreted. Nevertheless, Mother Lucy had come to understand how persuasive written materials could be, and with all the damage that Eunice's book had done, the Shakers felt they had little option but to respond in kind.

Through several rainy days, the three men shut themselves up in the trustees' office to write, stopping for an occasional run into Albany to consult with lawmakers about Eunice's bill. They worked fast. Just two days after Calvin Green and Elder Seth had commenced their literary labors, their "Remonstrance" was complete and ready for signatures. Significantly, it was not Mother Lucy who signed the document, but three male leaders, including Elder Seth and Jonathan Hodgson. The decision to feature these men was consistent with the Shakers' occasional practice of downplaying Mother Lucy's role in their society—a practical maneuver given the unorthodox nature of feminine leadership and outsiders' prejudices against publicly assertive women. Yet this move was surely strategic in another way. Given all that Eunice had done to dramatize the dangers represented by Shaker women, the Believers needed to show that men were at their helm.

With the signatures gathered, Calvin Green and James left for Albany in the bitter cold, the statement carefully stored in their carriage. They headed for the offices of their staunchest ally in the senate, someone who also happened to be the most powerful man in the legislature, Martin Van Buren.

The thirty-five-year-old state attorney general had recently fathered a fifth child and was known as a charmer of the female sex—credentials that might have been in Eunice's favor, given the basis of her personal appeal. Not surprisingly, Eunice went out of her way to court him. But if Eunice was capable of "magic," as it was reported, she met her match in "the little Magician," as Van Buren was known. This skilled trial lawyer and statesman was famous as a shrewd reader and manipulator of people, and Eunice's charms fell flat before him. Van Buren remained faithful to his Shaker friends and promised to introduce their statement at once to the legislature.

On the morning of March 21, representatives from the society rode out to Albany to attend the scheduled reading of their work—they were most likely Calvin Green, who had lobbied successfully for the society's military exemption, and Elder Seth, who knew the situation better than anyone else. The scene they faced in the senate was far from inspiring. A number of tedious bills came first, including "an act for the inspection of fish" (which was read three times before being reassigned to a committee) and "an act to amend the third section of the act relative to turnpike companies" (which was passed). By the time the Shakers' statement was finally put on the table, the senators were as bored and antsy as schoolboys, nodding off, passing notes, flipping through newspapers, and even chattering in low voices with their neighbors.

But as the clerk roused himself for a lively reading of the Shakers' written defense (with the Shakers keeping quietly to themselves, watching and listening intently as a stranger took possession of their words), the hall grew still. Lawmakers now heard a view of the Chapman dispute that was wholly at odds with all that they had previously been told. The Shakers immediately rejected any suggestion that they violated liberties, separated married couples, or destroyed homes. Instead, they offered a detailed presentation of their beliefs that was meant to discredit and ultimately to subvert Eunice's charges. According to the Shakers, they were not the perpetrators of the crimes Eunice alleged but, rather, its victims.

The Shakers began with a clear statement of their policies regarding families. They boldly declared that married Shakers were free to "live together all their days" and raise their children as they pleased, without any interference. And when a family was divided over faith, the Shakers insisted that they tried their best to help the family stay together. Wives had to have their husbands' approval to join the society, while husbands were forbidden to desert their families. A Shaker man had to fulfill his duties as a husband and father, as law and morality required, and any assets he possessed had to be divided fairly.

But what were they to do, the Shakers asked, when a man did his best to support his family, only to be rebuffed by his willful, intransigent wife? And what was a man to do when his wife refused to live with him unless he would "violate his religious faith"? Was he required, by the laws of God or man, to put himself under her rule? What choice did he have but to assume the care of his children, as was his right and duty, and leave his wife to herself? Such was the case, the Shakers maintained, with the Chapmans. It was not James, they said, who had violated his marital contract, or their sect that had robbed Eunice of anything, but Eunice herself who had forsaken her marriage vows and stood to deprive James of his rights. (How, specifically, she required that he "violate" his faith was left ambiguous for now, but the impropriety was clear.)

The Shakers challenged their listeners to investigate matters fully. "We shrink not from investigation," they proudly declared. "Let them find those many women abandoned by their husband and left to suffer, while their property is carried among the Shakers. Let them find those children who are abused and brought up in ignorance." "Eunice Chapman," they avowed, "is the only woman that we know of, in this state, whose husband is among the people and she is not with them herself."

According to the Shakers, the Chapmans' dispute was an exceptional domestic quarrel in which they had merely been charitable bystanders. They had urged reconciliation, and in the end, it was solely as an "act of charity"—and at the father's request—that they had agreed to take in the Chapman children. When even this move failed to appease Eunice, James, they said, took matters into his own hands. In the Shakers' words, he "took the children and went where he thought proper, and we had no right nor disposition to controul [*sic*] him in the matter." Dismissing rumors that they had "concealed" the children, the Shakers declared that two years had passed since James had taken the youngsters away, and they had "never been here since."

The Shakers ridiculed the idea that they had any interest in hanging on to children such as the Chapmans, claiming that they could have hundreds of youngsters simply by taking in those who were offered to them. Just recently, twenty children had been brought to Watervliet, and of these the Shakers finally accepted three, only because the children would have otherwise starved. In short, it was hardly the case that the Shakers had need of the world's children: If anything, it was the world that needed them.

The Believers went on to rebut other accusations, such as their alleged tyranny, in a way that pointed to the fundamental irony of passing the recommendations of last year's senate committee. The principal "crimes" with which the Shakers had been charged were the restraint of liberty, the violation of family laws, and the unjust seizure of property. It was precisely these crimes, the Shakers suggested, that the state itself would be guilty of by declaring their society civilly dead.

The Believers expressed shock that the state would even consider passing a bill that would turn the Shakers into criminals—and for what? According to them, the only difference between their faith and others' was their celibacy, which could hardly be considered a crime. "Through all the ages of papal tyranny," they cried, "we do not find so persecuting a law against any people, for merely following the example of Christ," who had also led a celibate life. "Must a man, in this far-famed asylum of liberty, be compelled to sexual cohabitation, on pain of being deprived of every earthly inheritance? Of all natural and civil rights and privileges?"

The Shakers exaggerated—surely there was more than their sexual abstinence which set apart their faith—but their angle was highly effective. For if celibacy was all that really distinguished the Shakers from other Christians, then why, one might ask, was Eunice Chapman so opposed to their faith? What did it mean when she demanded that her husband "violate his conscience"? Was it possible that what she really wanted from her husband was the one thing forbidden by his religion? The Shakers did not fully articulate these points, but others less constrained in speaking about sex would soon draw out, with scandalizing frankness, what the Shakers hardly dared to suggest.

The Shakers concentrated for now on what, in their view, was truly on the line: the freedom of religion and even liberty itself. If the previous year's proposals were passed into law, they warned, "then in vain did the liberal framers of the Constitution affix such plain barriers to guard the liberty of conscience: For when the example is once set, there will never be wanting a specious pretext for a law against religion that stands in the way of popularity." The Shakers suggested that such a law would be a loss for the state for more practical reasons, as well. How, after all, could dead men—or dead societies—pay taxes?

In the end, the Believers expressed their faith that lawmakers would recognize the senate's proposed measures for what they truly were: a violation of the Constitution and of "the very principle of civil and religious right." "We trust," they remarked in closing, "that such a law can never stain your honorable code."

*   *   *

Afterward, Elder Seth would marvel that it had been as if "the power of God" had been attendant at the reading. As the clerk had begun speaking, the senators had looked up from their writing, laid down their pens, put away their newspapers, and ceased to chatter. Some nudged one another in agreement or disbelief, others stared with wonder, and those who were friendliest to the Shakers brightened as they focused on the clerk's vigorous tones and the serious, odd-garbed Shaker men who sat before them. The Shakers, it seemed, had redeemed themselves with their frank, rational arguments, reinstating their image as the upright pacifists their neighbors had known them to be.

By the time the reading was through, the Shakers' fortunes seem to have reversed. Their allies were newly motivated to speak for them, while others were far less certain of their positions than they had been before. That day, James Chapman, perhaps seeking to take advantage of this change in mood, met and spoke with various lawmakers to prepare them for his side of the story, next to come.

6

JAMES

Eunice was crushed to learn of James's plans to testify against her—and furious that the Shakers would bring him out now, after they had repeatedly denied any knowledge of his whereabouts. She had a final chance to avoid public humiliation, and possibly to work out an agreement, when James sent emissaries to propose a meeting. But Eunice saw nothing to gain by private negotiations. She rebuffed these overtures and most likely stayed home on the day her husband was scheduled to make his case in the capitol. She had hardly any other option, given the damaging statement he was likely to make against her character. As a woman, she would be unable to speak out in her own defense; if anything, her public presence would worsen matters, confirming for all that she was a woman prone to wandering out of her proper sphere.

But even if Eunice was not present to hear James's words, she had ample opportunity to see them in print, for the Shakers published numerous copies of James's "Memorial" as well as their own "Remonstrance." His words rounded out the

Shakers' political arguments with a far more intimate story and, as expected, formed a searing indictment of Eunice's character.

In her own writing, Eunice had made a powerful case that she had been deprived of her rights as a wife and mother. James shrewdly countered these claims by charging that it was *she* who had abused these roles and that she had caused an ever-broadening circle of damage against her family, her community, an innocent society, and now the state. In James's telling, it was Eunice, not the Shakers, who needed to be tamed and controlled.

It had all begun, James said, with Eunice's vicious temperament and "calumniating tongue," whose withering effects had been felt not just by the family, but by her church. James openly confessed to his past drinking problem, but he contended that Eunice drove him to drink, ruined his estate, and effectively ran him out of her life. In this depiction, James played to popular expectations about marital roles, portraying Eunice as the opposite of the supportive, subservient wife she was supposed to be.

According to James, the Shakers had only encouraged him to do right by his family, but Eunice stood in his way. She spurned his help while at the same time applying for public assistance. She refused to give him the children but complained that she could not support them herself. All she wanted was for him to live under her rule. Even when the Shakers took in their family as an act of kindness, she did not desist from her abuse. As James said, she "neglected no opportunity to abuse me and the people, to make the children unhappy, and, if possible, to create confusion and discord wherever she went."

As a final resort, he had driven Eunice to Albany and ordered her to stay away from him and the children for three months, warning that they would leave the state if she did not. He had hoped that fear might help control her and her "abusive tongue." Eunice, however, returned to Watervliet to brag of her powers with the legislature, and threatened violence. "Thus, in fact," James complained, "she not only set at defiance my authority, but threatened me with imprisonment, and the society with fire!"

James claimed that he had no choice but to follow through on his pledge. Eunice's threats against himself were hardly new, but he refused to allow the Shakers, who had shown such charity to his family, to suffer. He described his fateful move as follows: "Accordingly, I took my children and removed them out of state, to a place of safety, where they have ever since been well provided for, and are contented and happy." James assumed full responsibility for this decision. He was adamant that he had acted entirely on his own and that if anyone should be blamed, it should be himself.

James's presentation of his departure as a personal remedy for a personal problem was convincing on many levels. Not only did he clear the Shakers from all blame, but he reinforced the idea that his problems with Eunice were a private matter, which had been needlessly publicized by his wife. He closed his statement by questioning her motives for doing so, wondering whether it was "her children that the woman is so anxious about"—or whether, in fact, her actions originated in "an inherent propensity to slander and defamation, and a malignant spirit of persecution."

On the day that James took his statement to the legislature, the capital was soaked with midspring rains. That evening, satisfied that his presentation had gone well, James set off for

Enfield. For a man who had spent the last two years confined to a remote country village, passing most of his waking hours in a workshop or in the fields, the past several weeks had no doubt been exciting, if not exactly enjoyable. He had labored alongside his Elders, using his pen rather than his hands, traveled into and out of the city, met with politicians, and heard his own writing read in the domed capitol—all of which may have meant little to a Believer but should have pleased the adventurous businessman that James had once been.

The excitement continued on his journey home. James did not return to New Hampshire directly but stopped in New Lebanon for a few days to share the good news with leaders of his society. There, in the candlelit dimness of the meeting-house, encircled by curious Brothers and Sisters who had convened for a special evening meeting, James read his statement aloud, along with Calvin Green, who presented the Shakers' "Remonstrance." The Brothers reported that they had had a "hard scene of it," as it had seemed that all of Albany was set against them, but they felt that their labors had been worthwhile, since matters were finally beginning to turn around.

Believers in Albany, meanwhile, felt that a burden had been lifted. Like Eunice, they had papered the city with their writings. They left copies of their "Remonstrance" on the desks of every legislator and handed out still more to their friends and neighbors. Almost immediately, the furor against them began to settle down. Freegift Wells registered the hope that his people felt in these days, writing that the society's presentations "appeared to have a good effect in removing the prejudices which had been imbibed by reading Eunice Chapman's pamphlet—Believers had been much abused and insulted in Albany, but the tone of the public mind was now greatly changed."

For a short while, at least, it seemed that the legislature might be transformed, as well. Thanks to the strenuous lobbying efforts of Martin Van Buren, lawmakers agreed to remove the proclamation of civil death against the Shakers—in the Believers' view, this was the worst of the measures proposed against them by the senate committee the previous year. Yet in the long run, the Shakers' appeal probably hurt them. While their statement had successfully dispelled myths about their society, it subverted their claims to innocence, proving that they had known where James had been all this time. Elder Seth now appeared to be a perjurer. The fact that (because of time constraints) James did not provide depositions to contradict Eunice's witness statements also put them at a disadvantage. In the end, the society's credibility was profoundly undermined, and even Martin Van Buren, "the sly fox of Kinderhook," as he was also known, was not able to prevent the senate from passing an anti-Shaker bill.

On April 28, after nearly a month of wrangling over the terms, the senate voted 18 to 9 in favor of passing an "act for the relief of Eunice Chapman, and for other purposes." This act granted Eunice an immediate and full divorce, allowing her to remarry, while denying James the same right. But it also enabled *any* person to apply to the chancellor for a divorce when his or her spouse joined the Shakers. If the petitioning spouse was a woman, the chancellor could further grant her "other relief"— a broad provision that empowered women in Eunice's position.

The legal ramifications of these measures were breathtaking. First, the instant dissolution of the Chapmans' marriage was an unparalleled use of legislative power. Normally, to be convicted of any crime, an accused person received a trial by jury and was presumed innocent until proved guilty. In this case the legislature would "punish" James Chapman by depriving him of his civil right to remarry, without a court hearing, and on unprecedented grounds. These grounds in themselves should have been enough to give lawmakers pause. The passage of this act would mean that in a state where even extreme cruelty was thought insufficient reason for divorce, the mere fact of entering Shaker society was considered "criminal" enough to dissolve a marriage.

The act was similarly punitive when it came to custody. A woman like Eunice, whose husband became a Shaker, now had lawful grounds for seeking full guardianship over her children—or, to put it slightly differently, to deprive her husband of his custodial rights. And, she could seek a writ of habeas corpus forcing the Shakers to bring her children forth for a custody trial. If the Shakers failed to comply, or appeared to be hiding children, she could make a further appeal to the chancellor, who was empowered to issue search warrants authorizing sheriffs and other officers to enter Shaker homes at any time of day, search the premises, and even search individual Believers.

Elder Seth went to the capitol to obtain the verdict in the senate, accompanied by another Brother. Immediately afterward, the Shakers confronted lawmakers, only to be told by some of them that they had previously promised their support to Eunice and had to stand by their word. The fate of Eunice's bill, however, was still far from sure. It had succeeded in the senate, but it would have to be approved by the house, as well, if it was to become law. The Shakers could only send their prayers to the assembly and hope that there the act for Eunice's "relief" would face more debate—and fiercer resistance.

7

AN ACT OF RELIEF

Early on the morning of April 4, 1817, there was one gentleman on the assembly floor—or "within the bar," as this space was described—who was not a bona fide lawmaker: the newly anointed editor of the *Albany Gazette*, William Leete Stone. Not yet twenty-five years old, Stone was boyish in appearance, with a plump, handsome face and full head of feathery brown hair. By Thurlow Weed's description, he was "a half-grown and half-learned itinerant printer, without friends or money."

As youthful as he may have appeared, however, Stone was a veteran in his profession. He had launched his career at seventeen, walking all night from his father's house in New Paltz to Cooperstown, New York, with only a "single Mexican quarter in his pocket and a small bundle of clothes in his hand," in search of work as a printer's apprentice. Two years later, he had bought and taken control of his first paper. His current position at the head of Albany's first daily was now his third editorship in a row.

As a writer, Stone was feisty and opinionated—a style that would lead to a spate of libel suits in his future, including two from his onetime friend James Fenimore Cooper. Stone's own father, a Congregational minister and Yale graduate who had furnished his son with all the education he had, had once warned: "You write, my son, with a pen dipped in vinegar." But in Albany, the young man's acidity had yet to be felt. He was well respected and was granted a special reporter's seat in the legislature—the first of its kind.

On this day, the house had been expected to resume its debates over the Erie Canal bill, which had come to a head after months of argument. The fate of this controversial canal—which would provide a "wedding of the waters" between the Hudson and the Great Lakes, transform New York's economy, and become known as one of the chief advances of the early nineteenth century—was weighty indeed. Stone, who heartily supported the project, was one of many who were eager for an answer. But, as the newspaperman was soon to report, yet another issue had "excited considerable interest and curiosity in the minds of the public," and managed to shunt aside all talk of even the great canal —and that was the case of Eunice Chapman.

Interest in this case had been mounting all season, from the moment that the lady had laid her writings on the desks of all the legislators and sold her books throughout the city. Her story had inspired much talk of changing the divorce laws, as well as a flurry of other divorce petitions that Stone, among others, had endured day after day. Now the woman was halfway to having her own law—and the first legislative divorce in New York history—the senate having gratified her with a bill in her name. Whether or not she actually succeeded, however, was yet to be seen.

This was just the sort of story that interested the young editor, who loved uncovering scandals, exploring religious truths, and studying issues of civil liberty—although in this case he was personally inclined to be sympathetic to the opposition. As Horace Greeley observed, Stone was a true "conservative," mindful of "the restraints of the law and the deference due to rightful authority." Stone's way of thinking probably reflected the teachings of his puritanical father, who had held religious and civil liberties in the highest esteem.

Moreover, Eunice's writings, with all of their captivity drama and sentimentalism, were not likely to have had much of an impact on a man who had grown up sympathetic to Indians, and who was later to debunk a narrative very much reminiscent of hers. In the 1830s, Stone published an exposé called *Maria Monk, and the Nunnery of the Hotel Dieu*, addressing a young woman's claim that she had been held captive and abused in a convent. Maria Monk's allegations against the Catholic Church, which included charges of rape and infanticide, were far more salacious than any Eunice dared to make against the Shakers, but the sensationalizing impulse was the same, and Stone's work, as his son wrote, "put an effectual quietus upon that extraordinary mania into which divines and laymen were led by the fictions of a silly, profligate woman."

Soon enough, Stone would use similar language to describe Eunice, but at this point, he found the woman fascinating, and he could not help noticing her frequent comings and goings in the capitol. For some reason, he had not written about her case in his newspaper the day before, when the house debates had begun. As the discussions recommenced, however, he took down as much as he could, and it is fortunate that he did, since his transcripts provide the only record of them that is available today.

Stone's biases are evident, though he made some effort to conceal them. He favored old-school Federalists, conservatives who believed it prudent to centralize authority in a wise, judicious few—unlike Republicans, the party of Thomas Jefferson, with their glorification of the common man. Federalists were a dying breed in the nation, but they still held sway in New York. They also formed the basis of Eunice's opposition—not surprising, since her proposed act went so far to advance the cause of a single individual over the larger law. This is not to say that support for Eunice's cause fell strictly along party lines; her staunchest opponent, Martin Van Buren, was a leading Republican. Moreover, party affiliation counted for little at a time when the Federalist Party was in shambles. Allegiances tended to revolve around individual leaders, such as Van Buren or his soon-to-be adversary, DeWitt Clinton, more than anything else. However, it is a fact that those who still called themselves Federalists consistently ranked among Eunice's most vocal and powerful adversaries.

It was a conservative of this cast, William Duer of Albany, who launched the attack on Eunice's bill. Knowing that emotions ran high, Duer tried to refocus his colleagues' attention on the legal issues at hand, calling the actions against the Shakers unconstitutional. Yet it was the commanding presence of Duer's mentor and fellow Federalist, Nathaniel Pendleton, that stirred up the assembly and captivated Stone's pen.

The house stood in attention as the Virginia native, celebrated Revolutionary War veteran, and onetime New York City lawyer took the floor. Pendleton's own personal life was not without controversy. It was said that he had committed adultery with the widow of his commanding general and that he had fled to New York to avoid damage from that affair. Pendleton was also famous as the man who had held the dying Alexander Hamilton in his arms after the former treasurer had been shot in a duel by Aaron Burr. The sixty-one-year-old assemblyman was now more bent and gray than he had been during those days, but he still spoke with eloquence and verve.

Pendleton narrowed in on the fact that Eunice Chapman already had a solution to her problems in the present laws. For flair, he drew up a bundle of papers containing the state's divorce statutes and quoted several passages. New York, he reminded his audience, made adultery the sole criterion for divorce. But the state *did* have a remedy for other complaints, such as cruelty and abandonment: divorces from bed and board. These partial divorces saw that wives and children were provided for, even if they did not, Pendleton added with emphasis, permit remarriage. Turning from the statutes, Pendleton squarely faced his colleagues. "The case now before the committee is of that class already fully provided for, in relation to everything, but that of giving the liberty to the lady to marry again." As he saw it, the bill before them was nothing more than an authorization for Eunice Chapman to find herself a new husband.

If his fellow lawmakers actually saw value in this plea, Pendleton advised, they should pass a new divorce law, not a special bill, because as far as he could see, this case was not exceptional: A man had left his wife after drinking away his fortunes and joined a religious society with his children. The sect was eccentric, maybe even fanatical, but it was also known for being "sober, industrious, and inoffensive." No further charges appeared in the bill. In her writings, Eunice had suggested adultery, but she had given no evidence, and this was also troubling. If Eunice's husband were truly an adulterer, she might have obtained a divorce through the chancery—assuming, of course, that she was "innocent herself." Why she had chosen instead to come to the legislature remained a mystery.

To Pendleton, this was clearly a flawed case, and he deplored the proposed bill, which he said would "open a wide door for divorces" and "be productive of infinite mischief." He then reminded his fellow assemblymen of all the women whose similar requests they had denied, even though many of them made stronger cases. His colleagues surely murmured with assent, thinking of the many divorce bills that had come to them that season. How could they forget Laura Hall, who was married at sixteen and remained unable to consummate her marriage five years later? After endless examinations, medical experts had concluded that sexual relations would not be possible without the loss of her life, and the poor woman had begged for a release from her marital duties. Then there were Sophia Griffen, whose husband had abused her with a "barbarism" that everyone deplored; Mary Pardee, another "victim of caprice to cruelty"; and Catharine Barnum, a teenager who had been forced into marrying a man she despised.

Not one of these cases had resulted in a legislative divorce. And Eunice Chapman, Pendleton maintained, would have suffered the same fate, had it not been for the tremendous impact of one object: her "artful pamphlet." It was this little book, he suggested, that had riled people to such a degree that they had lost sight of the laws. Pendleton warned his colleagues to resist its influence and leave this case to the courts.

The younger assemblymen next to speak, however, ignored the senior statesman's counsel and picked up where Eunice's book left off. John Treat Irving, a New York City lawyer, would never be as well known for his writing as his brother Washington Irving—later famous for "The Legend of Sleepy Hollow." But this Irving, too, had literary talents, which he put to work in his arguments for Eunice's cause.

Embracing Eunice as a sentimental heroine, he described her ordeals in "pathetic terms," dwelling on her abandonment as a wife and her losses as a mother. (William Leete Stone, for one, listened skeptically from his corner.) The ardent assemblyman rejected the idea that Eunice Chapman should be denied a divorce simply because she had not proved adultery. Irving believed that divorce should be permitted in all cases where the marriage contract was breached. And what greater violation could there be than here, he asked, "where a man had joined a society who held all carnal intercourse between the sexes, even between man and wife to be sinful?" This was a terrible principle, he said, one that would cause corruption among Shaker youth and harm to society at large.

Irving admitted that the legislature could pass a more general law to help Eunice Chapman. "But as this case was now before the legislature," he said, "they might with propriety decide upon it." He then addressed the question of motive that Pendleton had raised. Eunice Chapman, he argued, lacked the means to file a lawsuit, and there were sure to be other delays. What would become of the woman and her children in the meantime? Even her earnings could be seized, and she would have no means of defense. Irving implored his fellow assemblymen to have pity on the woman and closed his speech with one last, weepy appeal, vividly evoking how they might feel if their own "bosom friends and nearest relations" were to suffer as Eunice Chapman had suffered. If the state did not act now, he implied, their loved ones, too, could share her fate.

Nathan Williams, a Republican from Oneida, responded by exclaiming that he would, by all means, "restore the child to the parent who had been deprived of it by fraud, under the pretext of religion." And to bring back children who had been "kidnapped" in this manner, he would "go to all lengths—if necessary, even to level the buildings to the ground." But he protested the other provisions in the bill, namely those concerning divorce.

"Shall we, sir," he cried, looking to Irving, "undertake to say, that because one party has joined the Shakers, the marriage contract shall be annulled? The principle would apply equally well to a Jew." By this reasoning, any marriage could be dissolved; any religion could come under attack.

Irving, he acknowledged, had treated the case with "much feeling." But Williams urged his colleagues to return to the one fact that should bring this case to a close: Eunice Chapman already had a legal solution. Williams challenged his hearers with a final statement, which closed the debates for the day: that the "man who did not feel for the distresses of a helpless woman, was a villain—but that the man who let his feelings sway his judgment, was unfit for a legislator."

According to Nathan Williams's criteria, a majority of his colleagues should have lost their jobs. The next day, ignoring all arguments that the bill set a dangerous precedent, upended the divorce laws, and was unconstitutional, the house passed "An Act for the Relief of Eunice Chapman" with a vote of 53 to 43.

Although it was too late to change the vote, Elder Seth spoke once more to legislators to understand what had happened. He discovered that Eunice's sentimental appeal had trumped all. In the assembly, just as in the senate, a number of lawmakers had been bound by their promises to Eunice, which they had made under the influence of her writing. Some of them had approved the bill, despite their misgivings, while others had fled the house to avoid voting. (A man, it seemed, was only as good as his word—especially when the defense of a woman was involved.) For still others, Eunice's appeal as a heroine had been impossible to overcome. Abraham Van Vechten—the Shakers' lawyer, as well as a senator—expressed it this way: The "enticing little woman" had not "spent two years in courting the members for nothing."

However, Eunice's act had to pass one last test before it became law. All acts of legislature required approval from the Council of Revision, a supervisory tribunal composed of the governor, chancellor, and justices of the supreme court. Luckily for the Shakers, there was not enough time left in the season for the council to give its verdict. The final judgment would be postponed until the next session, which was not until January of the following year. For Eunice, a long nine months lay ahead.

Finalized or not, if the public papers were to be believed, the act was a done deal. Newspapers small and large—from the *Farmer's Repository* in West Virginia to the popular *Niles Weekly Register* in Baltimore, Maryland, and countless other journals in Maine, Kentucky, New York, New Hampshire, and beyond— spread news of Eunice's case across the country. Most of these papers erred in their reporting. Some presented Eunice's act as if it were already a law. Others published a previous version that featured the civil death clause, provoking outrage from luminaries such as former president Thomas Jefferson.

In a letter to George Ticknor in May 1817, Jefferson referred to Eunice's act, which he read about in the papers, as one so preposterous that "it would puzzle us to say in what, the darkest age of the history of bigotry and barbarism, we should find an apt place for it." "It is said," he mistakenly reported, "they have declared by law that all those who hereafter shall join in communion with the religious sect of Shaking Quakers, shall be deemed civilly dead, their marriage vows dissolved, and all their children and property taken from them; without any provision for rehabilitation in case of resipiscence." Jefferson dismissed the act with his hope that "this departure from the spirit of our institutions is local . . . and merely momentary." Still, he could not get it off his mind. A month later, the former president wrote worriedly about Eunice's act in a letter to Albert Gallatin, describing it in nearly the same terms he had used in his letter to George Ticknor.

For Eunice, of course, this matter of public anxiety was cause for personal celebration—even more so, because after more than two years of searching and waiting, she finally learned where George, Susan, and Julia were.

Around the time that Jefferson first wrote about Eunice's case, roughly a month after the legislature had approved her bill, a troubled man in his twenties came wandering into Albany, restless and more than a little vulnerable, hoping to leave behind his past with the Shakers. At first he had been drawn to Watervliet, for Shaker life was all Josiah Terry had known since he was sixteen years old. He had hoped that given his history with the society, the Believers might be persuaded to help him start up a business making whips. But the Watervliet society had been alerted to keep him at a distance by their Brothers and Sisters in Enfield, New Hampshire. Josiah was known as a "very bad character" who was prone to extreme and unpredictable behavior—he had once tried to freeze and starve himself to death—and the Watervliet community would have nothing to do with him.

Josiah was angered, for as he saw it, he had spent nearly a decade laboring in their society, free of charge. However, he resolved to build a new life for himself in New York's capital city, whose crowded harbors and wide, grand streets promised something different from the close, chill woods he had left behind in New Hampshire. And it was there, in Albany, as Josiah began forming acquaintances, making inquiries, and speaking of his past employment with the Shakers, that he met Eunice Chapman, whose stories about the Shakers had saturated the city.

For Josiah, it was a marvel to meet this exquisite little woman face to face, especially after reading her book, which presented a fascinating contrast to the accounts he had heard in Enfield. Naturally, as a Believer, he had not been in the habit of meeting privately with members of the opposite sex, and it was surely with some nervousness that he accepted Eunice's invitation to visit. But the woman was excellent company; she was charming and graceful, and above all, seemed to understand the troubles he had endured as a Shaker. She called for him once, twice, and then even a third time, and he obliged her on every occasion, for if truth be told, she roused deep within him what he would later call an "impetuity of passion"—precisely the kind of carnal reaction that he had struggled to suppress as a Believer.

With Eunice's encouragement, Josiah unburdened himself of his entire Shaker experience. He told her of the pressures he had faced, as a young Believer, to comply with the Elders' constant exhortations to "walk by faith and not by sight," and to trust in them as God's messengers. He recounted the terrifying stories the Elders told to keep youngsters in line: tales of torture and damnation that would cause even grown men to shudder. And he spoke of the Shakers' abuse. One evening, he claimed, he had been sent out to a mountain, and though his work clothes were soaked through, and the ground was thick with snow, he had been ordered to stay outside for three days and nights, without food or shelter. All this, he said, was punishment for his alleged lack of faith.

Clearly, Josiah was not a reliable character or narrator, and his mental health was questionable. He would switch sides between Eunice and the Shakers repeatedly over the next few years and change his story to suit his audience. However, he was accurate in relaying at least one critical piece of information to Eunice. As Josiah told Eunice, James had arrived in Enfield with his three children one bleak February day, over two years ago. The boy had been sickly early on, but he and the girls were now well again. Josiah had not seen much of them, since the children had separate schedules, but he had had ample time to talk with James, for they had been assigned to the same workshop. Her husband had spoken highly of her, Josiah said, returning Eunice's flattery. "A volume could scarcely contain the praise I heard him give," Josiah reportedly said.

The young man's usefulness did not end there. Josiah further informed Eunice that there was another mother out in New Hampshire who, much like herself, was battling the Shakers for her children and was also going to her state legislature for help—a woman whom the Believers would later describe as a "more finished instrument of the devil than Eunice." Her name was Mary Dyer.

Mary Dyer's case differed from Eunice's in ways that Josiah himself may or may not have known. The most striking and most important difference was that Mary had once been interested in Shakerism. She had voluntarily joined the society with her husband, signed the Shaker covenant, and released all claim to her children. Soon after taking these steps, however, she became disenchanted. She had hoped to make something of herself as a Believer, and even wanted to preach, but she became resentful when the Shakers thwarted her plans. They would not even hear her suggestions for improving their orders—which allegedly included arranging for the very type of "spiritual marriage" that Eunice had hinted at in her book.

Discouraged in every way, Mary finally decided to leave, and hoped to take a few of her children with her. Too late, she realized that her husband and the Shakers would only permit her to depart alone—that by signing the Shaker covenant, she had agreed to give the Believers permanent title to her children. She began to protest in earnest, and then her story and Eunice's began to run a similar course.

Mary herself was never directly acquainted with Eunice's children, having left the Enfield community just before their arrival. She did, however, know James as her Brother in the North Family and later as an adversary. James had helped Mary's husband drive her away from Enfield; he provided similar assistance when she returned to the village sometime later. By Mary's account, James and her husband had forcibly removed her from the Shaker church, and then, when she sat down in the road, vowing that she would rather die there than leave her children, they had dragged her to the trustees' office, tearing her dress in the process. Eunice would learn these details as she and Mary Dyer began a relationship, initially by mail, that was to sustain them for months and years to come, and help Eunice in ways that she could never have foreseen.

Eunice initiated the relationship, writing to Mary of her troubles and sending a copy of her book, which she hoped would

be useful to the other mother as Mary pursued her own legislative suit in New Hampshire. Eunice saw their efforts as part of
a shared, God-given quest, and hoped that if one of them succeeded in winning a law, similar measures would be enacted
across the nation. Eunice also asked Mary repeatedly for news
about her children. Now that she had contact with someone
who lived within miles of her children, she was anxious for
any details about them—how they looked, how tall they were,
if they appeared healthy, whether they seemed happy or
distressed—anything to make them real to her after an absence
of two and a half years. Unfortunately, Mary was not very helpful
there. She had once briefly glimpsed one of Eunice's daughters,
but at the time, she had not been aware of the girl's identity
and could not oblige Eunice with much of a description.

Eunice was tempted to go straight to New Hampshire and
see her children for herself. Wisely, however, she refrained, well
aware that her bill was not yet law, and the Shakers could at any
time decide to move her children yet again. It had to be enough,
for now, to know that her children were alive and together.
Eunice would not hold herself back, however, from contacting
the Shakers. She vowed that even if it was not yet time for her
to reclaim her children, it was high time for her to confront the
woman who had replaced her as their mother: Lucy Wright.

8

MOTHER AGAINST MOTHER

Thirty miles from Albany, just over the border between Massachusetts and New York, Lebanon Valley was the picture of rustic reverie. Fragrant meadows and lush woodlands spread out for miles, and a series of dramatic hills, all bright and tender green, embraced the land. All through the countryside were signs of careful cultivation: wooden cottages surrounded by well-tended kitchen gardens and summer blooms, orchards, groves, and field upon field of ripening grains.

When Eunice traveled to this region at the end of July, a ride was not hard to come by, despite the remote locale. It was prime tourist season in Lebanon Springs, where warm mineral waters, bubbling forth year-round at an even seventy-three degrees, drew droves of invalids and pleasure seekers from New York City and a large number of visitors from the South.

These waters were not as restorative as those of Ballston or Saratoga Springs, but what they lacked in mineral content was offset by other benefits, such as the quality of the air, the serenity of the scene, and the "opportunities provided for sport." Horseback riding was a favorite pastime (as was betting on horses), but there was another activity, considered a sport by some, which was almost unique to the region: visiting the Shakers.

The two communities of Lebanon Valley, the resort town and the Shaker village, were a study in contrasts. Lebanon was known as a "marriage market," where the young ladies, flushed from their baths, regularly "angled for husbands." When not enjoying the waters, the well-heeled visitors who dominated the town at this time of year would amuse themselves with leisurely walks, horse races, and games of checkers. At night, they lounged in their boardinghouses, smoking, drinking, and playing cards. Even to non-Believers, some of these nighttime activities appeared unsavory. As one international visitor observed, "the orgies of the evening crowd at an American inn" were known to be "disgusting," and formed such a contrast to the "serenity and decency" of the nearby Shakers that he could hardly believe that he was but half an hour's walk from the "Society of Union."

The leisure in Lebanon Springs may not always have been wholesome, but it offered Eunice a perfect opportunity to hawk her story. Here, among a populace that had ample time to read, Eunice's books found a ready market. Just as in Albany, people in Lebanon Springs had no trouble believing that the unassuming folk beside them were actually cunning captors in disguise. Even locals, who were beholden to the Shakers for taxes and tourism, joined in the fray and contributed their own stories of Shaker abuses. There was a Shaker named Riley, for instance, a formerly devoted husband who tried to run off with his infant child to the Shakers. Neighbors had come to the rescue in the middle of the night and hidden the child in order to save it from its father.

Encouraged by her success at Lebanon Springs, Eunice rode out seven miles over the Massachusetts border to the town of Pittsfield—Mother Lucy's hometown, which bordered another Shaker community—to distribute more books. However, she was stopped by a group of Shakers who had followed her out from the springs and threatened to sue her for libel if she dared to circulate any more of her writing.

Eunice remained undaunted. Not long after returning to Lebanon Springs, she set out for the Shakers, accompanied by a local man and his daughter whom she had met in town. The gentleman had encountered Mother Lucy once before and recalled that the elect lady had come before him, dressed from head to toe in white, like some kind of angel or goddess, leaning heavily on the arms of her minions. Eunice had heard other stories about the Shaker Mother—that she was a good-looking woman who had had trouble letting go of her husband. Such tales encouraged Eunice. If the "goddess" at the Shaker helm had once harbored strong "natural bonds," perhaps the memory of these, in addition to legal pressures, would move her to change her society's course.

The travelers descended into the valley before taking a winding dirt road that brought them up to a "noble mountain terrace." Here, as one visitor described, "halfway between the deep green valley and the bending sky, lay the Shaker village . . . half hidden by trees and a vail of blue smoke," with the meetinghouse standing out, bright and white, "like a cluster of stars."

At the trustees' office, however, the Shakers refused to allow Eunice near their Mother. They rebuffed her when she visited

yet again, this time observing that it would be "of no use" for
Eunice to see Mother Lucy, who had nothing to do with her
children. Eunice argued that if Mother Lucy only gave the
word, her children could be free at once. Then she drew a harder
line. Handing the Sisters a copy of her book, she warned that
there were five hundred people ready to descend upon the
Shakers to take her children away.

The Sisters steadily replied: "If you have so many men at
your command you had better come out and show what you can
do." Yet they were obviously not at ease. Several of them refused to give their names when asked, and as Eunice and her
companions turned onto the immaculate stone path that led
them back to the springs, Eunice could see that, from under the
shade of their broad Shaker bonnets, the Sisters were "gaz[ing]
after her."

Lucy Wright might have come out to see Eunice and confronted
the woman for whom motherhood meant something entirely
different from what it meant for herself. She had been in New
Lebanon at the time of Eunice's visit and was fully apprised of
the other mother's activities. The Shakers had been tracking
Eunice closely. They knew that she had begun writing again
in Albany and even that she was in touch with "a smart, capable woman from North Enfield," none other than Mary
Dyer. Yet the Shaker Mother had decided to remain indoors—
probably no more than a street's distance away from where
Eunice had stood.

A month later, the Shakers received more upsetting news,
that James Chapman had probably "renounced his faith." They
learned that the man had an "excessive appetite for cider" and
"was often overcome"—a state that was likely to lead to "other

evils." With James missing and in bad shape, the timing of Eunice's next move could not have been worse for the Shakers. It came in the form of a letter, penned in a cramped hasty script and addressed to "Mrs. Lucy Goodrich."

Albany, December 4, 1817

Mrs. Lucy Goodrich,

I have been twice to your village to see you, hoping an interview with you would induce you to be satisfied it would be best for your people to restore to me my children. I now call upon you to take the matter into serious consideration, and judge whether you had not better hastily restore them, and grant me some compensation for all my trouble on account of your society's abuse of me and my children, and thereby prevent your complete overthrow —You know on what a foundation you stand. The sword of justice is lifted against you, and you cannot sheathe it, unless you comply with the above speedily.—Remember that a woman can be as mighty to pull you down, as a woman was to build you up. If you think it is for revenge; remember that a woman can dive deep in *that* art, even to exceed an army—I shall wait till Christmas for an answer from you, before I proceed any farther; mean time I shall be making preparations, as I now am—If you treat this letter as your society has every other they have received from me, you will not hear from me again very soon, only through the hands of others as an *instrument*.

Eunice Chapman

Eunice's aggressive stance in this letter could not be more different from the vulnerable posture she assumes in her published writings. No longer is she a cowering victim, "tortured in the whirlwind of affliction and woe." Empowered by her legal successes, by public support, and by her conviction that she is an "instrument" in God's hand, Eunice boasts of "overthrowing" the Shakers, holding the "sword of justice" to their necks, and even "exceeding an army" in her ability to exact revenge. The sentimental heroine has given way to a terrifying warrior, one who knows full well her power. Facing a worthy female adversary and no longer constricted by the demands placed upon her gender, Eunice glories in her powers as a writer, woman, and political actor.

The significance of this discrepancy, between Eunice as she appeared in her book, and Eunice as she was in reality, was not lost on the Shakers. They made sure to preserve her words, carefully folding the letter back in its wrapping and storing it away. In the meantime, Mother Lucy resolved to address Eunice directly.

The Shaker Mother was not in an enviable position. She had the power to return Eunice's children, but there were political issues to consider, and these were particularly delicate for a female ruler who was hardly as unquestioned in her authority as Eunice assumed. Like Eunice, Mother Lucy had faced repeated challenges on account of her gender. Early in her reign, there were mass defections by young men such as Angell Matthewson, who resented being subject to a female leader. Later, the Shaker Mother was repeatedly snubbed by certain Brothers in her own community, who put off her request to relocate a building so many times that she finally marched over to the site and began taking down the house herself.

Male resistance took a more insidious turn in the form of Father John Barns. Barns, who once led the Shakers in Maine, had recently begun an outright rebellion against "petticoat government." He was doing all that he could to undermine Mother Lucy's authority, arguing that "the lead being in the female brings great distress upon the body." Barns had been stripped of his power, but he continued to make inroads among the rank and file, especially young Believers.

Now, Mother Lucy faced additional pressure on account of the newly published biography of Mother Ann, edited by Seth Wells. The book contained some details that looked not quite right, even to those in charge—for example, it recorded that Mother Ann would occasionally grab bad Believers by the nose. It would further hurt the Shakers' case if a copy of this book in its raw, inspired state got into the hands of their enemies— particularly Eunice Chapman, who, the Shakers knew, was coming out with a book of her own.

But Lucy Wright was a skilled and savvy leader who, like Eunice, knew how to use her femininity to her advantage. In her smooth, stately hand, she wrote:

> New Lebanon, Columbia County, New York State
> December 12, 1817
>
> Eunice,
>
> I have received thy letter of the fourth instant and read it with due attention, and can see no consistent way for me to fulfill thy demands. Thou callest on me to "*restore thy children, and to grant thee some compensation for thy trouble on account of the society's abuse of thee and thy children, and thereby prevent my (or our) overthrow.*" I can wash my hands in innocence before God and all men, respecting any abuse to thee or thy children; and if any abuse to thee or thy children hath been done by the society, it is unknown to me. I have

neither the will nor the power, either to hold the children
or to give them up to thee; for I have nothing to do with
them.

Their father, as I have been informed, took them under
his own care—he acted [in] his own pleasure in the matter. Thou must, therefore, look to him for thy children,
and not to me nor the society, to which I belong, for we
are not responsible for him nor his children, for they are
not with us, nor under our care.

I think it would be inconsistent with law and gospel
for me to try to wrest them from under the government
of their father—I want no authority in such matters.

Lucy Goodrich

It is indeed a pointed irony that the head of the Shakers, who
was among the most powerful women of her day, would declare herself not just innocent but powerless to affect Eunice's
circumstances. Signing off with the married name she had
abandoned decades ago, Lucy Wright outdid even Eunice in
using a demure feminine posture as a shield. According to
the Shaker Mother, it was not within her rights to interfere
with the "government" of the children's father; she deferred
entirely to his authority on this matter and suggested that
Eunice do the same.

In reality, of course, Lucy Wright was hardly as helpless as
she claimed. In 1819, she would step in to resolve a similar conflict over children in New Lebanon. This crisis divided the
Shakers along gender lines: The Sisters wanted to return the
children to their unbelieving parents, while the Brothers preferred that the society stand by its legal right to its charges.

Mother Lucy ultimately sided with the Sisters and, in effect, a mother like Eunice.

Where the Chapman children were concerned, however, Mother Lucy's hands were tied. Were she to order the release of Eunice's children at this moment, all the Shakers' prior claims of ignorance—Elder Seth's legislative testimony, the Shakers' written statement, and James Chapman's insistence that he had acted alone—would be exposed as a sham. The Shakers' credibility would be ruined, and with it, all their hopes of defeating Eunice's bill. The Shakers' militia exemption was sure to be compromised as well, and there might even be national repercussions. In addition to fighting Mary Dyer in New Hampshire, the Shakers were staving off further attacks in Ohio. In July, an Ohio Shaker community had been mobbed over an escaped child, and a newspaper editor named Abram Van Vleet was inflaming the masses with violently anti-Shaker propaganda. If Mother Lucy were to concede to Eunice, a domino effect could very well follow.

As things stood, there was a decent possibility that Eunice's bill could fail, or so the Shakers' allies assured them. It was true that the Council of Revision did not often exercise its veto power over the legislature. Of the hundreds of bills passed by the state every year, only one or two were ever rejected. But the council was also famous for its conservatism, dominated as it was by die-hard Federalists who saw it as their duty to "check the ravages of the demagogues." Chief among these hard-liners was the illustrious Chancellor James Kent (the so-called "American Blackstone"), whose family occasionally dined at Watervliet. With its questionable curtailment of civil and religious liberties and expansive use of legislative power—on behalf of a single petitioner, no less—Eunice's bill was just the kind that the council was most likely to strike down.

But Eunice, too, had her connections and reasons for hope. Her brothers were friendly with the new governor, who presided over the council. DeWitt Clinton was a fellow Mason with Elijah, who named one of his sons "DeWitt Clinton Hawley." The governor also owed a debt to Jesse Hawley, whose writings on the canal had inspired Clinton to back the project that would become the defining accomplishment of his career. Family law, moreover, was changing at such a pace that no one's vote could be counted on for sure. Chancellor Kent himself had recently issued an unusual judgment in favor of keeping children with their mother. Another council member, Chief Justice Smith Thompson, had determined the Waldren case of 1816, which set the precedent for the "best interest of the child" as an approach to custody that was to define American family law in years to come.

Christmas came and went, and when the Shakers ignored the deadline that she had set for them, Eunice moved ahead as promised. She taught all day, while staying up much of the night to work on the latest version of her book—a schedule that was making her more than a little bleary-eyed and sometimes sloppy. She also hustled depositions from as many sources as she could, writing to Mary Dyer for a statement and asking Thomas Brown to write on her behalf.

By now, Eunice had already succeeded in getting the ex-Shaker Josiah Terry to sign a statement that she may have written herself, if his words are to be believed. Josiah later claimed that after repeatedly calling for meetings, Eunice had presented him with a statement which was based on his words but to which she had added "her own glosses." She then asked him to sign the statement, whereupon the bewildered, entranced young man could only agree.

In the critical days leading up to the council's judgment, Eunice put her charms to work on the governor, as well, having been introduced to him by her brothers. (Unfortunately, no records exist to describe this meeting between "Magnus Apollo," as Clinton was known, and his diminutive petitioner.) The Believers, meanwhile, prepared for the conflict to come, apprehensively awaiting the "dreadful bundle of trash" that was sure to emerge from Eunice's pen. Eunice also braced herself. In a letter to Mary Dyer, who was gearing up for her own legislative battle, Eunice had warned the other mother "to be prepared to meet with all the slander from the Shakers, that an evil spirit can invest." To overcome this onslaught, she advised: "You must set your face like a flint."

9

THE COUNCIL
OF REVISION

On the opening day of the legislature, January 27, 1818, the Council of Revision returned a terse judgment. Eschewing all talk of constitutionality, marital responsibility, and rights to religious expression, the council rejected Eunice's bill because it would deprive James Chapman and all Shakers of the right to remarry, without a trial by jury. Believing that these reasons alone were enough to deny the act, the council went no further, and left all other questions—including whether or not joining the Shakers might be a legitimate rationale for divorce—unanswered.

William Leete Stone considered the case closed. In order to become law, Eunice's bill would now have to repass both houses of the legislature by a two-thirds majority *and* earn the approval of the dubious council. As he printed the verdict in the *Albany Gazette,* Stone observed: "We hope this subject is put to rest, and that the members will no longer be harassed by the pressing importunities of this fair and fascinating petitioner." A few days later, the senate voted 14 to 12 against overturning the council's veto, and the Shakers celebrated the apparent death of Eunice's act. As Elder Seth crowed in a letter, "The hussy failed of her purpose." Still, the Elder did not rest easy. Eunice had sworn that she would pull down the Shakers, and given that they were still standing, he knew that she was probably "not done with us yet."

The Elder's instincts were right. The day after the senators voted to uphold the council's veto, Eunice's supporters in the senate revived her bill, rewriting it to address the council's criticisms and retooling it as a personal act of relief—as a means to help Eunice rather than as an indictment of the Shakers. By the terms of this new bill, Eunice would have her divorce, but James would not lose his right to remarry. Gone, too, was any indication that others could apply for a divorce on the same grounds. These changes were significant, for by removing the "punishment" previously imposed on James and the Shakers, the proposed act freed all parties from blame (this was rather odd from a legal point of view, since divorce was considered a remedy for a crime). The remaining general provision made it possible for Eunice and other Shaker wives to obtain custody. Later, a habeas corpus provision was added, as well.

With these changes in place, Eunice was gratified by a rare overturn of the council's verdict. In a remarkably small window of time, she managed to persuade every single senator who had previously pledged to help her to stand with her again. She also persuaded others who had never supported her before to vote in her favor. Thus on February 2—less than a week after the council's veto—the senate passed Eunice's new act by a landslide: 19 to 3. Two weeks later, announcing that this was to be

"POSITIVELY HER LAST APPEARANCE THIS SEASON," Stone registered a similarly spectacular triumph in the house, where the act passed "EIGHTY-FIVE to NINETEEN!" "We have only to remark," he wrote, "that we were astonished at the result."

How did Eunice effect such a dramatic transformation? Onlookers were hard-pressed to explain. Stone, for one, posited that "some strange infatuation—some magic—some invisible influence" must have been at play. He also pointed to Eunice's aggressive tactics. He accused her of stalking lawmakers to make her point, of even following them into their bedrooms late at night. Regardless of how and where Eunice pleaded her case, her grit and charisma were undoubtedly vital ingredients in her success. But there was more to her success than her personal conquests: Eunice had finally released the latest version of her book, which reinvigorated her phenomenal appeal as a sentimental heroine.

This new book, *No. 2, An Additional Account of the Conduct of the Shakers*, was even craftier than the first. Eunice did not generate new lies about the Shakers, as Mary Dyer would in the years to come. (Mary charged, for instance, that Shakers were sterilized—an allegation that would result in humiliating medical examinations of Believers in New Hampshire.) Instead, Eunice intensified her portrayal of herself as a helpless heroine in need of saving and the Shakers as cruel, unknowable captors, thus honing a strategy that had proved irresistible before. She also provided more depositions against James and the Shakers, and a refutation by Thomas Brown, the celebrated anti-Shaker author whose name had made Elder Seth jump from his chair during his senate hearing. She did not, however, include statements by Mary Dyer and Josiah Terry, which revealed her knowledge of her family's whereabouts. If the Shakers were to obtain a copy of her book and read these ex-Shakers' words, they might be tempted to move her children yet again. Eunice could not take that chance. Nonetheless, she shared Mary's and Josiah's stories with key legislators, leaving pages for them at various boardinghouses.

Eunice's book was an impressive feat of editing and republication, but what made it even more effective at this crucial juncture was that for many in the legislature, it was entirely new material. Recent elections had brought in a whole new class of lawmakers, political rookies from across the state who had not been privy to the earlier debates on Eunice's bill, were unfamiliar with the Shakers' point of view, and finally, were vulnerable to the influence of a newcomer to the assembly, a man who would become Eunice's strongest, most vocal, and most controversial advocate to date: the Brigadier General.

It was said of Erastus Root that when he found himself laid up with a broken leg in Coxsackie, a staid little village peopled by Dutch folk on the west bank of the Hudson, the mighty legislator roared in despair to a visiting friend: "Think of it, here I am in this miserable, God-forsaken hole with nobody to talk to and nobody to drink with; and if I were to die here and be buried among these Dutchmen, when I rise at the resurrection, I would not be able to understand a damned word which these Hollanders have to say!"

The forty-five-year-old Brigadier General, so named for his role in the state militia, was a "great fierce obstinate-looking creature," as Elder Seth described him, with a warm, leveling gaze and a most "scandalizing" manner of speech. To his opponents, he was a demagogue of the worst kind. Although

by birth a genteel Yankee—a Dartmouth-educated, schoolmaster turned attorney who was as well-versed in the classics
as any of his peers—Root considered himself a man of the
people and befriended those whom his high-class peers openly
disdained. Critics dismissed his associates as vulgar, drunken
hooligans who knew nothing of restraint or religion. In the capitol, as William Leete Stone observed with contempt, Root held
court among the yokels, "back-woods members who, delighted
with his virtues and his eloquence, [would] gaze with silent
admiration upon his greatness" and hang on his every word.

Yet even his enemies could not help liking Root. The voluble
hunk of a man was famously affable—and persuasive. Root enjoyed a reputation as a skilled debater who knew how to work
up a crowd with wit and passion. From his first days in politics
as the youngest man in the house, he had been known to play
dirty, skewering his opponents with off-color quips. But invariably all was forgiven because his speeches were so entertain-
ing. Years later, when his love of drink got the better of him (he
would be mocked for allegedly nodding off drunk in his senate
chair), the General's personal charms were insufficient to carry
him above the ranks of congressman or lieutenant governor, and
he was politically stymied. In 1818, however, Erastus Root was
a man in his prime.

Anything that smacked of privilege was fair game for attack,
as far as this brash assemblyman was concerned. As Stone put
it, "No matter what the bill—if it says anything about money—
whether it be for the support of officers, of government, or for
the payment of our debts, or for rebuilding a bridge, or increasing the toll of a turnpike gate . . . we are sure to have a speech
from General Root upon the subjects of prodigality—waste—

extravagance—taxes—oppression—tyranny, etc.—the whole concluding with the most passionate protestations of love for the people, and an abhorrence of high salaries and speculation."

In Root, Eunice had found the perfect defender. How the two first met is not known (it is possible introductions were made through Asahel Paine, whom Root replaced as representative from Delaware County), but one thing is evident: they had an explosive personal chemistry. Although Root was a long-married father, to outsiders, at least, it became obvious that he was infatuated with Eunice and was far more invested in her case—and her—than was appropriate.

But personal affinity was not the only force at work. Eunice's case fell perfectly in line with Root's outrage against the forces of aristocracy. He despised the Council of Appointment, which conspired behind closed doors to dole out public offices, from those of postmaster to mayor, without so much as a word from the people. He opposed restrictions on suffrage, which put the vote out of the reach of too many men, merely because they lacked property. And most of all, he hated the Council of Revision, which may have represented the greatest affront to his egalitarian values.

Among New Yorkers in general, the council was unpopular and was especially resented for its authority to reject any and all acts of the legislature. To Root, it was appalling that the council would dare to pass judgment on the will of the people, and so for him, as for many others, Eunice's case came to stand for much more than the interests of one beguiling petitioner. To this ardent assemblyman, democracy itself was on the line.

If Eunice had depended on the Brigadier General to help overturn the council's veto, she now needed his help more than ever. The council had one more chance to assert its authority, and this time its focus would be personal. Whereas previous versions of Eunice's act had a broad orientation, addressing the existing family laws or the dangers posed by the Shakers, this latest incarnation concentrated on the needs of a single petitioner. And with this narrowed lens, it would not be the laws or the Believers who would go on trial so much as it would be the heroine at the center of the story. Inevitably, the focus would shift to this: not just whether the petitioning damsel was truly in distress and the state should help her, but whether, in fact, she was worth saving.

On February 27, exactly one month after it first rejected Eunice's bill, and in a highly unusual move, the Council of Revision delivered a second veto. This time, it did not lack for words. In a rambling message that filled three dense pages of legislative journals, the council laid out three reasons for its decision. The first was insufficient grounds for divorce. "The institution of marriage," it grandly declared, "by legalizing and regulating sexual intercourse, has greatly multiplied the sources of rational enjoyment, and exalted the human character. It is the only basis of domestic happiness, and the firm foundation of social order." And while the council acknowledged that the permanent state of marriage sometimes led to misery, it countered that "many thousands of families" were saved by the "mutual forbearances and concessions between husband and wife" that resulted from their knowing that marriage had no exit. Only in the case of adultery should the marital contract be revoked. In all other situations, matrimony should be defended at all costs.

The council further rejected the bill because it allowed the legislature to terminate a marriage contract without a trial by jury, an unprecedented abuse of power. Whether or not James Chapman suffered punishment by being denied the right to remarry was beside the point. The council also objected to the act as unconstitutional. James Chapman was guaranteed his religious rights, and as a father, he was entitled to the custody and services of his children, "without accountability." Yet, under the proposed act, he would lose these rights simply for being a Shaker. Echoing the Shakers' argument, the council warned that by this logic, the state could deprive a man of anything else, "banish him, or even put him to death."

The council next went beyond these essential arguments to launch an unusually personal attack, one that betrayed a curious preoccupation with sex. According to the council, the existing laws were capable of answering to Eunice's complaints in almost every way. If her husband had abandoned her without cause (and on this point the council had its doubts), then she could seek a divorce from bed and board. The same could be said for cruelty. If James had abused his rights as a father (and here again the council was skeptical), she could ask the chancellor to intervene on the children's behalf.

What, then, was left of Eunice's complaints? Now the council made a tremendous leap in logic, borrowing again from the Shakers' arguments. As the council saw it, the only thing that the woman seemed to be missing, which could not be provided elsewhere, was sexual fulfillment. And, "if the mere privation of sexual intercourse is the real subject of complaint on the part of this woman," they wrote, "the Council feel constrained to remark, that such an application is offensive to public decency."

Here, the council seized upon the Shakers' sole criterion for differentiating their religion from all others—their sexual abstinence—not to judge the sect, but to censure Eunice, turning her portrayal of herself as a sentimental heroine on its head. A character like Charlotte Temple may have been preyed upon as a sexual object, but she herself was always innocent of sexual desire. The reason for her "fall" was not that she lusted but that she was lusted *after*. Eunice, the council suggested, was entirely the opposite—a woman of gross sexual appetites, who was therefore far more dangerous than the Shakers would ever be. In the council's view, the Shakers' "notorious" stance on sexuality, repugnant as it was, actually safeguarded them from being any real threat to society. "The absurdity of that tenet," the council wrote, "is so plain and obvious, as to prove an antidote and security against any serious danger of its prevalence. It may be pitied as a delusion, but it ought not to be regarded as a crime."

The council's report was handed out to every member of the legislature and given top billing in the *Albany Gazette*. From there, it was reprinted in more distant newspapers such as the *Columbia Gazette* in Utica and the *Commercial Advertiser* in New York City. William Leete Stone expressed the public backlash against Eunice when he wrote the following:

> We charge her with no crime; but we do say . . . that any female who would so far lose sight of the dignity of the sex, as literally to dog and harass the members of the legislature, year after year—who will visit the bed-chambers of members, necessarily strangers, at all hours of the day, and alone—cannot expect, with the better part of community, to enjoy that influence or to command that indulgence, attention, and respect, to which a virtuous and amiable woman is entitled. Eunice Chapman may be chaste,

for aught we know; but to turn a figure of Sir William
Draper's round—a woman's honor must be like a soldier's
—not only pure, but unsuspected.

The council's report and all the bawdy talk it inspired were
crushing for a woman who considered her reputation her "only
dependence for existence." Even so, infamy was not without
its benefits. The legislature had one last opportunity to overturn the council's judgment. If both house and senate rejected
the veto, Eunice's bill would be law; if one of them did not,
however, the bill would be lost. With word of Eunice's case
having spread so far, all of Albany and beyond were attuned
to her problems, ensuring a wide audience and potentially a
more sympathetic hearing as the legislature pondered its final
response.

10

AN OBJECT
OF DISGUST

On the eve of the legislature's final consideration of Eunice's case, Albany was awash in a flood storm, the likes of which had not been seen for nearly half a century. Shopkeepers sealed their doors and secured their wares, and the townspeople nervously watched from behind fogged windows as the waters of the Hudson swelled, surged, and finally overran the shuttered city. Wild and engorged, the normally hospitable river knocked great sloops against the docks, swept away unmoored objects, and hurtled a horse ferry halfway down residential Pearl Street. The night of the third was the worst. On Church Street, a number of families would have drowned if they had not been pulled to safety. Even in the sheltered barroom of the Eagle Tavern—Leverett Cruttenden's towering hostelry, which boasted views of the ravaged harbor and was not far from Eunice's home—the water came up past a grown man's knees, and politicians who lodged there were forced to imbibe their spirits elsewhere.

As the storm cleared, the people of Albany began to pick their way once more along what was known as the "ladies' turnpike," narrow footpaths that linked one sidewalk to the other. Raging alongside the mincing pedestrians and occasionally spraying them with clay-rich mud were hightailing teamsters who would steer their overloaded wagons to the edges of the street, reckless in their eagerness to unload their goods. Ladies' skirts were rimmed brown, and it must have seemed as if only the street hogs could enjoy such weather. Still, the streets grew crowded again, with townspeople eager to leave their dank quarters for some fresh air.

On the morning after the storm's peak, the senators once again took up the matter of "an act for the relief of Eunice Chapman." They were anxious to proceed. Days earlier, when they had first received the council's veto, some senators had been so outraged by the council's audacity in checking the legislature's authority —and by its attacks on Eunice—that they had sought to overturn the verdict right then and there, without even printing the council's statement, as was customary. They had been persuaded to wait; then came the storm. Now, with little debate, the senate voted to reject the council's second ruling, and re-passed Eunice's act by a wide margin: 20 to 6.

The fate of Eunice's bill thus came to rest entirely with the house. With such a weighty decision at hand, Erastus Root proposed that Eunice's case be made the special order of the day for Wednesday, March 11. His motion was quickly approved. For Eunice, the stakes in these debates could not have been higher. With defeat, she could lose her children forever; with victory, she would make history.

*　*　*

The appointed day was unexpectedly warm, and in Albany, where fast-melting snow streamed downhill toward the harbor, the capitol was thronged as never before. Toward midday, crowds worked their way up State Street, converged on the capitol steps, and passed under the forbidding gaze of Themis before crossing the marble halls into the hall of assembly, which was packed to its capacity.

On the floor, the lawmakers' seats formed concentric semicircles before a raised speaker's area, to which plush chairs and heavy drapery lent an air of finery. Also opposite the speaker, suspended high above the ornate chandeliers that brought scant light to the hall, was a long balcony with rows of boxed-in stadium seats for the public. On this day, this balcony was crammed to the ledges. Looking up from their seats, lawmakers were surely astounded to see the number of faces peering down at them. Every last seat was taken, and those who were not fortunate in securing one jostled one another for the remaining standing space between the aisles.

For Eunice, this was truly the performance of her life. Dressed in her finest gown and sitting at demure attention among the onlookers, she now had to completely embody the heroine she had promised to be in her books, all this under the unforgiving glare of the public spotlight, where every blemish and misstep would be magnified and examined. Eunice already had at least one hostile observer on the floor: William Leete Stone, who studied the "modern enchantress," as he called her, pen in hand, barely disguising his contempt. As fascinating as he found Eunice personally, Stone had come to believe that her bill was "fraught with the most dangerous consequences to the people of this state." No one could be deserving of such perilous rewards.

The Shakers were notably absent from the scene, much to the disappointment of their supporters and, no doubt, the crowd. During the past several weeks, numerous visitors had driven to Watervliet, eager to see for themselves whether the sober-eyed, oddly garbed people who sold them quality brooms and seeds were really the villainous wild-dancing, sex-obsessed, child-stealing pagans Eunice Chapman had made them out to be. Two weeks ago, seventy-eight carriages, conveying four hundred visitors, had arrived for public worship. The past weekend, two hundred more had arrived at their doors.

The Shakers' friends—neighbors and business associates of long acquaintance—had also called on them, eager to rouse them from what seemed to be a kind of stupor. Two days before, a group of these supporters had confronted Elder Seth, taking the Shakers to task for being "idle" at home when their friends were working so hard to help them. The Elder had shrugged—the society had delivered its "Remonstrance," after all—but was chastened when he learned that Eunice and her friends had suppressed these materials, and that it was popularly believed that James and the children were hiding in Watervliet. Yet when he had traveled to Albany a day earlier with fresh copies of the "Remonstrance," he had been told by house members that there was little that the society could do at this point —that they might actually hurt their cause by attempting to further it, and that their best defense lay in the words of the Council of Revision. With this, the Shakers had decided to stay home.

On the floor, in their place, were the lawmakers who had vowed to defend them. Thomas J. Oakley, a Federalist from Dutchess County, was a relative newcomer to the house, but he

knew the Shakers personally, as did his wife, who had been
among the group that had chastised Elder Seth two days earlier.
Henry Meigs, a father of seven and a recent veteran of the War of
1812, was a Republican from New York City. A second Federalist to lead the defense was Albany's William Duer, who had opposed Eunice's bill ever since he had sat on the first committee
on her case, led by Asahel Paine in 1815. (Paine was no longer in
the assembly.) There was also the Republican Nathan Williams,
who had declared during last year's debates that the "man who
did not feel for the distresses of a helpless woman, was a villain—
but that the man who let his feelings sway his judgment, was
unfit for a legislator." He planned to make a similar case today.

The Shakers' defenders knew they faced a difficult battle.
Oakley and Meigs had personally confided to Elder Seth that
Eunice was likely to prevail. However, they were bolstered by
the presence of the illustrious Council of Revision, whose members had attended the short debates in the senate and were
unlikely to have missed the final arguments in the house.

Towering over this group was the forceful, jowl-faced new
governor, DeWitt Clinton. Unlike Erastus Root, who was liked
even by his foes, Clinton was known to be capricious and self-
serving, and had even betrayed his fellow Republicans by courting Federalists in years past. Eunice surely felt deceived by
Clinton, who, despite his loyalties to her brothers and to her,
had signed off on the council's venomous statement. With so
much on the line in his new term as governor—including the
Erie Canal, which some opponents called "Clinton's Ditch"—
Eunice's cause was simply not worth the fight. Six other men
flanked the controversial governor, including Chancellor James
Kent, a small man who looked swallowed up next to the gar-
gantuan Clinton but was in fact the ringleader of the group.

Near him was Jonas Platt, a thin, reserved, and intensely pious judge and the purported author of the council's statement. These men grimly awaited a hearing that promised to be a referendum on their power as much as on Eunice Chapman.

Their many enemies took their seats on the diamond-patterned assembly floor, some studying the council's report, others rehearsing their statements or consulting the materials that Eunice had given them. Still others ambled in on their own time, flushed from having sampled the house's ready supply of spirits. Erastus Root, however, was sure to have entered the hall promptly as he prepared to defend his petite charge. Never far from him was Dr. Isaac Sargent from Washington County, Root's ally on virtually all issues and a man whose personal attentions to Eunice had also become a subject of lewd speculation.

In circulation around this time was an anonymously written two-act farce that ridiculed the two men's connections to Eunice and her command over the assembly. Entitled *Indoctum Parliamentum*, or "the unschooled parliament," the play shows Eunice bewitching Root, Sargent, and others—including the devil himself—with her seductive story and ultimately throwing the legislature into lawless upheaval. In her last appearance in the play, Eunice is seen celebrating promiscuously with "eighty-five wiseacres" clad in homespun, who take turns dancing with her and drag in a hogshead of whiskey. (The play was probably not intended for performance.)

To the many gathered in the assembly hall for these final debates, the anarchy that the farce predicted must have loomed as a real possibility. When, at noon, the chairman of the committee on Eunice's case, George Brayton, took the lead, he looked out on a vast and motley congregation straining the house walls, spilling beyond the public viewing area, and taking up the aisles. There was a strange and unquiet energy in the overbooked arena. People who read anti-Shaker books— particularly books, like Eunice's, that evoked witchery and torture—were known to become violent. And there were simply too many people in a space so poorly ventilated that even on normal days, assemblymen commonly complained of "dizziness in the head." The potential for violence was great; the crowd was worked up with that unsettling mixture of greed, hostility, and delight common to public reckonings, carnivals, and hangings.

The hall grew momentarily tame, however, when Brayton announced, in the strongest voice he could muster, "The Act for the Relief of Eunice Chapman and other purposes." For a second time this year, Brayton declared, the Honorable Council of Revision had rejected this bill, and for a second time the senate had favored it. It now fell to the assembly to decide whether to stand with the senate or the council—and whether or not to make this bill law. He then called for a reading of the council's objections.

Eunice could only have winced as the house clerk stood to read the council's report. However difficult it had been to see the words in print and know that they were being circulated in public taverns, in homes, and everywhere else that papers were read, it required a new kind of endurance to hear them spoken aloud in view of an audience. As the clerk pronounced the council's grandiose statements about marriage and rattled off the arguments against her divorce, Eunice braced herself for its distressing conclusion: "If the mere privation of sexual intercourse is the real subject of complaint on the part of this woman, the Council feel restrained to remark, that such an application is offensive to public decency."

At a time when public discussion of sexuality was taboo, such commentary was sure to have ignited the house and to have turned heads toward the notorious woman who had inspired it. Eunice, however, had no direct means of defense. The house was in session and her sole means of vindication lay in the assemblymen who competed to speak on her case that day.

The first to address the house was New York City's Henry Meigs, one of the politicians whom Elder Seth had consulted the day before. To the Elder, Meigs had expressed his fears that his colleagues would vote with emotion, rather than reason. Today, he sought to have reason prevail by making constitutionality the issue of the day. Meigs opened by strongly asserting that the Shakers were a harmless religious people, well known for their industry and order. No charges, he said, could be brought against them—except, perhaps that they banned sexual intercourse. But did this practice qualify as an "act of licentiousness" or as a threat to the public—the sole conditions under which the state had a right to interfere in matters of religion?

"The constitution of this state," he proclaimed, "guarantees equally the religion of all. The Jew, who believes the blessed Savior an imposter; the Egyptian who worships a crocodile or an onion; the Pagan who worships the sun; the Indian who pays divine honors to sticks and stones; the worshipper of Odin; the Chinese or the Mahometans. All persuasions, denominations or religions are equally protected." Meigs's listeners twittered, and Stone scrambled to take down the droll examples. But Meigs's point was clear: It did not matter how absurd a sect's professions were. The state had no right to meddle with a religion unless it was proved to cause public harm—which was hardly the case with this benevolent sect.

By granting Eunice Chapman a divorce, Meigs further observed, the state would set a dangerous precedent. New York had always assumed a protective stance toward marriage. Since its early days as a colony until the present, not a single legislative divorce had been passed. History raised the question: Why should the state change its ways now?

As soon as Meigs resumed his seat, a like-minded colleague arose. This was Nathan Williams, who had implored his fellow assemblymen to heed their better judgment the year before. Williams proceeded to reiterate well-rehearsed arguments—that the proposed bill represented an abuse of power and a threat to matrimony and that the capitol would be overtaken with divorce bills featuring cases "infinitely more cruel." Husbands and wives, he said, would not try to work out their differences but would flee to the Shakers in order to obtain divorces. Innocent children would be "torn" from their father's arms. Justice would be overrun.

But then the lawyer from Utica took a new tack. By this bill, he declared, "we are now attacking and attempting to break down" not just "the laws," but "the ordinances of God." And for whom was all this to be done? Williams cried, turning toward the mortified woman sitting in the audience. "For *Eunice Chapman*!" he spat, "the very name of whom excites disgust. Eunice Chapman," he repeated, "who has been figuring away at the capital these three years."

At this, the public glare fell on Eunice. It was all she could do to stay in her seat, given her natural inclination to stand up for herself, but she was required to remain as she was. She had to stay true to the role in which she had cast herself, since the least protest would only confirm the charges against her.

"Sirs," Williams called, beseeching the assemblymen, "this Eunice Chapman is not one of those modest, retiring, deserving women, for whom we should entertain a sympathy. She has been boldly courting public opinion for years, instead of concealing her griefs, if she has any. No modest woman would conduct herself thus. No modest and virtuous woman would be harassing the legislature year after year, and barely and avowedly for the purpose of obtaining the liberty of marrying another man. Such a female can only be an object of disgust—nothing else, for her impudence."

At this, Eunice's supporters roared in objection, but Williams was not yet done. "By passing this bill," he announced to the crowd, "we shall give boldness to the female character. Those who are now apparently amiable, encouraged by the success of Eunice Chapman, would become emboldened. The vermil-tinctured hues which modesty casts upon the cheek at the least indelicate expressions or action, would be chased away. They, like Eunice Chapman, would leave their retirement, and by familiarity with gentlemen would soon become emboldened, and would be haunting the members—for divorces!"

By now, the assemblyman could barely be heard in the riotous hall. Erastus Root clamored to speak his turn, as did Dr. Sargent. All the while, as people cried out around her, objecting, laughing, and pointing, Eunice "set her face like a flint," as she had advised Mary Dyer. It was a moment before Williams could offer his conclusion. His tone was somber. The day that this bill became law would be the most unfortunate he could ever imagine and one that history would mourn.

By the time Williams finished speaking he was hoarse, having projected outward to an audience of hundreds for more than two hours. As he prepared to leave the floor, he courteously apologized to his listeners for having "thus trespass[ed] upon their patience," adding, however, that he had "felt it a duty he owed society to use every effort to prevent the passage of the bill."

There was no time left for anyone else to speak. One day had not been enough for Eunice Chapman; the discussion on her case would have to continue tomorrow. The session was called to a close, and the house slowly drained of its audience. Those who had been standing vowed to come earlier the next morning to secure a good seat, and everyone was eager to know what would be said in Eunice's defense.

11

AN ORNAMENT
TO HER SEX

The following morning, a Shaker known only as Brother David headed for Albany, assigned the task of learning what had become of Eunice's act. While Elder Seth remained at home and other Brothers prepared for a day of laying floors and splitting wood, this lone Believer settled himself behind a team of well-fed horses for the tortuous road ahead. He got off to a good start. The weather was mild and pleasant, just right for travel. In the skies, spring birds hovered for the first time, giving him hope for warmer weather.

In the city, however, Brother David encountered chaos.

Instead of finding a tidy message of failure or success in the assembly, he faced crowds of spectators in the galleries who studied him with as prurient a gaze as they had cast upon his adversary the day before. If Eunice had been on trial as a heroine, the Shakers were now under scrutiny as potential villains—ones who robbed parents of their offspring, whipped their young, and either engaged in no sexual relations at all or took turns with one another's husbands and wives. To onlookers who knew little more about the Shakers than what they heard whispered, the Shaker Brother was a deviant, a laughingstock, a ghoul, or at best a curiosity.

With the broad brim of his Shaker hat offering him some means of protection, even as it betrayed his identity, Brother David made his way to the public seating area, determined to await a judgment. It was sure to come later that day. The next day's session had its own special topic of consideration, a grisly murder case that also starred an ill-matched couple. Five years after he had abandoned his wife on their wedding day, Abraham Kessler had allegedly returned home to poison his spouse, knowing that death was the only way to end his marriage and wed someone else. The Kessler case provided yet another reminder of the limitations of New York's marriage laws, trumping even the Chapmans' in its degree of tragedy.

Below the gallery where Brother David and the other public spectators were seated, the legislators also took their positions. Standing out among them like a modern-day quarterback was broad-shouldered Erastus Root, followed by his associate, Dr. Isaac Sargent, or "the Disorderly Sargeant," as he was caricatured in *Indoctum Parliamentum*. All eyes were surely on the Brigadier General, but he would not be the first to take up Eunice's defense. This honor fell instead to a rookie: twenty-eight-year-old Simon Throop of Chenango, a "brilliant but dissipated man," a contemporary recalled, whose wit made him another popular favorite.

Throop started off by announcing his plan to limit his arguments to the council's objections, as he claimed his colleagues should have done—but then he said he could not help himself:

He *had* to address the personal attacks on Eunice. He proceeded to fall off topic as much as everyone else.

Eunice Chapman, he said, was hardly the "loathsome and disgusting object" that others had made her out to be: Indeed, she was a "pattern of virtue and an ornament to her sex," a woman who deserved to be heard "if not with sympathy, then at least with impartiality." If anyone merited disgust, Throop argued, it was not this "pure, spotless" woman but her "drunken wretch" of a husband and his even more debauched associates.

Surely, Throop acknowledged, no one could disagree with the council's statements on the importance of marriage or on a father's right to his children. "But," he wondered, "are we to tolerate the abuses in the exercises of that right? Are we to allow him to withdraw them from society, and incarcerate them in the walls of a—" and here he chose his words carefully, "Shaker prison?"

Throop went on to reinforce Eunice's portrayal of the Believers as evil captors, expressing outrage at what would become of children raised by such "an infatuated set of enthusiasts." He was adamant that youngsters could not possibly resist becoming indoctrinated by the Shakers' unnatural tenets—the most harmful of which, in his opinion, was what the council had deemed harmless: celibacy. He exclaimed, "It is made our duty by the imperious mandates of holy writ, to be fruitful, multiply and replenish the earth." The Shakers' "rigid avoidance of sexual intercourse" was thus, as he saw it, "in direct violation of the commands of God himself."

"I have seen enough of this society," Throop concluded, "to convince me, that all their professions of religion are hypocritical." Even "the Fountain Head, the Polar Star, the worshipful

Grand Master of their society," as he called Elder Seth, had been caught telling "four falsehoods in ten minutes" before a senate committee. "He is one who has been looked up to as a parent for their conduct," Throop noted, "and if the fountain be thus impure, the streams will be impure also. We ought therefore to do all in our power to discountenance and destroy their society."

When Erastus Root rose to speak, striking a fine appearance in his slim-fitting coat, with his dark hair swept to the side, as was the fashion, all gravitated toward him—not just the "honest back-woods members" who fawned over the great man, but even his critics, including the house reporter. On any given day, "the General," Stone wrote, could be seen "making love to the people, weeping at their losses, and sighing at (not after) every dollar exacted by the tax gatherers." And yet, despite the "eternal ding-dong" of these professions, not even Stone could resist taking pleasure in the General's theatrics. "Sham patrio" he may have been, but Erastus Root—Brigadier General, Masonic Master, Everyman, or Demagogue, depending on one's point of view—knew how to put on a good show.

Root began his lovemaking right away. "After [such a] flowery display of rhetoric by the gentleman from New York," he proclaimed, gesturing toward Henry Meigs, "and after the capacious display of the honorable gentleman from Oneida," he said of Nathan Williams, he "despaired of furnishing the committee with much information or novelty." However, he would certainly try.

"The bill upon the table," Root announced, was nothing short of a "temple erected to chastity and domestic felicity." In Root's view, those who argued that this bill was unconstitu-

tional ignored the fact that it was the *Shakers* who were the true
violators of the constitution. He proceeded to detail the crimes
of this "infernal society" with relish, introducing exciting new
evidence that had previously been unavailable to all but select
members of the house.

At his disposal were signed eyewitness statements—including
depositions by Josiah Terry and Mary Dyer—testifying to the
"licentiousness and debaucheries" of the Shakers in unprecedented detail. In her writings, Eunice had merely hinted at
what the Shakers did behind closed doors; Mary Dyer openly
proclaimed that the Shakers had selected a mate for her and
urged her to indulge in the very practice that they claimed to
denounce, saying, "you must not be so shy, the world's people
think we are afraid of each other, but they do not know the
liberties we take." Likewise, whereas Eunice had merely charged
the Shakers with mistreating children, Josiah Terry gave graphic
firsthand testimony of the society's brutality. As Terry deposed, the Watervliet Elders even had a special room, lined
with whips, meant for punishing the young.

Root quoted liberally from these documents, and his arguments on the Shakers' criminality were among the strongest
made that day, awakening the house to the Shakers' alleged
cruelty as nothing before and making a mockery of their claims
to piety, chastity, and order. Whereas opponents of Eunice's bill
had claimed that there was nothing to prove that the Believers
were licentious or dangerous, Root's accusations made it impossible to take this argument seriously, showing that it was not
just the lady but *the people* who needed to be defended against
the sect. As for arguments that passing this bill would result in
thousands of similar applications coming through their doors,
Root declared that he, for one, was ready to hold those doors

wide open. "If these thousands of applications were as just as this," he cried, he would "legislate a thousand days in deposing them!"

But then the Brigadier General launched into an even more memorable line of argument, which would bring him trouble in the days to come. Declaring his belief that "the marriage of Mrs. Chapman was dissolved by the Bible itself," Root used the scriptures to argue that sexual relations were a required part of the marital covenant, and that by refusing to maintain these relations, James Chapman had defaulted on his marriage. Suppose, then, that Eunice Chapman was seeking redress for her sexual needs, as the council alleged. As far as Root was concerned, even if this charge were true, it should hardly be cause for objection. For, in the view of this ardent assemblyman, the satisfaction of those vital needs was tantamount to a right.

As Root spoke with increasing ardor about Eunice Chapman's deprivations, mourning her unnaturally celibate state, the house erupted into mayhem. Spectators cackled at the General's ribaldry and shouted from the galleries or grimaced at the blasphemy and covered their faces. For some, it was simply too much. By the time Root returned to his expected lines of argument, blasting the council for its tyranny and exhorting lawmakers to assert their authority as the people's agents, the more sensitive members of the audience—including a number of assemblymen—had risen from their seats and walked out of the house.

Summing up Root's speech later that night, Stone himself was generous, writing: "The General . . . was generally eloquent —always ingenious, amusing and original, and his speech had much the charm of novelty." As for the more controversial turns, Stone would only say: "From the delicate nature of the subject, however—and the peculiar course he took in his argument, it will be obvious to all who heard it that anything like a general sketch of it would be improper."

But later, after Root complained that his words had been shortchanged and relations between the two men soured, Stone became more critical. The speech, the journalist wrote, was "too indelicate—too obscene for the public eye"—a "disgrace" to the speaker, and "an insult to every man of common sense and common feeling in the House." "Among respectable gentlemen," Stone concluded, Root's "indelicate language and obscene allusions, added to his monstrous profanity in perverting the scriptures, created but one opinion and one feeling—that of indignation and disgust."

Abraham Kessler, accused wife-killer, would have to wait longer than expected for his murder conviction. By the time all had had their say on Eunice Chapman and her bill, a total of three days had passed in the assembly. Finally, on March 14, just before three o'clock, a vote was called.

The house was filled to capacity, as it had been throughout, since Eunice's case had excited unusually strong feelings "not only in this house, but in this city; and indeed in every part of this country." On a full floor, the assemblymen waited to say their yeas and nays, all last-minute pleas for votes having been exhausted, while in the balconies, spectators strained to hear the final call.

No one could have been more anxious than Eunice, who struggled to maintain her composure as she awaited the conclusion to her three-year legislative ordeal. Always present in her mind were the faces of her three children, George, Susan, and Julia, though by now they must have been much changed.

She sent up final prayers to her Maker, while across the balcony, the lone Shaker no doubt did the same. Then, one by one the men of the house announced their votes, and the outcome was clear well before the end of the roll: In a final vote of 85 to 27, the house rallied to overturn the council's veto. The "Act for the Relief of Eunice Chapman" was now law.

The hall was in an uproar. There were shouts from the galleries and one particularly loud cry from the floor. "O Tempora, O Mores!" ("What times, what customs!"), William Leete Stone exclaimed in despair, invoking a Ciceronian saying that bemoaned society's moral decline.

The journalist's utterance perfectly captured the frustration of Eunice's opponents, to whom the passage of this act augured a changing political tide: the loosening of values, decline of justice, and triumph of mob rule. Day after day, they had argued against the bill, some wielding the Constitution, others resorting to scripture and delivering virtual sermons on marriage and divorce. Among the more creative arguments was the assertion that by divorcing the Chapmans, the state would deprive James Chapman of his ability to reform. "Call him if you please, a wild and infuriate maniac," one assemblyman said, but tomorrow he could regain his senses and wish to "claim the services and comfort of his wife." This law would make such a return impossible.

Yet in the end, these arguments were no match for Eunice's singular appeal as a "poor, defenseless woman" in need of the state's protection. Eunice's emotional portrayal of herself as a long-abused wife and a mother deprived of her children had proved irresistible to an American populace that was increasingly inclined to value maternal nurture yet also anxious to uphold traditional, patriarchal norms. Eunice's presentation of her dilemma as a Christian woman—one forced to choose between her family and her faith—also resonated in an era when free will and self-determination were on the rise as core spiritual values. Few went so far as to embrace the Shakers' belief that heaven could be had by asking, but more Americans had begun to believe that God could be called upon, and not merely for grace. In this climate, Eunice's insistence that a secretive people were indoctrinating children and demanding that mothers like herself relinquish their spiritual beliefs became a terrifying source of motivation—all the more so given the Shakers' identity as a celibate, separatist, communitarian sect.

Last but not least, there was Eunice herself—an "ornament to her sex," and "object of disgust," as she had been called—a woman who was astoundingly attuned to how others perceived her and what they wanted her to be. With great diplomacy, she succeeded in presenting herself as both an ordinary woman, typical of all wives and mothers, and an extraordinary one who demanded a rare intervention. Combining sentimental vision with a spiritual appeal, she created an unbeatable public persona.

With the announcement of her victory, however, this compelling character was transformed. After holding herself in check for so many years and enduring merciless public humiliation, Eunice abruptly abandoned all sense of decorum and openly gloried in her success. Pointing a finger at the sole Believer in the house, she declared herself God's instrument, and boasted that she would soon have her children and bring the Shakers down.

Eunice's zeal is understandable, given the intensity of her fight, but it was not a good time to let down her guard. Her success had depended on her credibility as a vulnerable, deserving character, and many were startled at the sight of this seemingly helpless mother crowing in such an aggressive, unladylike manner. As an anonymous Shaker Sister wrote: "After the passage of the act Eunice became so bold and brazen and her behavior was so utterly the reverse of all modesty, that many who had ruled in her favor became quite disgusted with her conduct . . . but it was too late to recall their votes." To many in the hall, it seemed that Eunice had been acting all along and that it was only now that her true nature was finally exposed.

Eunice would eventually face consequences for her temerity. For the moment, however, she had every cause to celebrate. After fourteen unhappy years of marriage, she was free from any obligation to her husband, thanks to an unprecedented legislative divorce that would be the first and last to pass in New York State. The act stopped short of granting Eunice immediate custody over her children but gave her a promising way of obtaining it. Under this law, Eunice could go to the chancellor or a judge of the New York supreme court who, using a writ of habeas corpus, could demand that the Shakers produce the children and then award her custody. If the Shakers failed to cooperate, the judge could authorize a search of any Shaker premises in New York State. There were further penalties if the children were moved. The last clause of Eunice's act made it a "high misdemeanor" for the Shakers to send children across state lines, and anyone convicted of doing so could be fined $200 (roughly $3,500 today) or sent to prison. By the terms of this law, James, Elder Seth, Joseph Hodgson, and even Mother Lucy could face trial for their "crimes."

But there was yet another level of significance to Eunice's act, which was not explicitly stated but was evident to all present, and that was the resurrection of her civil identity. As a married woman, Eunice had been a nonperson, her identity "covered" over by that of her husband—a "feme covert," to use the legal term. With the successful passage of her act, she now regained her status as "feme sole," or woman alone. She had full title to herself, her possessions, and potentially her children. As a citizen in her own right, Eunice was born again.

Following the verdict, Brother David exited the house as inconspicuously as he could. He mounted his wagon, taking along two useful items: a copy of the *Albany Gazette*, which described the recent debates, and a collection of unbound sheets from Eunice's latest book (including a part of Josiah Terry's testimony), which he had received from a sympathetic local. He passed these on to Elder Seth, along with a report of the day's events, upon his return home.

The following day, Elder Seth was pensive as he gave his own report to Mother Lucy. "What effect the final decision of this Bill will have," he mused, "time must determine." As always, however, the Elder tried to make the best of the situation, observing: "Tho' the devil may rage for a season, I believe his weapons will finally fall upon his own head, and E.C. will get her reward." Perhaps, he suggested, there was a lesson to be learned. "It seems at present to strike a kind of damp upon our feelings," he admitted, "but I hope it will teach us humility, and I think it ought to teach us wisdom."

Yet as he closed his letter, the tired Elder could not help playing the child to his spiritual mother. Many among them were sick, he complained, probably with the flu. "We want to hear from Lebanon," he pleaded, "we want Mother's love."

12

O Tempora,
O Mores!

Although Eunice wanted to go after her children, she was unable to take action quite yet. Her law was enforceable only in New York State. She might request searches of Shaker villages in Watervliet and New Lebanon, and have Believers in these communities put on trial, but none of this would help her in New Hampshire. The Enfield Shakers were under no obligation to abide by her law, and if Eunice tried to take her children from their village by force, *she* would be the outlaw, since the children were there by their father's authority. She needed to put additional pressure on the Shakers so that they would finally understand that it was in their best interest as a society to comply with her demands.

Eunice also had to make sure that her children remained in Enfield, lest she travel the distance only to learn that they had disappeared yet again. And so she waited for further news, doing all she could in the meantime to hurt the Shakers the best way she knew how. She began lobbying the legislature again, this time for a repeal of the Shakers' military exemption. She also issued a dire warning to the Shaker leadership, but she ignored Mother Lucy and addressed Elder Seth and other male heads of the sect:

> Albany, March 20, 1818
>
> To S. Y. Wells, Joseph Hodgson, and Peter Dodge.
>
> I have thought I would not warn you again of my intentions, but it is revealed to me that I must warn you as Moses did the Egyptians, that for your stubbornness your overthrow may be the greater—Think not that the battle is over after such a victory is gained—I am consulting my friends, COLLECTING MY FORCES FOR A NEW INVASION. You see what I, as an instrument in the hands of God, have brought to pass—You see that all your money and lawyers, nor your Gods could not save you—You have fallen before a poor weak woman. You will soon see what will become of your boasted Military Law,—I shall convince you that my children is my object—And my children I will have—I have told you before, that if you will restore to me my children, I will be at peace with you, I do not wish to spend the best of my days in contending with you—You see that the more you oppose me the more you expose yourselves: I have looked to God for direction, and still look to God; HE has crowned me with SUCCESS, and BLESSED be his name.

Eunice goes on to claim that it had been "revealed to her" that she had been "chosen" to bring about the Shakers' "complete overthrow." She states that she has "few minutes to write," as she is busy putting together yet another publication against the Shakers, one that is eagerly awaited not only by the public but also by distinguished heads of libraries in various cities, who want it for their collections.

But the Shakers, she repeats, have a way out. If they will only give her back her children or promise to return them by a certain time, she vows she will desist—a great promise, given the intensity of her hatred for the Shakers. Yet if the Shakers fail to comply with her demands, she warns, her friends will not only bring about the repeal of the Shakers' cherished military exemption, but also "bring in a bill before the Legislature granting *me* power to imprison as many Shakers as I have children and keep them in close confinement, until my children are restored to me, and THEY WILL CARRY IT, BY A CONSTITUTIONAL MAJORITY!" This new bill will also force the Shakers to provide support for all "Shaker wives"—whether their husbands have property or not.

Eunice's language is telling. Now *she* is the potential captor (with the ability to "imprison" as many Shakers as she pleases), a Moses figure, a military commander, and even a royal character "crowned" with success—the chief emblems of male authority. (Note that her only reference to her vulnerability as a "poor weak woman" is delivered in sarcastic tones.) Her threats are severe, even violent, and substantiate complaints that she was a harassing figure with a delusional sense of her dues and capabilities. However, without such a large sense of self-worth and purpose, Eunice would not have been able to achieve all that she did. It was her extraordinary faith in herself and God, along with her awareness of the gender expectations of her times—the understanding that women were the frailer sex, in need of male protection—that empowered her to exploit these expectations and, ultimately, to subvert them.

In the conclusion of her letter, Eunice declares her intention to "go into every state in the union to get a similar law passed." "I shall send my books into every state," she says, "and every principal town." There would be no stopping until she reached her goal: "My children I will have," she swore, "not by a *Mob*, but by the *law, and you* shall not have the power of breaking up families any longer."

The Shakers took Eunice's letter, along with her previous correspondence with Mother Lucy, and went directly to the press offices of William Leete Stone on North Pearl Street in Albany. Stone was only too happy to receive them. Ever since he had exclaimed "O Tempora, O Mores!" in the assembly—and printed these words in his paper—he had been hounded by legislators, especially the two men he had dubbed "those choice spirits of jacobinism and disorganization," Erastus Root and Isaac Sargent.

Root was particularly angered by what he considered Stone's lack of journalistic objectivity. The newspaperman complained that had the General "swallowed a barbecued Delaware catamount stuffed with ten-penny nails and basted with aqua-fortis, he could not have been more furious, or, had he breakfasted upon fried vipers and scorpions, more venomous." As a result of this assemblyman's punitive efforts, Stone had lost his seat as house reporter. The newspaperman was also suffering from an undisclosed ailment that made it difficult for him even to take notes anymore. He was sick, angry, and vengeful.

Thanks to the Shakers, he could finally exercise his revenge on Eunice, whom he blamed for his misfortunes. Although

Root and other legislators had demanded that he show greater deference and objectivity in his reporting if he wanted to reclaim his seat in the house, Stone resolved to do the opposite in a full spread on Eunice and her case.

On March 28, the people of Albany opened their papers to an unusual piece of reporting under the header "EUNICE CHAPMAN." To introduce the subject, Stone wrote: "The public have by this time become so familiar with the name of this lady"—at a time when women were supposed to stay out of the public eye, familiarity suggested indecency—"that we presume they will not startle at seeing it again. . . . We introduce her again to the public, both as an act of justice to ourselves, and also to a peaceable class of our fellow citizens, against whom the arm of persecution has been raised through the instrumentality of this woman."

Of the Shakers, Stone contended, little ill could be said: Some of their views might be ridiculous, but they were nevertheless reputable. Their adversary was another story. "Mrs. Chapman," Stone observed, "has been repeatedly clothed by her champions and advisors, pending her bill, in all the beauty, loveliness and purity of a Christian. Her piety and saint-like virtues have been standing themes of her orators." Yet there was strong evidence to the contrary—letters in the woman's own hand that revealed her to be the very opposite of the consummate heroine.

Stone published Eunice's letters to the Shakers in their entirety, including her recent letter to the Elders and the letter to Mother Lucy, in which she warned that "a woman can be as mighty to pull you down, as a woman was to build you up." He also printed Mother Lucy's response, and asked his readers to compare the "arrogance and the malignity" of Eunice against "the meekness and civility" of Lucy. He then inquired of his fellow Christians "whether a bosom within which rankles such vindictive passions as are here displayed, can have much room for the pure, undefiled and lamb-like religion of the blessed Savior?" Eunice Chapman was a woman, Stone insisted, who would "prostitute the name of the Almighty"—not to mention herself.

After this stunning assault, Eunice hurried to the journalist's office with a bundle of testimonials, hoping that he would publish a different view of her character. But he refused, and she was forced to bluff as lawmakers and others in Albany questioned her about her letters. Eunice finally retaliated by printing her own attack on Stone in yet another version of her book, which she planned to take with her when she went to get her children. In it she accuses the newspaperman of being paid by the Shakers to "publicly insult the endearing affection of a bereaved mother for her tender captive offspring." She also smugly reports on Stone's own sufferings—both his loss of his reporter's seat and his struggles against a "truly alarming" disease—which she sees as retribution for his actions against her.

In the end, however, Eunice could not remain occupied with Stone for long, since she had a promise to keep with Mother Lucy. In order to encourage the repeal of the Shakers' military exemption, she actively urged people all around Albany to sign a petition against the society. Eunice allegedly employed questionable means: Although Elder Seth admitted it could not be proved, he was sure that some signers "were coaxed and flattered and others heated at taverns." Many of them could barely write their names, and some who had signed were known to be illiterate.

Eunice's efforts were once more rewarded. In April, the legislature passed an act that repealed the Shakers' military exemption and required instead that all able-bodied Shaker men pay a hefty annual fee in place of their military service—or face imprisonment. Then came another triumph. "Mysterious providence," as Eunice later wrote, allowed her to learn where her children were. Possibly from a sympathetic local or Mary Dyer, Eunice had confirmation that her children remained in Enfield, and she resolved to take them from there, legally or not. Providence had yet to reveal, however, whether or not they would be there when she arrived—or whether the Shakers would willingly give them up.

PART III

REWARD

There is no man that hath left house, or brethren, or sisters, or father, or mother, or wife, or children, or lands, for my sake, and the gospel's, but he shall receive a hundredfold now in this time, houses, and brethren, and sisters, and mothers, and children, and lands, with persecutions; and in the world to come eternal life.

—Mark 10:29–30

1

CAPTIVE BABES

The Enfield Shaker community lay sixty miles northwest of Concord, the state capital of New Hampshire, on land that had once been the site of terrible geological violence—volcanic eruptions, glacial freezing, and destructive floods. Before the Shakers' arrival, the terrain had still been wild, so dense with foliage that to walk there was to travel in near darkness. But the Believers had worked their magic: There were at present over 250 Shaker buildings, including a dental office, an infirmary, a boathouse, an icehouse, barns, shops, dwellings, and a church, as well as expansive gardens, orchards, and pastures. There were canals to bring fresh water to their village and dams to control the water's flow. There were long galleries of sugar maples and butternuts, which stretched far across their acreage up to the encircling hills.

Though distinctively Shaker, with a gambrel-roofed meetinghouse identical to those in Watervliet and New Lebanon (and even built by the same hands), this Shaker settlement was different from others in significant ways. Because the Believers here had begun developing their land simultaneously with other settlers of the New Hampshire frontier, their community was far less isolated than other Shaker communities. In fact, the Enfield Shaker village lay along a major road—the Fourth New Hampshire Turnpike—and on the shores of a central lake. The nearest town, also called Enfield, was just two miles away. The Shakers' property holdings were also more scattered than they were elsewhere. In addition to their villages and farmlands, they also owned some of the nearby hills, where fallow pastures and empty barns awaited further use.

For the past three years, George, Susan, and Julia Chapman had called this unusual Shaker enclave their home. Their friends in Durham would scarcely have recognized them. At thirteen, George may already have been instructed by the clean-shaven Shakers on how to trim his thin whiskers. Eleven-and-a-half-year-old Susan was also close to puberty; if she had not yet joined the ranks of women lining up monthly to turn in their dirty rags for clean ones, she would soon be there. Julia was only eight, but her mother might well have mistaken her for her older sister, who had been the same age when the children had left home.

By now, the children were bona fide Believers. They awoke every morning in their tightly strung beds, followed the Brothers and Sisters in their daily chores, danced and sang in meetings, and confessed their sins to their Elders. George had grown his hair out long in the back and kept it cut short in the front. For the girls, the white Shaker cap, which their mother once scorned, had become so much a part of their bodies that they would have felt naked without it.

As in Watervliet, the children had been separated. This time, Susan and Julia went to the Church Family, where there was a girls' order, while George lived in the North House with his father. Nevertheless, the youngsters did not lack for company. There were enough children in Enfield to form two separate youth orders. And there were others there who knew what it meant to be in a divided family—including the five children of Mary and Joseph Dyer, the youngest of whom was near Julia's age.

Concerning the children's health, safety, and general well-being, Eunice's worst fears were unfounded. The children were not starved, beaten with special whips, or forced to flagellate one another's naked bodies, as apostates said was common practice. Not that the Shakers forbade corporal punishment as a rule: According to one Shaker account, Elder John Lyon, who was in charge of the Family where George lived, once caught a badly behaved boy by the arm and "shook him as a dog would a woodchuck." But the shaken woodchuck grew up fine and later reflected that he had deserved the punishment, as was usually said to be the case when the Shakers resorted to force. Moreover, at a time when beatings were the norm, the Believers preferred gentler methods of discipline. For instance, children who were tardy for meetings were required to stand in front of a clock for as long as they had been late.

The Chapman children also attended school, where they learned skills such as reading, writing, spelling, arithmetic, grammar, geography, ciphering, and "good manners." They enjoyed pitchers of fresh milk and had lots of protein: Supper, as one later ex-Shaker recalled, "usually consisted of good rich meat hash with nice juicy apple pie with tender crust and fat insides, with plenty of rich cheese to go with it." And, although children worked hard, they also had time for play. Records are scant for the period when the Chapmans were Shakers, but later Believers reminisced about sledding, berry picking, and making popcorn, among other pleasures.

There was one aspect of her children's lives as Believers, however, where Eunice's fears proved valid, and that was regarding Shaker teachings about love and family. As expressed in a Shaker hymn:

> *Love not self, that must be hated,*
> *Love not satan, love not sin;*
> *To the flesh, tho' you're related,*
> *Love not flesh, nor fleshly kin.*
> *Love not riches, honor, pleasure,*
> *Love no earthly vain delight;*
> *But the gospel's hidden treasure,*
> *You may love with all your might.*

For three years, George, Susan, and Julia had been taught to distance themselves from all earthly connections, especially their family. They were supposed to love everyone, but no one in excess: Friends who became too close were taunted for being "married," and, if necessary, broken apart. Dolls were expressly forbidden, although at least one sneaky girl managed to keep a makeshift one hidden in her dress, made from an old corncob and wrapped in a scrap of discarded muslin.

The children knew very little about their mother. They had heard something of her aggression against the society the previous year, when their father had stood up before the entire community to read aloud his "Memorial," but they had no idea that Eunice had also published *her* story. All they knew was that she had fought hard to obtain a divorce in order to remarry—a sure sign that she was a woman of deep earthly appetites and bound for hell. Eunice, as they understood, had become a "common and very base woman," whom even outsiders refused to allow into their homes. In their eyes, this woman was no longer "Mother"—a term they now used exclusively to refer to Mother Lucy—and their home was no longer Durham. All told, being "rescued" from the Shakers (something they had once begged their mother to do) could not have been further from their thoughts—or their desires.

Roughly 150 miles away, separated by two states and a formidable mountain range, Eunice made her preparations. She wrapped up copies of her latest book and sent them ahead to Enfield in order to whip up the locals, whose support would be crucial if she were to have any hope of retrieving her children. She then dismissed her pupils and packed her trunk, tucking away gifts for her children, including a finely dressed doll for her girls and a writing tablet for George. She enclosed with special care a small pocketbook that jingled with a dollar's worth of change—once George's prized possession, which she had refrained from spending all this time.

Eunice worked in secret, not even trusting her closest friends. She told everyone that she was going to visit her parents. The one person who knew otherwise was an unnamed ally who bought her an advance ticket for the stagecoach under a false name. And she scheduled her trip for an hour when few people (and certainly no Shakers) were likely to be on the streets: 2 AM on the ninth of May.

The night was full of storms. As rain poured over the darkened streets of Albany and thunder crackled overhead, Eunice hurried out of her quarters on South Market Street, past the deserted docks and trash-strewn alleys, to mount the eastbound stage. Soon the coachman lashed his whip overhead (too loudly, as it was publicly complained), and the lone mother—packed between strangers, her identity known to no one, and damp in her floor-length gown—began to close the gap of three years, and many miles, that stood between her and her children.

It could not have been a worse time of year to travel. Normally, the mud season would have come months earlier, but this year, as in several years past, the seasons were out of sync, and winter trespassed into summer. As Eunice and her fellow travelers journeyed beyond the easy, sloping hills of Albany and crossed the border into Vermont's abruptly mountainous terrain, they met what appeared to be bottomless mud, alongside piles of snow, as much as three feet high. What passed for roads in these times added further terror to the travel. Some were little more than paths, laid over with logs to prevent sinking—"corduroys," they were called, for their texture—and when the frail stages passed over them, or hit a muddy rut, passengers would be thrown about, and even hurled out of the moving vehicles.

Early in the journey, Eunice's crew changed to a larger, open-air wagon, which was supposed to provide greater stability, but this, too, tipped and slid and became mired in mud, so much so that Eunice feared she would be "dashed in pieces" against the steep rock ledges beside the road. Deep in the Green Mountains, somewhere between Bennington and Brattleboro, Eunice despaired, fearing that she would die before she saw her children again. Yet she dared not confide her feelings to anyone, increasingly worried that someone might betray her when she was nearly within sight of her goal.

At last, twenty-four hours and seventy-six miles from where they had begun, the travelers pulled into Brattleboro, Vermont —a pretty little village with a handsome white Congregational church. A long row of shops crested over Main Street, and a sheer mountain face loomed sublimely over the rooftops. Despite knowing that the stop would be short, Eunice decided to rent a room, where she was finally able to stretch out her limbs and rest. Just one hour later, however, her journey resumed.

That day, the rain fell hard. Crammed with new passengers, the stage lurched and nearly toppled to its side. Eunice, her nerves already worn, fell into a faint and had to be revived by the other travelers. The coach pressed on for many more miles before arriving at Hanover, New Hampshire. This handsome town, the home of Dartmouth College, was a welcome sight, with its distinguished campus square and white clapboard houses. Eunice rented another room, hoping to recover somewhat before reaching Enfield, but got little rest. Her temporary landlady was an "old maid," as Eunice called her, who was no doubt more accustomed to hosting young male students than older single women. She accosted her guest with unnerving questions, which Eunice, exhausted and fearful, was unable to answer.

By the time she reembarked for the last leg of her trip several days later, Eunice was deeply unsettled and more fearful than ever. Enfield was only ten miles away, and she could not be sure whether the Shakers had gotten wind of her arrival. To be safe, she decided to claim that she was headed for a farther destination. She would feign sickness as the coach neared Enfield, in order to have a reason to stop.

From Hanover, the stage passed through the town of Lebanon along a relatively new road, the Fourth New Hampshire Turnpike, which provided steady relief after the tumult of the Green Mountains. Hills were all that Eunice could see for miles around, until glistening waters abruptly came into view.

Here was an expansive glacial lake called Mascoma, whose farthest point she could hardly discern as they turned the corner and proceeded down its shores.

The stage road hugged the lake for about a mile, offering glimpses of blue through a thick fringe of aspen, pine, spruce, maple, and birch. Then, before she knew what was happening, Eunice found herself passing a milk-white meetinghouse, a trustees' office, and eerily familiar dwellings. The pike road cut straight through the Enfield Shaker community, and from her seat, Eunice could see three Shaker Families pass by in succession—the North, the Church, and the South—at least one of which was certain to have her children.

When the stage reached the center of Enfield, minutes later, Eunice hardly needed to pretend that she was unwell. She had only to announce that she felt sick, and was unable to travel any farther, and her anguished face said the rest. With exaggerated difficulty, she descended from the coach to find herself in front of Willis's Tavern—Enfield's central lodging establishment, occasional meeting hall, and main watering hole.

The town of Enfield was small, with little more than a cemetery, a few stores, public houses, and private homes. To most travelers, Enfield was a resting stop, a place to change horses, sleep, or have a hot meal before traveling on. For Enfield's residents, however, the arrival of the stagecoach was a central event, a kind of daily show, and they peered out their windows or strode toward the tavern as soon as they heard the driver blow "lustily on his horn," calling for fresh horses and dinner. On rare days, when the British guard, resplendent in their regalia, came through on their way to Canada with the mail, the townspeople were treated to a spectacle. Today, however, they saw little more than a sick woman in a rumpled gown alighting nervously from the carriage with a well-worn trunk.

When she set foot in Willis's Tavern, Eunice did not advertise her identity, but it was not long before she was recognized. As she was settling into her room, a thin woman about her own age, with dark hair, a sharp nose, and shrewd black eyes, rushed in and exclaimed, "Mrs. Chapman, can this be you?"

"We met like two unfortunate sisters," Eunice later recalled. The woman she embraced was Mary Dyer.

Thirty-eight-year-old Mary Dyer was an ambitious woman of many frustrations. She was born on the frontiers of northwestern New Hampshire, a land of hardscrabble farming, which was vulnerable to Indian attacks. At eighteen, she married Joseph Dyer, a widowed farmer who was nearly a decade her senior. Two years later, Mary bore a son, the first of four children. From the start, Joseph and Mary Dyer had differences, but what they did share in common was a revivalistic faith and dreams of preaching. Both were also intrigued when a wandering preacher named Lemuel Crooker happened to come by with a copy of the so-called Shaker Bible. Before long, the Dyers decided to join the Enfield Shakers, bringing their children. But Shakerism failed to satisfy Mary, and it separated her from her family in ways that she had not imagined. In 1814, within a year of signing the covenant, she was ready to leave.

Even greater frustrations followed when Mary tried to reclaim what she had lawfully given up. Her husband refused to give her any of the children, and still worse, the youngsters themselves did not want to leave. For the next several years, Mary lived here and there, initially close to the Shakers and then as far as one hundred miles away, her board paid by her husband and the Believers. During this time, she tried to lobby her state legislature, but with far less success than Eunice. Although New Hampshire briefly considered passing a law similar to Eunice's, Mary was not able to muster the same kind of support as her fellow mother-in-arms, and the bill died.

During the very month that Eunice claimed victory in New York, Mary had returned to Enfield, eager to be reunited with her children, whom she had not seen for more than two years. She began boarding at Willis's Tavern, supporting herself as a teacher and seamstress. She also brought her troubles to the attention of one of the town's selectmen and a justice of the peace, Joseph Merrill, who mediated a meeting with her husband. But despite the presence of public officials, and the support of some neighborhood women, the meeting had resolved nothing.

A month after this latest failure came Eunice Chapman with her legislative success, her books, and her gumption. As the women huddled together in Willis's Tavern, sharing meals and stories, Mary gave Eunice the lay of the land as only an ex-Shaker could, and the two mothers plotted their course.

The Enfield Shaker village was protected, bordered by hills and water, but it was not remote. As Eunice had already seen, the pike road ran through the Shaker lands, directly past the North Family, where Mary had once lived, and where James and George were now. If the children could be brought to the edge of the village, closest to the road—say, to the trustees' office, which stood at the border between the Shakers and the outside world, and where meetings with outsiders were supposed to take place anyway—it would not be hard to take them to safety. Mary would enter the village first, accompanied by a group of trustworthy women, and ask to see all the children, hers and Eunice's, while Eunice remained hidden. Then, when the children were brought forth, Eunice would jump out and whisk them away to a waiting carriage.

This was a plan for abduction, as both women knew, but given their failure to accomplish anything through negotiation with the Shakers, they were willing to bypass the law. If Eunice could only get her children back to New York State, she could win full legal title to them and pave the way for Mary to do the same with the Dyer children.

For ten days Eunice stayed hidden at Willis's Tavern, making her plans with Mary Dyer while she awaited confirmation that her children were in the village. She learned that the Shakers had been terrified by the effect of her writings in Enfield, and were fearful that people would "shoot them down in the street." She had to consider the possibility that the Shakers had moved the children on the basis of these fears. At last, she received word from another parent, presumably a mother visiting her children among the Shakers, that George, Susan, and Julia were there, two miles from where she was. All she would have to do, Eunice assumed, was find a way to get to the "dear little captives"—hardly anticipating that the captives themselves might not wish to be saved.

2

AN ELDER AND
AN EMISSARY

On Monday morning, May 25, 1818, the Believers at Enfield returned to their daily chores after a day of rest and worship. Sisters stoked fires to heat vast pans of bread and sorted through piles of laundry. Brothers drove their herds to open pastures. Then word began to fly through the aromatic kitchens and the still-dewy fields. A mob was gathering at Willis's Tavern, planning for an attack at 8 AM the next day. Commanding this group, the Shakers learned, were two women: James's wife, Eunice; and Joseph's wife, Mary.

To John Lyon, the Elder of the North Family at Enfield, these women's names were very familiar. James Chapman and Joseph Dyer were both members of his Shaker household, as Mary Dyer had been before leaving their society. Mary had been a special thorn in his side, having developed a particular affection —a "carnal affection," as the Shakers would have called it— for the Elder, who, at thirty-eight, was exactly her age. When

Mary Dyer had proposed starting "spiritual unions" for certain members, she had Elder John in mind as her "mate."

The women's planned aggression could not have come as a total surprise to the Shakers, since the arrival of Eunice's books in town had sounded a warning. Even so, they had no idea that Eunice had been in the neighborhood for over a week, and they were taken off guard. All of the heads of the community—not just the New Hampshire Ministry, but also the Deacons and even Trustee True Heath—were away on business, and so it fell to younger leaders like John Lyon to take charge of a crisis that was virtually unprecedented in Enfield.

To be sure, the Shakers there had had their share of troubles, like Believers anywhere else. Two Sisters of marriageable age, now in Elder John's house, had been so badly hounded by their neighbors that they had resorted to shearing their hair in an effort to appear less attractive to the outside world. Another Sister in the North Family had arrived at the village with a single pillowcase stuffed with clothes, after being tortured and finally spurned by an unbelieving husband who had once "fasten[ed] her with cords" to their marriage bed in order to force her to submit to his lust.

But the only incident of mass public violence against the society had occurred thirty-five years earlier, when Molly Andrews had come to the Shakers with her infant, fleeing her abusive husband and seeking to join the faith. A mob headed by her husband had chased her down at a Believer's home and whipped her until she tumbled to the ground, nearly dead. There they left her, fearing that they would be accused of murder. After she had barely recovered, they came for her again. While Molly clung to her baby, the mob threw the young mother on a bare-backed horse, tying her legs to the horse's belly. The mob then captured and tied a second Shaker to the horse's tail, and "secured the services of a negro" to drive them back home. Over the course of twelve miles, as the awful caravan proceeded to Hillsboro, the woman's native town, the mob called for the black man to abuse the bound Believers in ways that were, as the Shakers wrote, "shameful obscene and brutish and too filthy to relate."

Molly Andrews was still alive when Eunice arrived at Enfield, seventy-eight years old and living in the Church Family along-side Susan and Julia Chapman. But for the average Enfield Shaker, trials like hers were unknown. Whereas most other Shaker communities had seen mobs (most more than once), for the Believers in Enfield such episodes had been thankfully rare.

John Lyon, however, had a personal frame of reference for such attacks, and the propsect of another one surely filled him with dread. During his boyhood in Worcester, Massachusetts— when his family had embraced Shakerism but before they had moved into a Shaker community—he had been forced to huddle indoors with his brothers and sisters, parents, grandmother, and cousin while two hundred men and boys surrounded his home. Wielding pistols and, oddly, a goose quill as a weapon, the men and boys banged drums, honked horns, and roared that they had "come to drive the Shakers away." The cousin had wanted to fight, but John's father insisted on pacifism, and he and his wife sang songs instead. Finally, his uncle came charging at the crowd on horseback with a broken fence rail as a lance; only then did the mob finally disperse.

Elder John's family had moved in with the Shakers not long after this incident, and so he had spent most of his life as a Believer—which is not to say that he was always steady in his faith. As a teenager, he had even fantasized about leaving the society and "participating in the pleasures of sin," until an angry voice from the heavens interrupted his sexual reveries and commanded him to mind his conscience. (Thereafter, whenever he lapsed, he would recall that voice and tremble.) Yet he had eventually passed these various tests of faith, which primed him for his work in the Novitiate Order, or North Family. Initially, he had served as an assistant Elder in the Family, but later, when the senior Elder began to ail, he had assumed the lead.

This work had required talent, since an unusually mischievous group had populated the order nearly from its inception. The North Family counted among its members not just Mary and Joseph Dyer and James Chapman but also Josiah Terry and a man named Benjamin Green, who would publish a troubling tell-all after apostatizing. To date, none of these conflicts had amounted to much. The most vindictive of the group, Mary Dyer, had failed in all of her efforts. A separate lawsuit, filed by an apostate seeking to recover wages, had also come to naught. Thankfully, the Shakers' neighbors had always been willing to recognize that the Believers were law-abiding citizens who deserved the law's protection—that is, until now.

Sighting Joseph Merrill in the village, John Lyon took the opportunity to ask the selectman, or town officer, for his help. Although he could hardly be counted on as a friend, Merrill had shown some willingness to reserve judgment against the society. When Mary Dyer had gone to him with her complaints a month earlier, he had resolved to organize a meeting between husband and wife, rather than simply pressing charges against the Shakers, as the woman would have preferred.

The Shaker Elder told the selectman all that he had heard about the coming mob and beseeched him as an officer to

"suppress such proceedings if it came within his knowledge."
But Merrill insisted he knew nothing, and would make no
promises.

Later that evening, when Judge Edward Evans happened to
come by, the Shakers expressed their fears once more. The
judge, too, was doubtful: "It could not be," he said—he "did
not believe it." Nevertheless, he agreed to look into matters on
his way home.

The Shakers could not have chosen a better emissary than
Judge Edward Evans. Mary Dyer also trusted him: In the past,
she had chosen him to voice her complaints to the Believers,
and she had even stayed with the judge's family. Evans had
yet another qualification in his favor as he approached downtown Enfield on behalf of his neighbors. Long before he had
acquired his legal title, he had been the town's first minister
—a position he had managed to hold for many years despite
unorthodox Methodist inclinations that put the Congrega-
tionalists on edge. When he entered Willis's Tavern to face
Eunice Chapman, Mary Dyer, and whoever else might be
there, Evans would be recognized not just as a man of the
people but as a man of God.

Personally, Evans felt that the Shakers were being overly
fearful. And from a distance, Willis's Tavern, its windows like
beacons in the dark town square, would have betrayed few signs
of agitation. Perhaps a number of carriages were pulled out in
front, hostlers patting down their horses, but this would hardly
have been an unusual sight for a public house along the turnpike.
However, when he entered the place, Evans found that it was
"all tip toe raised up in arms." Smelling of sweat, tobacco, cooked

foods, and ardent spirits, the main hall reverberated with the sound of restless feet and urgent voices. Many more people were assembled there than Evans had thought possible, a host of countrymen swirling around two feminine forms: black-eyed Mary Dyer, whom the judge recognized immediately, and a second, smaller figure, from whom the rancor seemed to emanate—Eunice Chapman.

The judge worked his way to the women, and after an introduction was made, he managed to pull Eunice aside. He told her she "had better be calm," that he had just been to the Shakers, and he did not think that she would have any trouble seeing her children. Eunice replied that she did not care about seeing them: She wanted to *have* them.

The judge preached prudence. He said that, as Eunice was a stranger in town, he would take her to the Shakers himself, along with three or more of her friends—if she would only be peaceable. He gave her his word that she would be allowed to see her children and vowed to help her and James come to an agreement so that they might settle their troubles in peace.

In the close quarters of the tavern, with the candlelight flashing and strange faces gathered all around, Eunice considered the offer. To the judge's relief, she agreed.

The following morning, Judge Evans dressed and calmly prepared to meet Eunice, "thinking," he later recalled, "that matters were going on well." His chaise ready, he drove his team toward Willis's Tavern, where Eunice should have been waiting with two or three friends. What he found instead was the woman half hidden in a crowd of a dozen or more men and women—not quite a mob, yet large enough to be intimidating. Among those waiting was Joseph Merrill, the selectman, who stepped up as the woman's spokesperson. Merrill demanded to know whether Evans had talked to the Shakers since the night before and charged him with being "interested" in the Believers.

The stunned judge answered that his only interest was in "truth and equity," but then Eunice interrupted to declare her terms. She would go to the Shakers with no fewer than twelve companions, including Mary Dyer. The judge replied that he could not promise that the Shakers would admit her with such a group; as it was, the Believers were fearful of an attack. However, he would take down a list of names, show it to the Shakers, and see what he could do.

The list in hand, the judge rode off to the Shaker village, where he conferred with a small group of Believers, including Elder John Lyon, James Chapman, and Deacon Nathaniel Draper, who had thankfully returned from his travels. The Believers shook their heads. There were far too many people on the list: A company of that size could too easily encircle the children and carry them away. Better to admit a select few, including Mary Dyer, if need be. James himself marked the selections, which included Joseph Merrill and his wife, as well as a second local officer, state legislator Jesse Fogg and his spouse.

The judge had hardly turned back toward town when he spied a stagecoach hurtling toward him in the distance. Taking up the best seats were Eunice and Mary, who led a parade of attendants, some leaning out of their gigs, others on horseback, all of them determined to see the women's children. When they reached him, the judge tried, for a moment, to hand over his marked-up list. It had been changed, he said, and Mary Dyer was welcome to come, but his voice proved feeble against the crowd. No one wanted to hear what the Shakers had to offer, and the judge saw that he would be of little use. Thus while Eunice, Mary, and their followers charged on toward the Shaker village, the judge shifted his own course and crept home.

3

LITTLE
STRANGERS

The Believers were probably in the trustees' office, still conferring over the judge's latest list, when they learned that Eunice was on her way. Through curved glass windows, they watched as a stagecoach clattered down the road and stopped outside their doors. Smaller vehicles and more men on horseback followed behind. The Shakers gazed upon the procession with astonishment. This was a far larger group than they had agreed to, and Judge Evans's chaise was nowhere in sight. As Eunice was helped out of the stagecoach, Mary Dyer beside her, James prepared to come forward.

Years had passed since Eunice and James had faced each other directly. By the standards of his time, James was an old man, fifty-four years old, and past his life expectancy. His hair was gray, and his workman's hands were creased and calloused. Nearing forty, Eunice, too, was considered past her prime, and she was also past putting on appearances. No longer was she the winsome heroine everyone had admired in Albany. Now she was a seasoned warrior, ready to pull the Shakers down. She made this clear as she swept through the Shakers' doors and confronted her ex-husband.

She hailed him with these words: "Woe, woe, woe, to you James Chapman and to all your society throughout the land if you do not give up my children."

Glaring at his companion, Brother James Pettengill, she then warned, "I will scare you yet and make you tremble; it is a mercy you are not all dashed to pieces. You know," she added, "what I have done in the State of New York."

James Pettengill conceded, "You do look some scarrish."

"Scarrish," Eunice scoffed, "I could scare you to nonexistence. I have scared six men smarter than you are," no doubt referring to the Council of Revision.

Then James Chapman came forward to size up his ex-wife, and he saw that she, too, was much changed. Enticing as she had appeared as recently as two months ago—a "modern enchantress" was how William Leete Stone had described her—her trials had taken their toll on her appearance. Her former husband was quick to point that out.

"I think it is a pity," James said, "that the United States are so reduced as to be stirred up by two old women running up and down the street."

But Eunice's looks were not all that had hardened. "I have written a great deal about you," she replied, "and I shall write more if you do not give up my children. What I have purposed to do, *that* I will accomplish." She then demanded that the children be brought forth.

James responded that he did not want "all the town to come on so small an occasion, just to see the children"; next thing, "the whole country would want to come." The Merrills, the Foggs, Mary, and Eunice could go to the Family dwelling, where the children would meet them, but no others.

Eunice refused. She wanted to meet her children in the trustees' office, as she and Mary had planned, and there she sat, unwilling to move. At first, Joseph Merrill, Jesse Fogg, and their wives remained with her, but after some time, they decided to go down to the Shaker dwelling to see the children. Then Mary Dyer could not bear it any longer, and she, too, crossed the threshold into the Shaker world, leaving Eunice alone.

It must have required extraordinary fortitude for Eunice to resist running to see her children—who were hundreds of yards away—after finally bridging the distance of so many miles and years. The last time Eunice had seen George was on a snowy winter day, three years and four months ago, at the Church Family in Watervliet. At that time, he had begged to know when she could bring him home; choking back her tears in order to spare him further anguish, she had promised that she would fetch him soon. She had lived with his question all this time. When Eunice had parted ways with her daughters one month later, with her brothers-in-law looking on, the girls had beseeched her with the same question. Now, nothing prevented Eunice from answering her children's call except her determination to see them on her own terms.

Nearly two hours later, Eunice was still waiting in the office by herself when a polite boy in plain dress—not quite a man, yet no longer a child—entered the building and came into her view. Eunice stood and stared at "the little stranger," but could not recognize him.

Then George spoke.

"Eunice," he said, "how do you do?"

* * *

Eunice burst into tears and tried to embrace her son, but the firstborn child who had once rolled about the floor screaming for his mother recoiled from her touch. To remind him of their past life together, Eunice produced his old pocketbook, with its dollar's worth of change. She told him how much she had cherished it, as it had carried memories of him. George, however, showed no interest.

Next, Eunice produced a notebook and pen, and asked her son to sign it with the date he had been taken from their home in Durham. The exercise would reveal to her what sense he had of the time that had passed and whether he could still read and write. It would also serve to conjure his previous life. This time, George accepted the offering. He correctly marked the year he turned Shaker, 1814, and wrote beside it, "when I was kindly taken from my mother," before handing it back.

Eunice read the words with disbelief. The son she knew had cared for her when she was sick and would drop whatever he was playing with at the sound of her call. She had entertained all sorts of terrible scenarios during their years apart, but never had she imagined that her child would disdain her. She hardly knew what to feel as this creature she barely recognized addressed her as "Eunice" and quietly but insistently pushed her away.

Eunice struggled to rekindle some feeling in George, to have him remember the life that they had once shared, but in vain. George's only interest was in bringing Eunice to see his sisters. The devoted son who Eunice had believed would care for her in her old age had become stiff, "unnatural," and even "impudent"—a Shaker to the core, as he proved with his parting words.

As the boy moved to leave, Eunice tried to press his old pocketbook into his hands, only to be repulsed again. Proving his worth as a Believer, he said, "I shall leave my money for my mother."

Having seen what had become of her son, Eunice could wait no longer to find her girls. She walked down to the dwelling house where she had seen her friends heading hours before and entered the meeting room. She saw everyone comfortably assembled, Mary with her children, all in a line, the Foggs, and the Merrills, looking placid enough. And then she saw them; standing there dutifully before the group, dressed in formless shifts, with their hair tucked into plain, tight caps, were two joyless figures—her daughters.

The older child, nearly twelve, came toward her first, and as Eunice gazed at her in wordless amazement, she greeted her mother just as her brother had done, with a gentle, "Eunice, how do ye do?"

Once her mother's pride, with much of the good looks, outgoingness, and personal charm that had served Eunice herself so well, Susan appeared "like a shadow." Her previously glowing features were pale and wan, and even her accent had changed. Anxious to reconnect with the child she had once known, Eunice pressed the girl's cheek to her own, crying, "Can this be my Susan, my dear Susan!"

Eunice tore off her daughter's Shaker cap, which half hid her face, but Susan became so upset that Eunice quickly replaced it. There were tears in the girl's eyes.

Then Eunice saw her youngest—her baby, as she continued to call Julia—and was dumbstruck. The child had been only four when her father had stolen her from Durham, and she was still playing at her mother's feet. In her place was a grown girl, who looked upon Eunice as a stranger. Julia approached her mother primly, uttering the now familiar greeting: "Eunice, how do ye do?"

Seeing her favorite child up close, Eunice was overwhelmed with both pain and pleasure, as she later recalled, and became even more emotional than she had been with the others. Pulling her youngest into her lap, Eunice wept, "Oh, my dear Julia, my long-lost babe," and rejoiced that she could hold her child once more in her arms. But Julia wriggled her way out of her mother's embrace, informing her that sitting in laps was against orders.

For a time, Eunice cried uncontrollably. The Shakers stood or sat stiffly: attentively, but betraying no emotion. The visitors, however, "wept like children" at the scene—the men included.

Finally, James could not stand any more and said, "Eunice, don't make such a racket, you disturb the Brethren and Sisters."

Her face wet and swollen, Eunice gazed eagerly at her daughters and asked if they wanted to leave with her. The girls, however, replied that they preferred to stay with the Shakers. Their mother warned that they must not say such things, asking if they were told what to say, but the girls insisted that they were speaking for themselves.

Desperate, Eunice pulled out gifts that she had brought for them, extending a beautifully dressed doll—a forbidden treasure —to Julia.

"It is handsome," Julia admitted, "but I do not want it here."

The two girls told their mother how happy they were among the Believers and how much better off they were there than with her. Their answers perplexed Eunice. She had anticipated resistance from the Believers but hardly expected it from her own children. How was she to rescue the youngsters when they showed no desire to leave?

Eunice might have benefited from some lessons from Mary Dyer. Across the room, Mary was concluding her meeting with her children, and having spent more time as a Believer, she knew precisely what to say to produce a desired effect. Drawing her youngest boy near, she coaxed, "Would you not like to have me take the care of you as well as anyone, if it was the gift?"

The boy smiled and replied, "Yea," as a good Shaker should, for anything that was a "gift" was both a blessing and an order, a requirement among the people of God.

The Shakers saw at once that Mary had tricked the child—in the presence of worldly witnesses who would not understand the full significance of the exchange—and rushed to end her meeting. Mary's oldest children, seventeen-year-old Caleb and sixteen-year-old Betsey, grabbed hold of their younger brother while Mary clung on—a necessary precaution on the Shakers' part, since Mary had managed to run away with her youngest child once before.

At this moment, Eunice looked out at her sister-in-arms and, not having witnessed all that had happened before, was bewildered. All she could see was that one of the leading Shaker men, Nathaniel Draper, was standing behind her friend's children, apparently encouraging the older ones to fight their mother and drag their little brother away.

Eunice glanced at James, catching an expression on his face that she had not seen for many years, a look both strained and remorseful.

"James Chapman," she demanded, "can you remain insensible through all of this?"

But the moment had passed. At Eunice's words, James quickly recovered himself and betrayed no further emotion as a group of Shakers surrounded Mary's children, covering them like a cloud, and hustled them from the room.

By evening, with both Eunice's and Mary's children insisting that they wanted to remain where they were, the mothers were at a loss. The Shakers, meanwhile, became increasingly open. Following the initial meeting with the children, James personally invited Eunice's companions to take the youngsters aside for a private interview, promising that if the children said they wanted to go with their mother, they would be free to do so. Eunice, however, rejected the offer, certain that the children would continue to act like "parrots," dutifully repeating what the Shakers had coached them to say.

Then, when the dinner bell rang, the Believers invited everyone to join them for supper. Eunice initially refused this, too, saying, "No, my meat and my drink is to do the will of my Father" —a brave gesture, given that she had probably not eaten since leaving Willis's Tavern that morning and the meal would have saved her some expense. But when everyone else eagerly accepted the invitation, unable to turn down a tasty Shaker supper, Eunice "consented to have some," as well, declaring that she "meant to eat as much as she could."

Mary's daughter Betsey good-naturedly replied that she was welcome, to which Eunice snapped, "Welcome, I do not want anybody to make me welcome," before digging into her meal.

At dusk, the party finally headed back to town, their bellies full, and with an odd semblance of peace among all but the mothers. Everyone but Eunice and Mary had thanked the

Shakers for their hospitality, and the members of the group as a whole were in far different spirits than they had been when they had marched down Shaker Road that morning.

Eunice herself was evidently chastened, for she listened carefully as her husband offered this parting advice: Don't trouble us tomorrow about seeing the children, he said, for the Brethren and Sisters had been in "a perfect hell" all day and needed rest.

Eunice would take his advice and wait until the day after to return.

The next evening, Mary Dyer traveled back to the Believers, joined by six or eight friends, minus Eunice. This was a desperate move. Whereas Eunice had a law behind her, and drew sympathy as an outsider who had come from far away, Mary enjoyed no such support. Her relative weakness showed in her present company. Mary and her group were only women, as the Shakers observed—a far cry from the impressive company assembled the day before. But when the Believers saw their silhouettes in the darkness, the women's faces looking ghoulish in the candlelight, they were alarmed enough that they forbade the intruders to set foot in their yard.

Mary informed the Shakers that she had no intention of giving up, that she would fight for her children even if she had to die trying. When the Shakers continued to block their gates, Mary offered her most provocative threat, one that would have serious consequences for her friend Eunice. There were a great many people who were prepared to descend upon the village "at a minute's warning," she alleged; the Shakers would soon see what she could do.

The Shakers could be sure that Mary herself did not have the power to stage such an attack, not alone, at least. The fact that no men joined her on this occasion suggested as much. Yet her threat reminded the Believers of what they had heard whispered for days, that people were gathering around another woman who could command a mob, and would.

Mary eventually turned back, but she had made her mark. Already on the alert, James Chapman became fearful that no doors would be strong enough to protect his children, and he made plans to relocate them.

Although the Shakers must have given their approval, the initiative to hide the children may have come from James himself. An unstable character who drank heavily even as a Believer, James would have been willing to take desperate measures to ensure that his children did not end up with his ex-wife. Moreover, the Shakers' Deacon, Nathaniel Draper, had returned, but other senior members of the society were still missing, giving James all the more impetus to push for an extreme solution. The Shakers hardly shared James's desire for vindication, but they had another powerful motivation for supporting his mission. George, Susan, and Julia had become faithful Believers (more dedicated, in fact, than their erratic father), and they had expressed their wish to remain. Because of them, the Shakers were willing to make a last stand against Eunice. They agreed to give the children shelter in a remote part of their property, hoping that their assailants would be thwarted and eventually go away.

James had to tread carefully. A voluntary sentry had been set up around the village, watching the Shakers from all sides and at all hours to make sure that they did not try to move the children. Meanwhile, the Believers themselves had also set up a rotating number of Brothers to watch over their property and sound an alarm in case of attack. How the group evaded detection is unknown, but at midnight, George, Susan, and Julia were spirited out of their dwellings, unseen. For the children, it was surely déjà vu as they rose groggily from their beds and joined their father in the dark. But on this May night, they were not headed far, and, anxious to avoid being captured by their mother, they were much more compliant.

Up on the hill, George, Susan, and Julia had company in the Dyer children, who had also been roused from their beds. Now the youngsters were scattered and hidden well, some tucked into deserted barns, others given shelter on the ground. (George was once again separated from his sisters.) There were no homes for at least a half a mile around, and the children were made as comfortable as they could be in the woods. They remained there for hours, shivering in the spring chill, listening to their own hushed breathing and the sounds of the night around them.

4

FIVE HUNDRED MEN

Eunice may have refrained from disturbing the Believers, as promised, but she had not allowed herself to rest. All day she had canvassed Enfield, going from house to house with her story, and when she headed back down the Shakers' road, it was with new friends: Samuel Cochran and his latest wife. Forty-four-year-old Cochran, a storekeeper, was a man whom nature had repeatedly robbed of his kin. His first wife, Mehitabel, had died five years earlier from a "wasting sickness," following to the grave the couple's one baby boy. Cochran had remarried, but in a short time he had lost his second wife, as well. Soon after his bereavement he had wed again, and thus it was his third wife—a young widow named Hannah—who was by his side when Eunice asked him to accompany her to the Shakers.

Once Eunice, Cochran, and his wife reached the trustees' office, Cochran asked to see James. Cochran said that he wanted to sit down with the Chapmans and help them reach a compromise, for news of this painful affair, he had heard, was speeding across town and even state lines. The Deacon promptly directed the group to the North Family, where James lived. There, Elder John Lyon sent at once for James. His dispatcher returned, however, to say that James was not home. He claimed not to know where James was or where the little girls had gone.

Now it was Eunice who had a terrible sense of déjà vu, and she refused to leave until James was found. The Shakers invited her to wait in the trustees' office as before, but Eunice had another agenda. As Samuel Cochran headed back to town for support, Eunice boldly marched into the street—the same public road along which she had first come into town—and proceeded to hail down every passing wagon, gig, and stagecoach to proclaim how the Shakers had abused her. For two hours she carried on in this way, while the Shakers looked on helplessly, unable to persuade her to come indoors.

The road was well trafficked: The Fourth New Hampshire Turnpike serviced freight and passenger coaches traveling along the East Coast between Canada and the Massachusetts shore. And all along that road, word of Eunice's troubles spread quickly—past Canaan, Grafton, and Danbury to Salisbury, New Hampshire, in the east; to Champlain, Vermont, near Burlington, in the north; and even out to Boston.

Before long, many of those who had heard of Eunice's story began milling around the Shakers' grounds, eager to help her or simply to attend the promised spectacle. By six o'clock, a more official company joined them: a group of twelve to fourteen men, led by Samuel Cochran and Selectman Joseph Merrill. Merrill first approached Elder John, beginning peaceably. He said that he and his company had "not come for a riot" and that he would personally pledge that Mary Dyer's children would

not be touched. What they wanted, quite simply, was a conference with James Chapman.

But when Elder John responded that James was not there
and that no one knew where he was, the selectman abruptly
changed his tone. Merrill's voice rose like thunder before the
shifting crowd as he demanded that the Shakers produce James
Chapman at once. He said that he could raise "five hundred
men in a short time" and that he would not leave until Eunice
had her children.

The Elder looked steadily at the selectman from whom he
had requested assistance several nights ago—the same man
who had sworn he knew nothing about people gathering—and
appealed, once more, to Merrill's sense of duty. Reminding him
of his responsibilities as a justice of the peace, the Elder beseeched him to dismiss the crowd or at least to calm them
down.

Merrill openly rejected his pleas. "The people are all stirred
up," he replied, "and I am too, and I will do nothing about it."

Then, as more and more insurgents gathered around the village, standing guard on horseback, trolling about the grounds,
and even slipping under fences to keep a better eye on the
Shakers' doors, the officer himself began to whip them up.

James Chapman had escaped the gallows in New York, Merrill
cried, and he had run to this state in order to evade his own
state's laws. This, he declared, was "too much to be borne."
Could such a crime be suffered? Could such a man be allowed
to escape? James Chapman, he said, should be run out of town
and removed from the state—and there were men to do it.
People had been calling in from all around to demand why no
one would help this disconsolate woman, and hundreds could
be gathered in no time.

Turning to the Shakers, the selectman warned, "You won't have much sleep tonight, I will warrant you." Five hundred people, he said again, could be "assembled by tomorrow at nine AM."

Darkness had come upon the village. The Shaker grounds were overrun with worldly intruders who had spread themselves out to the farthest fences—about a hundred people in all, as far as the Shakers could see. Inside the dwelling houses, the Brethren and Sisters prayed and sang, and hid the little ones from public view. For who knew how the mob might rise up at the sight of a youngster—any youngster, even if it was not a Chapman?

Then James Chapman appeared, as if from nowhere. He said that he was willing to speak, but not before a crowd. A smaller group of visitors and Shakers moved into the North Family shop. There, with candlelight casting shadows upon the Brothers' mounted tools and obscuring the features of those within, Eunice and James confronted each other for what, unbeknownst to them both, would be the very last time.

Eunice's companions proposed a compromise. Keep your boy, they told James, but give the woman one of the girls; then, cast lots for the third child.

James, however, growled that he would "sooner tie his children to a log and set them adrift in the river, than . . . give them to a crazy woman who was wandering from town to town, among strangers, and unprotected."

These strangers, he continued, had no idea who Eunice really was. She was a woman of questionable character—as were her family members and all the other deponents who had testified to her virtues in her book. But Merrill and his company stood by Eunice, declaring that they believed everything she had said, as well as her witnesses' statements. Moreover, they argued, the New York State legislature would never have been "imposed upon by a woman" if she had not truly been deserving of redress.

Eunice now turned tearfully to her former husband, resuming the posture of a sentimental heroine, a strategy that had served her so well in the past.

"Mr. Chapman," she pleaded, "when I was married to you, you [were] respectable; your relations are still so. I am now an unprotected wanderer, and expect to wander until I obtain my children, though I ought and might have been under the protection of a kind husband."

"Though you may have some claim to the son," she continued, "can you withhold my daughters, my dearest self from me?"

This was now the third time Eunice had offered to divide her children along gender lines, and it showed that despite all of her successes, Eunice recognized that the culture of custody would continue to weigh in James's favor. She may have won *access* to custody rights in the state of New York, but she would have to bring her children before a judge in order to claim these rights. In New Hampshire, moreover, her law had no effect. By the laws of this state, she was trespassing on private property and setting herself up as a kidnapper of her own children. James knew this, too, and he remained unmoved. He insisted that as a father, he had a lawful right to *all* of his children.

As Eunice and James continued to go back and forth, the Shakers declared their neutrality. They claimed that they had no control over James or the children—that it was up to the father to set his course. Eunice, however, was deeply skeptical, and she watched angrily as James repeatedly leaned in toward the Shakers, or they drew him aside and appeared to advise him what to do.

Eunice was certain that the Shakers were urging James to stand up to her, but it is possible that they were encouraging him to settle: A hundred intruders had besieged their property, and who knew how many more might gather at dawn. But the Shakers had never forced James's hand, as they might have done, by threatening to release him or leaving him to resolve his problems by himself, and it seems that they did not do so now. Unity was their guiding principle, and it prevented them from turning their backs on members in critical moments such as this. Unfortunately for the Shakers, the outside world would never understand the complexity of their dilemma. To outsiders, the Believers had become complicit, at the very least, simply by standing beside James.

By eleven o'clock that night, Eunice's supporters could take no more. Sheriff Moses Johnson came forward with a warrant for James's arrest. James was then cuffed and forced from the workshop, while the Believers, bewildered, tried to protest. They soon learned that he was being taken in on charges of abuse—not against Eunice, but against Mary Dyer. Months ago, James had assisted Joseph Dyer in carrying Mary off the Shaker premises. According to Mary, he had dragged her away from the meetinghouse and left her in the street, ripping her gown. At the time, she had not pressed charges, but now the incident became a ready excuse to remove James from the village.

With James taken prisoner, the village erupted in chaos. After being encamped for hours, some of the visitors decided to leave the scene, but others ran over the grounds with new zeal, led by Eunice, who proclaimed that she would not leave the premises until she had her children.

"What hinders our laying all these buildings flat?" the Shakers heard her cry out to the throng. "Are we not able to raise men sufficient to do it?"

The Believers, meanwhile, stood alert behind barricaded doors, drawing their children close.

For nearly two hours the mobsters searched the yards, the fields, the barns, and every available building, sparing the church, whose doors they did not dare break down. Then, suddenly, Eunice was inspired with a vision—a conviction, from a source unknown, that her children were in a barn up on a mountain, half a mile from where they stood.

No one thought it possible, but Eunice was certain as she pointed to a distant hill.

Two nights had passed since George fled the village with his father and sisters and hastened up one of the encircling hills. On the first night, he had been left to sleep by himself in an empty barn. Near daybreak, his father had come and taken him nearly a mile farther up the mountain until they reached another deserted hay barn. James left the boy with cold food and drink, and told him to stay low.

He was still waiting when he heard the crowd's approach—the sound of shuffling shoes, the swish of garments, low-toned voices, and twigs snapping underfoot. Terrified, George submerged himself in hay, neglecting in his haste to hide his supper dishes, still laden with the food he had been too unnerved to eat.

Among the first to enter was Sheriff Moses Johnson, who saw the food and helped lift George out of his hiding place. The boy struggled, but Johnson was a man who, even in his old age, carried a whip and two pistols to fight off woodland bandits, and the

boy was no match for him. Johnson and the others seized George
and brought him out to Eunice.

It was well past midnight when the boy met his mother. He
turned away from her under the glare of torchlight and trembled,
as she recalled, "as though he had been taken captive by the savages." This was hardly an ideal reunion, but for Eunice it was
good enough. She pushed George toward a carriage, ignoring his
cries of protest and those of the Shakers. Joined now by their
lawyer, a dozen or so Believers trailed after Eunice, demanding
to see James and a copy of the writ under which he had been
seized, yet they hardly dared to do more.

But George, like his mother, had a mind of his own. Just as
Eunice had gotten him into the coach, he tried to hurl himself
out of the vehicle. Eunice held tight, and despite the fact that
she was up against a vigorous teenager, and though George
pulled so hard that he yanked her headfirst out of the carriage,
she managed to drag him back into the coach. There, as the
carriage took off, they sat in an awkward half-embrace, Eunice
continuing to grasp her son in spite of his resistance. There
were flecks of hay imbedded in his shirt, palpable in the darkened coach, and both mother and son were out of breath.

As the village began to recede in the distance, Eunice was all
business with George. She told him that he had no choice but
to go with her and that he would have to remain with her until
his next birthday, when he would turn fourteen. But after that,
she said, he could decide for himself whether he preferred to
stay with her or return to the Shakers. Hearing this, the boy
finally ceased his struggling.

With George safely within the carriage and no longer fighting her, if far from content, Eunice considered what to do about
her girls. She had learned that Susan and Julia were barricaded

in the church. The only way to get them would be to break down the doors. She decided to leave George in a safe place before taking matters any further. She hid him among strangers, several miles from the Shaker village, before returning to the village in pursuit of her daughters. But when she learned that James had been released from the local jail and was on his way back to the scene, she turned around at once, for it was either "flee," as Eunice saw it, "or lose the child I had got."

With a paid bodyguard for their protection, Eunice and George sped toward Albany. The trip took longer than usual, for Eunice directed her driver to take private roads and detours at extra expense in order to shake off possible followers. Eunice remained sleepless for the entire ride, keeping a close watch on both her son and the road behind her.

The Shakers also got little rest. That night and for several days and nights to follow, gunshots rang at irregular intervals, fired by a man Eunice had paid to keep the Believers from going after her—and to "let them know what they might expect in case they should."

5

MOTHER AGAIN

For forty hours Eunice neither slept nor ate, fearful that George would try to run off the moment she turned away. In Albany, mother and son "received congratulations from every class," but Eunice largely kept George hidden while she sewed him a new set of clothes. She was surely anxious that George would be identified as a Shaker, and every time she saw a Believer—a team of Brethren riding past in their wagons, or unloading their goods, or simply walking in the street—she shuddered and kept an extra-close eye on her son. "I trembled whenever he went out of my sight," she later recalled, fearful that the boy would make a run for Watervliet.

Eunice's suspicions were on the mark. When he first arrived in Albany, George was far from being reconciled to his life with his mother, whom he still insisted on calling "Eunice." Later, George himself would admit that he had been plotting his escape, fearful for his soul's well-being after all that he had been taught. For a young Shaker, the thought of being sent out to the world and being contaminated by its sins was a terrible prospect. George would have been all the more frightened knowing that he was now living beside a woman who was bound for hell.

But little by little, Eunice managed to interest her son in the pleasures of worldly life. As important as it was for her to resume working—she had depleted her savings in Enfield—Eunice set aside time to show her son "the different curiosities in the city" and indulge him in the "innocent luxuries and amusements" that Albany had to offer. And there was much to amuse a boy of George's age: lions, orangutans, and tigers on parade in "strong iron cages," a stunning array of musical performances, and "astonishing feats" performed by sleight-of-hand magicians. On display at Mr. Cook's Reading Room around this time was an especially breathtaking sight: "one hundred square feet of Canvass, forming a picture of Gloucester town, Cape Ann, and the harbour, boats, sloops and schooners, with an exact likeness of the GREAT LEVIATHAN, or, SEA-SERPENT, as she rose in search of her young one."

There were also the simple diversions that could be found almost anywhere outside Enfield. Without anyone to define the terms of their pleasure, Eunice and her son could linger in the markets. They could eat what they wanted rather than what happened to be served. And they could watch—for hours if they wished—the sloops and schooners and tall ships as they moored in the harbor.

For a country boy who had spent the last several years living among the Shakers, such sights were beyond imagining, and slowly but surely, Eunice won him over. At the end of several weeks in Albany, he turned to her, and instead of addressing her by her first name, he called her "Mother" for the first time.

* * *

James, too, was back in Albany, apparently on his own initiative. At the end of July, the leadership in New Hampshire wrote to Mother Lucy to say that things had calmed down in Enfield but that James had been determined to leave for New York so that he could go after George. The Elders were clearly troubled about James. He had exerted his personal will far more than was customary among Believers and showed little concern for the distress his affairs might bring. Fearful of further attack, the Elders had insisted that James either take his daughters with him in his travels or indenture them to outsiders who could assist in case of a crisis. James had finally signed one-year contracts binding the girls to local, non-Shaker men before leaving town.

Once in Albany, James arranged a meeting with the Shakers' lawyer, hoping to reclaim George at once. The lawyer warned James, however, that if he tried to take his son now, he would be subject to punishment by Eunice's law. When precisely Eunice obtained custody rights to George is unknown, but even if her rights were not yet official, James could be charged with interfering with custody hearings or attempting to take the boy out of the state, which it was now illegal for Shakers to do. In order to get the child back, James would first have to obtain a legislative repeal—and that, he knew, would be next to impossible.

James's course thereafter was unsteady, even more than it had been for some time. He returned to Watervliet and stayed there for a few months, but then even the Believers lost track of him. That winter, the Elders in New Hampshire wrote worriedly to Mother Lucy and her Ministry that they had not heard from James Chapman for months and that they "should like to . . . as two of his children are still at Enfield." Many months later, when James was still assumed to be in Albany, the leadership in New Hampshire wrote again. Over a year had passed since the mob attack, and the girls' indentures were soon to expire. This time, they addressed their letter directly to James. For Eunice, that choice would be fortunate.

For over a year, Eunice and George had been living on 40 Green Street—a backstreet located in an area formerly known as Cheapside, which was thick with workers and boardinghouses. They shared their quarters with a widow named Mary Warner who was a schoolteacher like Eunice. By this time, mother and son were a united front. When George had celebrated his birthday in February 1819, there was no question as to where he wished to live, and his mother could exult: "My son is now fourteen, and I can boast that he is much attached to me, and detests the name Shaker."

While George attended to his studies, Eunice continued to teach, not only to support her son but also to raise funds for her daughters' return. It was mainly because she had no money for the trip that she was unable to go back to Enfield right away: the town residents were ready to help her whenever she was ready, Eunice boasted to Mary Dyer. But there was yet another reason why she could not go back immediately. Once again, Eunice could not be certain where her children were. Given all the turmoil that had gone on in Enfield, and in light of Mary Dyer's renewed legislative suit, it would have seemed possible, even probable, that the girls had been moved out of the state.

There is reason to suggest that Eunice herself considered the possibility that her daughters had been taken to Ohio. In the spring of 1819, Josiah Terry was discovered making inquiries there, "begging for a privilege," as the Elders in Union

Village wrote. The Shakers suspected he was spying for Eunice. Eunice's writing was also circulating in Ohio—much to the Shakers' grief—thanks to the newspaper editor Abram Van Vleet. Eunice had sent Van Vleet a copy of her book, and he had been so impressed with it that he began reprinting it himself. Through Eunice, Van Vleet made Mary Dyer's acquaintance, and he published her writing, as well—a great boon for Mary, who continued to be unsuccessful in the New Hampshire legislature.

Eunice did what she could for her friend. She sent out books and letters to the governor of New Hampshire, and she had her brother Jesse, now of Erie Canal fame, do the same. She also wrote testimonials for Mary and tried to publish an article of support for her in a local newspaper. But Eunice's devotion to anti-Shakerism was soon to regain its single-minded focus, as news about her daughters reached home.

One day in September 1819, Eunice entered the post office in Albany. She did not always go regularly: In years past, Eunice's name had been listed in the papers among those who had neglected to pick up their mail. Today, however, her timing was perfect. In the letter box, filed under the letter *C*—Eunice continued to go by the name "Mrs. Chapman"—was a letter addressed to James.

As James's wife, Eunice had possessed the right to claim his mail. She claimed this privilege now, as she accepted the envelope from the postmaster and tore it open. The letter was sent from Enfield, and it was penned in the Shakers' beautifully curled script. Her eyes racing across the page, Eunice saw a request to James to renew the indentures of his daughters—*her* daughters, who had been in Enfield all this time.

With the letter to direct her, her son's word against the Believers, and—at last—the necessary funds, Eunice needed nothing more. She traveled at once to Enfield, where she hired a
lawyer and appointed an agent, perhaps a respected local such
as Samuel Cochran, to go to the Shakers for her girls. The Shakers balked when first approached, but once the agent produced
a letter from Eunice's lawyer, they allowed the children's guardians to release the girls without further protest. Even though
James had indentured his children to outsiders before leaving,
ensuring their right to remain in the area, it was simply too dangerous for the Believers to try to prevent Eunice from taking
them any longer.

There in Enfield, on a fine fall day, when the leaves were
tinged with crimson, Susan and Julia Chapman said good-bye
to their friends, their caretakers, and all their Brothers and Sisters in the faith. Then they dutifully followed their mother's
agent out of their village and crossed the Shaker gate for the
last time as Believers, to rejoin the world. Somewhere beyond,
their mother anxiously awaited them.

The girls looked like perfect Shakers, clad in their sacklike
gowns, their caps fastened to their heads. After all that Eunice
had gone through with George, she probably knew better than
to try to force them to embrace her all at once. But even if she
did, and the girls pushed their way out of her arms, Eunice
could rejoice that her extraordinary faith, against extraordinary
adversaries—which included not only her husband and the Believers, but the law and culture of her times—had finally brought
them together again.

An uncredited source in Lansingburgh, New York, provides
the last word on Eunice's journey, in a brief item that was reprinted in various newspapers: "Much credit is due to this lady,

for her fortitude and perseverance, against every species of opposition, in first interesting the legislature in her behalf, and in finally rescuing her children. . . ." Almost exactly five years since the children had disappeared from Durham, after a three-year legal battle, and a year and a half after she had regained her civil identity, Eunice had won her war.

EPILOGUE

In her letter to the Elders from March 1818, Eunice had sworn that all she wanted from the Shakers was her children—that she did not want to spend the "best of her days" contending with the society—and that if they were returned, she would make peace. She kept her word. Once her girls were home, and she was able to legalize her claims to all three children, Eunice dropped her anti-Shaker activities and devoted herself to creating a new life with her family.

For a time, Eunice remained in Albany, where she opened up a boardinghouse that promised to capitalize on her past political success. As one newspaper reported: "If all the members who voted for her divorce . . . now patronize her establishment, she will do well." That seems not to have been the case, however, because within a few years Eunice relocated to Auburn, New York, and embarked upon a new career as a milliner.

Launching a business in those times was no small feat. A financial panic swept the nation in 1819, the year that Susan and Julia came home. For a woman, the challenges were all the greater, and not surprisingly, Eunice struggled. At one point she had neither shop nor home, and she had to send her children to Rochester to live with her brother Jesse, who was described as "rather odd" and clashed with his young charges, especially George. But her past had toughened Eunice. As her elder daughter Susan wrote to her cousin: "I have this week received a letter from Mamma. She writes [that] when she takes a view of the past in her present circumstances she can say she has no trouble."

With some help from her family, Eunice was eventually able to get her business off the ground, and by the summer of 1823, it was thriving. The next year, Susan wrote: "Mother has a very pleasant situation on the main street: [She] has a commodious shop in front and a very pleasant room back of it." The house was crooked, but as Susan cheerfully observed, "we have vines in boxes which handsomely shades the windows," and "a full view of the prison," which was a mainstay in the town. Eunice's affairs were going well enough that she could afford to hire helpers, who also boarded with the family. "I felt very gloomy on my first arrival at Auburn," Susan admitted, "but now every day attaches me more and more to my house."

Susan's correspondence from these years reveals that her mother was finally able to provide a comfortable life for the family. When a circus caravan came through Auburn with elephants, lions, camels, llamas, and monkeys in tow, the girls got tickets to see them. Susan took dancing lessons and painted landscapes, had new dresses made in the latest styles, and became a belle, with the most dance partners and beaux of anyone around. George had bad eyes and continuing health problems but sharp business skills like his mother. In time, he embarked on a career as a merchant that took him all over the world.

Eunice seems to have had no further contact with the Shakers or James once her children were with her. Susan, however, did have contact. In May of 1825, five and a half years after the girls left Enfield, James wrote to his elder daughter. Susan was torn. Her father's letter was mostly filled with proselytizing. Even so, as Susan confided to her cousin, he seemed to "write with much sincerity and affection," which "awakens feelings most agonizing." He wanted her and Julia to pay him a visit.

A year later, the now nineteen-year-old Susan decided to honor his request—without, however, giving her father any notice. She recounts their reunion in moving terms to her cousin:

> Shortly after my arrival in Troy, he came there on business, not knowing of my being there—I remained some time in the room with him before I made myself known, and the scene that followed surpasses description—at first he could not recognize a feature, nor be impressed . . . that *his child* stood before him—but when recollection presented to him the features of her whom he never again expected to meet [on] this side the grave, Nature was overpowered and he sobbed aloud!

"He spent the day with me," Susan further recalled, "alternately conversing and weeping." Although James stood by his life as a Shaker, he no longer envisioned such a life for his child. As Susan wrote, "He was much delighted with my looks and appearances and advised me to live in the world, and marry if it was my choice."

Susan did go on to marry, but her domestic happiness was short-lived. She died not long after her nuptials, probably from childbirth, her newborn with her. There was a terrible irony in Susan's death that could not have been lost on her mother:

Eunice may have "saved" her daughter from the Shakers, but the girl ultimately died of a fate that she would never have suffered had she remained a Believer.

Eunice and her other children, however, went on to have long lives, and Eunice had the satisfaction of remaining with her kin for the rest of her days. Eunice and Julia shared a home until Eunice's death, residing for many years in George's house in Brooklyn, a respectable suburb of Manhattan. Eunice's last address on Pineapple Street was particularly nice—located in prime Brooklyn Heights, around the corner from Henry Ward Beecher's famous Plymouth Church and near the home of the celebrated minister himself.

Eunice's two remaining children negotiated their Shaker past in very different ways. Julia never wed and seems to have lived a fairly uneventful life alongside her mother. George, in contrast, became the ultimate capitalist—a fur trader, an art collector, a slumlord, and eventually a millionaire. He married more than once, fathered at least one illegitimate child, and became the subject of another sensational lawsuit, brought against his heirs by a daughter he never legally recognized. This case became the stuff of tabloids, and even the presiding judge called George a modern incarnation of Henry VIII—a far cry from the Shaker he had so nearly become.

As for Eunice, she became a wealthy woman in her own right. By the time she died at age eighty-five in November 1863, she owned the house on Pineapple Street where she lived with Julia, plus two other properties in Buffalo, New York. She could afford to provide an annuity of $650 to Julia and still leave more to George. She succeeded, in short, in taking full advantage of the rights that her divorce had conferred upon her. She owned land, signed contracts, and benefited from the services and support of her children. The only advantage she did not exploit was the right to remarry. Eunice remained single and went by the name "Mrs. Eunice Chapman" until her death.

Yet in spite of these successes, Eunice's story did not exactly have a fairy-tale ending. A divorce, no matter how hard won, remained a source of deep shame. The Shakers privately recorded that Eunice was charged with assault and battery in Albany and that she had been found "drunk in the streets." Eunice also continued to be litigious and was embroiled in multiple law suits that continued even past her death. Most of all, as her granddaughter, Louise Ellis, would attest, Eunice was scarred by her past. When asked to describe her grandmother, Ellis recalled, "She kept to her room a great deal. You know, [she was] divorced, and she was a recluse."

The ultimate irony in Eunice's story appears, quite fittingly, on her grave. Many epitaphs from the nineteenth century feature "beloved mother" or the like. Eunice's headstone, in contrast, does not name the role for which she had fought so intensely. Instead, it defines her life by her trials against the Shakers—though, in keeping with her promise to maintain her peace, the Believers are never named. Her gravestone reads:

She was a light in the age in which she lived.
After three years incessant labour she obtained from the Legislature of New York in the year 1818 the first law, ever enacted, in any country, which gives to married women rights over their children and property. This law has since been amended and adopted by most of the States of the Union. Woman call her Blessed.

*   *   *

In death, as in life, Eunice exaggerated: her law was hardly the first "ever enacted in any country" to grant custody or property rights to married women. However, the essence of her boast remains true. To fully appreciate the magnitude of Eunice's legal triumph in 1818, we need to jump ahead a full thirty years to the Seneca Falls Convention of 1848, the first national forum on women's rights. In their "Declaration of Sentiments," Elizabeth Cady Stanton, Lucretia Mott, and others complained that married women were condemned to a civil death, and that they could not own property or have any control over their children. Eunice, however, had regained her civil identity, property, and custody rights decades before most women could even dream of doing so. In 1839, a rudimentary Married Women's Property Act passed in Mississippi, but most states did not consider such laws until mid-century. New York's own comprehensive property act, which gave women the rights Eunice had won through the legislature, was not passed until 1860.

Eunice's divorce remained an even greater rarity. After 1818, a steady stream (if not a flood, as legislators had feared) of divorce petitions made their way to the capital, many of them heart-wrenching. But despite the awful tales they heard of beatings and incest, abandonment and cruelty, the lawmakers refused to grant another legislative divorce; neither would they change the divorce laws. Decade after decade, proposals to expand the grounds for divorce (to include cruelty, drunkenness, desertion, and "incurable insanity," among other causes) continued to fail. Well into the twentieth century, wives had to resort to hiring "professional perjurers" to give tearful confessions of having slept with their husbands, in order to end their

marriages. Not until 1966 would the divorce laws finally be re-
vised to include grounds other than adultery. As for Eunice's
act, it remained in effect until 1975, when there were no Shakers left in the state, and it was finally repealed.

All of this attests to Eunice Chapman's extraordinary capabilities: her uncommon ability to persuade the people of her
times to press for radical measures for *her*, well before they were
ready to do so for anyone else. Her story bears witness to what
a single person can accomplish with a single-minded goal, then
or in any period, and ultimately, to how history is made.

Today, precisely because of its exceptionality, Eunice's case
has become a footnote in legal history. Yet aspects of her story
endure. Eunice's subversion of the limited expectations for
women, as well as the tactics she employed of lobbying politicians and exploiting the press, all continue in one form or another. Moreover, in many parts of the world, where women's
rights are far from secure—where women are not at liberty to
end their marriages or where they stand to lose their children—
the problems she faced are ongoing. In America, too, the com-
peting issues of custody, marital, religious, and state rights
persist, as demonstrated by the furor over the removal of Mor-
mon Fundamentalist children from their family compounds in
2008. The questions Eunice raised about religious radicalism
and when government should intervene in religious life also
remain subjects of national and international preoccupation.
For these and many other reasons, Eunice Chapman's fight
against her husband, the Shakers, and her times remains richly
resonant in the present day.

If others lost sight of Eunice, the Shakers kept an eye on her
for some time to come. When another woman attacked their

society years later, they worried that she would become "another Eunice Chapman." Eunice's writings also maintained a
life of their own. Not only were her books reissued in the West,
but Mary Dyer would continue to republish Eunice's story for
decades. Because of the continued harassment they faced on
account of Eunice's writings, the Believers finally decided they
had to publish a full rebuttal. Entitled *The Other Side of the Question*, this hefty book offered a spirited if belated attack on Eunice,
as well as on other anti-Shakers.

In time, however, cases like Eunice's fell into the minor-
ity, even as the Shakers began taking in more and more children. By mid-century, Shakers became renowned not as captors
but as caregivers, as growing numbers of ex-Shakers dispatched
glowing accounts of their Shaker childhoods. These individuals may have chosen to leave the sect, but they remained profoundly grateful to the people who had raised them and, in
many cases, rescued them from lives of abuse or poverty. Some
even suggested that Shaker villages become official safe havens.
An article entitled "Giving Babies to the Shakers," published
in the *New York Daily Times* in 1855, approved of a proposal to
send impoverished children from Randall's Island to New
Lebanon for a proper upbringing. The article reported that
officials seemed to support this idea, "believing that the children could nowhere procure a kinder home than among the
Shakers."

Yet one custody complainant continued to haunt the Believers for years: Mary Dyer. Mary fought the Shakers until her
death, logging in roughly a half a century of anti-Shaker work.
Her efforts helped expand the divorce laws of her state, but in
the end, her own cause was lost. Although she did obtain a divorce, she was never able to claim her children, all but one of

whom remained Shakers for life. The most illustrious of these was her firstborn, Caleb, who became the senior trustee at Enfield, and, in a case of tragic irony, was shot dead by a worldly parent seeking to reclaim his children.

The other Believers in Eunice's story met quieter ends. Mother Lucy died just after her sixty-first birthday, in the middle of a February afternoon in 1821, two years after Eunice was reunited with her children. After appearing well for some time, she suddenly suffered from "a fit of the ague": a high fever and cold sweats. Her spiritual progeny knew that her end was near, and they drew about their Mother to be with her when she entered the next world. Mother Lucy had chosen Watervliet to be her final resting place, and there she expired, "calm, patient, and resigned" as always.

The next day, six wagons arrived from New Lebanon, bringing numerous Elders and Deacons and thirty-nine Brothers and Sisters. Together, they paid tribute to their beloved Mother, whose death brought an epoch of their history to a close. Lucy Wright was the last of a succession of charismatic Shaker leaders, beginning with Mother Ann, and she was the last Shaker leader to rule alone. Thereafter a group of four—two men and two women—presided over the society together.

Elder Seth Youngs Wells of the Watervliet West Family survived his spiritual Mother by many years, serving in a different capacity from the one he filled in Eunice's time. Before she died, Mother Lucy released him from his Eldership so that he could write, as well as run the Shaker schools. He died in 1847, at age eighty, of "dropsical asthma." Before his death, the former Elder was wistful and unapologetic as he looked back on his life. In a short autobiography composed for Shaker youth, he reflected that, in light of all the "difficult circumstances" and "trying scenes" he had endured during his "gospel travel," he could only conclude: "I do not know but I have done the best that I could."

James Chapman also remained a Shaker for life, though there is evidence that he continued to dabble in worldly business. For instance, he is listed as a shareholder in the Coxsackie Turnpike Company in 1825, alongside his brother Nathaniel. In Watervliet, James worked as a gardener and died in the West Family, where he had begun his Shaker path. Ironically, in his later years, James was able to provide his own mother with just the kind of life that Eunice had once tried to bargain for. Molly Chapman moved to Watervliet to live with the Shakers, but not as one of them—an exception to the rule that only those who believed were allowed to live in Zion.

Like Eunice, James lived an unusually long life. In October of 1852, after being unwell for two weeks and shortly after a mess of clams had been brought in from Albany to revive his spirits, he took his last breath at eighty-nine years of age.

The Shakers are commonly thought to have died out, too, but this is not quite accurate. Numerically, the society actually peaked in the decades after Eunice's case, owing in great part to the increasing numbers of children they took in from the world.

Sometime during her reign as Shaker Mother—possibly as a result of the crisis with Eunice—Lucy Wright began actively counseling her fellow Believers to accept children of only believing parents. Beyond the desire to avoid conflict, there were practical reasons for her advice. As the Shakers acknowledged early on, children tended to be a poor return on their investment, particularly those who did not have a family to root them in the society. After Lucy Wright's death, however, the Shakers began receiving such children at a rapid pace, in what has been described as a deliberate effort to enlarge their ranks.

If only the Shakers had heeded their Mother's advice. One scholar has recently speculated that the great influx of children was one of the prime reasons for the Shakers' decline. The presence of so many youngsters, who consumed much more than they gave back, sapped the Believers practically, emotionally, and spiritually. Although at mid-century, child visionaries provided the impetus for a powerful spiritual resurgence known as the "Era of Manifestations," this period was ultimately short-lived and led to even larger-scale defections, especially by the young. In the end, it was just as Mother Lucy had predicted: The Shakers' decision to accept children of unbelievers—essentially, children like Eunice's—proved to be a grave mistake, perhaps even their undoing.

Other factors contributed to the society's decline after the mid-nineteenth century, including the rise of industrialism and secularism; an aging population and a diminished leadership pool; financial insolvency; and even the society's improved relations with the world. As the nineteenth century progressed, the Shakers' model communes drew the notice of such luminaries as Ralph Waldo Emerson, Friedrich Engels, and Leo Tolstoy. The Believers corresponded with Abraham Lincoln and counted another American president, Franklin Pierce, among their friends. Such admiration, however, did little to yield converts. As the Shakers often said, persecution actually invigorated them. With enemies like Eunice, they became unified in self-defense. Without such opposition, they faltered.

By the end of the nineteenth century, the Shakers were dwindling as a group, and villages across the country began to close. Today, a single Shaker community remains in Maine.

There are few Believers left—three at the time of this writing
—and they little resemble those whom Eunice saw in her day.
Contemporary Shakers wear jeans, watch television, and run a
Web site. They hold meetings, at which they pray and sing
hymns, but they no longer dance. There are also no children in
the modern-day society. However, these Believers, like those of
yore, continue to live chastely together, sharing all their resources, and devoting themselves to God.

As for the dozens of other Shaker villages that were exemplars of ingenuity in Eunice's time, they have been razed, restored, or put to other uses. The grounds of the Watervliet
community, where Eunice first flouted the society's rules, were
partially cleared years ago to make way for an insane asylum and
now contain an airport, jail, nursing home, hockey rink, and
country club. All that remains of the Believers are a small Shaker
museum and a few scattered Shaker buildings, some of which
are private homes. Likewise, the picturesque site where the
mob stormed Enfield now features a conference facility, a gloomy
Catholic sanctuary, and a Shaker museum and archive.

At the Shaker museums in these and other communities,
parents and children and husbands and wives walk freely together through well-kept grounds, enjoy Shaker-style meals, and
tour the Shakers' meetinghouses (using whatever doors they
please). There are oval boxes for sale in the museum shops,
where Shaker herbs scent the air, and Shaker songs such as
"Simple Gifts" play softly in the background. In these preserved Shaker environments, there is little sign of discord—no
trace of the remarkable "little woman" who once threatened to
extinguish Shaker society and who, in legal terms, almost did.

SOURCES

Eunice Hawley Chapman's full story has never been told, and the Shakers' role in it has never been thoroughly recounted. Piecing together this story has been challenging, not only because no single source describes all of the events but also because those who published accounts in the period wrote with such distinct and contradictory agendas. When one reads Eunice Chapman's narratives next to statements by James Chapman and the Shakers, it is hard to know what to believe. Had the Shakers stolen Eunice's children and willfully moved them out of the state, as she alleged? Or were the Believers wholly blameless, as their leader, Lucy Wright, piously claimed?

That central mystery is the foundation for this book. I first encountered Eunice Chapman during the course of my doctoral studies. Long a fan of the Shakers, I was bewildered by the charges this aggrieved mother brought against the sect in her books—above all, because the historical evidence seemed to confirm the Shakers' wrongdoing or at least their complicity. For well over a decade, I studied newspapers, Shaker records, legal papers, legislative journals, personal correspondence, and other manuscripts to obtain a full view of what actually happened. This book is the result of my efforts to understand the crisis from all sides.

Existing studies on Eunice Chapman and her case are short but informative. The most detailed examination of the Chapman case to date is Nelson Blake's article from 1960, "Eunice Against the Shakers," which summarizes Eunice Chapman's legal ordeal. Blake's legislative citations provided a strong starting point for my research. Jean M. Humez and Daisy Sophia Miller have also analyzed Eunice Chapman's narratives in the context of married women's rights and writings about the Shakers. I am particularly indebted to Elizabeth De Wolfe's exhaustive study on anti-Shaker Mary Dyer, *Shaking the Faith*. De Wolfe describes Eunice's narratives and work as an anti-Shaker, but more importantly, her careful analysis of what she calls Mary Dyer's "anti-Shaker activism"—especially Dyer's use of print culture —stimulated my thinking about Eunice's writing and activities.

The bulk of my book, however, draws from work with primary sources. For part 1, which chronicles the Chapmans' early lives, their marriage, and Eunice's experiences with the Shakers, I have relied primarily on the printed eyewitness accounts: Eunice Chapman's *Account of the Conduct of the Shakers* (1817) and *No. 2* (1818), James Chapman's "Memorial" to the New York legislature, and the Shakers' "Remonstrance." These sources turned out to be more consistent than one might expect: The basic events correspond, even if the explanations do not. Eunice's works are also remarkably accurate: Small details, such as the weather, and dates and descriptions of Shaker meetings, are confirmed in the Shakers' daily journals. Her "sin" as a writer, if it can be called that, was not so much fabrication but omission, as I have previously analyzed in a dissertation chapter on her writing.

On Eunice's trial period in Shaker society, the Believers' direct contributions are scanty. Here, too, however, Eunice's writings prove to be surprisingly helpful. Eunice reveals more than she probably intended to in her literature, especially in the earliest version of her story. For example, although she claims that the Shakers could charge her with just a single disobedience during her entire stay, her *Account* betrays a whole series of rebellious actions. (Significantly, all evidence of misbehavior disappears in *No. 2.*) Thus, even when the Shakers do not impart their perspective, a close reading of Eunice's own writings yields other points of view. Inevitably, there are occasions when Eunice's account of her experiences clashes with that of the Shakers. In such cases, I have depended upon manuscript research whenever possible, but also my own judgment.

The central challenge of part 2, the legal drama, was that the original legislative papers were destroyed in a fire. The only legislative records that remain are published journals that tend to describe decisions, rather than arguments. Fortunately, William Leete Stone, editor of Albany's first daily, the *Albany Gazette and Daily Advertiser*, meticulously recorded the legislative proceedings, giving detailed descriptions of speeches that sometimes border on transcription. The Shakers' recollection of the debates, as well as Eunice's own reports, helped to fill in the holes. While trying to be faithful to the sources, I have occasionally condensed, reordered, or omitted parts of arguments made by individual speakers. On a few occasions, when Stone's reporting was spotty, I have bridged gaps in argument, relying on similar points made by previous speakers or offering an interpretation based on other documentary evidence. I have also interpreted audience reactions, using eyewitness reports whenever possible.

Documentation for part 3, which concerns the mob on Enfield, was the most straightforward. Eunice and the Shakers give detailed, dramatic accounts of this event. Eunice's appears in Mary Dyer's *Portraiture of Shakerism* and Abram Van Vleet's reprint of her book, *An Account of the Conduct of the Shakers*. The Shakers give an even fuller treatment in a manuscript entitled "A Statement Concerning the Mob at Enfield, NH" and in a deposition by Elder John Lyon.

Throughout this book, I have relied extensively on Shaker records, which include journals, diaries, correspondence, ledgers, legal papers, indentures, and spiritual writings. The Shakers maintained these records as impeccably as one might expect from a perfectionist sect. Especially useful were daily journals kept by Freegift Wells and Jethro Turner on behalf of the society in Watervliet, New York. These journals document much of what happened from the Shakers' side, even if they do not directly explain the Shakers' motivations. As I have shown in these pages, however, I believe that such an explanation can be found in context. I have chosen to filter my own reading of the Shaker response through the characters of Elder Seth Youngs Wells, who was James Chapman's immediate supervisor, and Mother Lucy Wright.

Although few works of scholarship address Eunice's own story, numerous studies have informed my reading of the Shakers, including the works of Priscilla Brewer, Elizabeth De Wolfe, Jean M. Humez, Stephen Stein, and Glendyne Wergland, which are most often cited in my notes. I am grateful to these and other Shaker scholars for the depth of their scholarship, as well as, in many cases, their personal insights. Regarding marriage and divorce in the nineteenth century—its history, practice, and popular views—I have relied heavily on Henrik Hartog's *Man and Wife in America*. My primary source for custody and family matters is Michael Grossberg's *Governing the Hearth*.

I should further note that while Eunice considered the Shakers her foremost adversary, many others had vastly different relationships with the society. Untold numbers of men, women, and children led deeply fulfilling lives as Believers, finding a haven from the spiritual and material poverty they encountered in the outside world. A short list of books that provide other views of the sect: Priscilla Brewer, *Shaker Communities, Shaker Lives*; Sister Frances A. Carr, *Growing Up Shaker*; Stephen J. Stein, *The Shaker Experience in America*; and June Sprigg, *Simple Gifts: Lessons in Living from a Shaker Village*.

A final note on style and content: I have written Eunice's story with an eye to drama, but this book is not a work of fiction. Details about the weather and descriptions of Eunice's thoughts and moods all originate in period sources. In particular, my discussion of Eunice's feelings is rooted in her books. I have limited page references to direct quotations, except for a few cases where her explanations are placed out of sequence in her writings. I have kept most of the original spelling and punctuation for these and all sources, making minor corrections to maintain clarity. In a few instances where I have expanded upon the existing evidence—for example, providing details of what Eunice was likely to have seen in Watervliet—I have listed sources. In the end, however, what I offer here is one view of Eunice, the Shakers, and the world they inhabited, my own interpretation of how the crisis unfolded, and why it played out as it did.

NOTES

ABBREVIATIONS OF SOURCES

AGDA   Albany Gazette and Daily Advertiser
BECHS   Buffalo and Erie County Historical Society Library and Archives, Buffalo, New York
CSV   Canterbury Shaker Village Archives, Canterbury, New Hampshire
LC   Library of Congress, Washington, DC
WM   Edward Deming Andrews Memorial Shaker Collection, Winterthur Museum and Library, Winterthur, Delaware
WRHS   Western Reserve Historical Society, Cleveland, Ohio

EPIGRAPH AND PROLOGUE

Live with me, my child! Rufus Bishop, Seth Y. Wells, and Giles B. Avery, comps., *Testimonies of the Life, Character, and Doctrines of Mother Ann Lee and the Elders with her, through whom the Word of Eternal life was opened in this day, of Christ's Second Appearing, collected from Living Witnesses, in Union with the Church* (Albany, NY: Weed, Parsons and Co., Printers, 1888), 243.

"I will scare you yet" Shakers, "A Statement Concerning the Mob at Enfield, New Hampshire," May 25, 1818, Hamilton College Library, Clinton, NY.

America in a time of revolution Debby Applegate captures the terrors of this era in *The Most Famous Man in America: The Biography of Henry Ward Beecher* (New York: Doubleday, 2006), 23.

people behind the objects have largely been forgotten Stephen Stein discusses the popular amnesia in *The Shaker Experience in America* (New Haven: Yale University Press, 1992), xiv. His book provides an excellent general history of the Shakers, as does Priscilla J. Brewer, *Shaker Communities, Shaker Lives* (Hanover, NH: University Press of New England, 1986).

"almost expect[ed] to be remembered" Stein *Shaker Experience*, xiv.

several thousand strong The Shakers peaked at more than four thousand souls in the mid-nineteenth century and eventually built more than twenty settlements in Connecticut, Florida, Georgia, Indiana, Kentucky, Maine, Massachusetts, New Hampshire, New York, and Ohio.

exclusive property of their father See Mary Ann Mason, *From Father's Property to Children's Rights: The History of Child Custody in the United States* (New York: Columbia University Press, 1994).

feminine weakness into a source of political strength Jean M. Humez, "'A Woman Mighty to Pull You Down': Married Women's Rights and Female Anger in the Anti-Shaker Narratives of Eunice Chapman and Mary Marshall Dyer," *Journal of Women's History* 6 (1994): 92; Other scholars have analyzed this capability: Daisy Sophia Miller, "Serpentine Advances in Sacred Places: Representation of the Shakers in American Literature," Diss., State University of New York at Stony Brook, 2000, 70; Elizabeth De Wolfe, *Shaking the Faith: Women, Family, and Mary Marshall Dyer's Anti-Shaker Campaign, 1815–1867* (New York: Palgrave, 2002), 87–88.

"modern enchantress" Quoted in Richard McNemar, *The Other Side of the Question. In three parts. I. An explanation of the proceedings of Eunice Chapman and the Legislature, against the United Society, called the Shakers, in the state of New-York. II. A refutation of the false statements of Mary Dyer against the said society, in the state of New Hampshire. III. An account of the*

proceedings of Abram Van Vleet, Esq. and his associates, against the said United Society at Union Village, Ohio. Comprising a general vindication of the character of Mother and the Elders against the attacks of public slander, the edicts of a prejudiced party, and the misguided zeal of lawless mobs (Cincinnati, OH: Looker, Reynolds and Company Printers, 1819), 18.

"ornament to her sex" AGDA, March 13, 1818.

Eunice Chapman was far more savvy Humez, "A Woman Mighty," 92.

"Think not that the battle" Quoted in McNemar, *Other Side*, 19.

"Well-behaved women seldom make history" Laurel Thatcher Ulrich has written a book by this name.

PART I: FAITH

"I know how to pray" Quoted in Campion, *Ann the Word: The Life of Mother Ann Lee, Founder of the Shakers* (Boston: Little, Brown and Company, 1976), 171.

CHAPTER 1: A CIVIL DEATH

eyewitnesses recount These include William Leete Stone, editor of the *Albany Gazette and Daily Advertiser*, and the Shakers, who comment repeatedly on her small frame. *AGDA*, January 29, 1818. Eunice's sex appeal is satirized in Anonymous, *Indoctum Parliamentum: A Farce in One Act and a Beautiful Variety of Scenes* (1818).

powerful temper Her husband remarked upon her temper most explicitly, but it is also evident in other sources, including her own writings. James Chapman, "The Memorial of James Chapman, to the respectable Legislature of the state of New-York, now in session" (Albany, NY: 1817), 1–3.

a well-settled world For the Hawley family's early history, I have consulted Elias S. Hawley, *The Hawley Record* (Rutland, VT: Tuttle Antiquarian Books, 1890), esp. 527–535; Samuel Orcutt, *A History of the Old Town of Stratford and the City of Bridgeport, Connecticut* (New Haven:

Tuttle, Morehouse and Taylor, 1886), esp. 490–493, 552; and William Howard Wilcoxson, *History of Stratford, Connecticut 1639–1969* (Stratford, CT: Stratford Tercentenary Commission, 1939).

"rude" "clownish" Timothy Dwight, *Travels in New-England and New-York*, vol. 3 (London: Charles Wood, 1823), 3.

settled by Connecticut natives . . . one eyewitness observed Ibid., 8.

chocolate and indigo Oriana Atkinson, *Not Only Ours: A Story of Greene County* (Cornwallville, NY: Hope Farm Press, 1974), 25.

Susquehanna Turnpike . . . stopping to rest These details appear in Atkinson, *Not Only Ours*, 51, 56; and Dorothy Kubik, *West Through the Catskills: The Story of the Susquehanna Turnpike* (Fleischmanns, NY: Purple Mountain Press, 2001), 29, 65, 70, 72.

"Aunt Sally has been here three months" William Hoyt to Elijah Hawley, January 25, 1817, box 1, folder 1A, #11, Hawley Family Papers, BECHS.

bridal pregnancy rate Ellen K. Rothman, "Sex and Self-Control: Middle-Class Courtship in America, 1770–1870," *Journal of Social History*, 15:3 (1982, Spring), 414.

"bundled" . . . "Bundling Song" Henry Reed Stiles, *Bundling: Its Origins, Progress and Decline in America* (Sandwich, MA: Chapman Billes Reprint, 1999), 13, 14, 86, 88.

leading members See *Commemorative Biographical Record of Hartford County, Connecticut* (J. H. Beers and Co., 1901), 12–13. Also see Frederick William Chapman, *The Chapman Family, or The Descendents of Robert Chapman* (Hartford: Case, Tiffany and Co., 1854), 196.

younger brother Asa Franklin Bowditch Dexter, *Biographical Sketches of the Graduates of Yale College with Annals of the College History*, vol. 6 (New Haven: Yale University Press, 1912), 6–7; *Commemorative Biographical Record*, 12–13.

admitted with full communion . . . laid to rest beside her "Index to Records from the Old Saybrook Congregational Church, 1736–1935," typescript from the Connecticut State Library, 1961, 54–55. On communion, see Applegate, *Most Famous Man*, 70–71.

troubled young ex-Shaker Eunice Chapman, *No. 2, Being an Additional Account of the Conduct of the Shakers, in the Case of Eunice Chapman and Her Children with Their Religious Creed* (Albany: I. W. Clark, 1818), 47.

feeling of intense sexual excitement James. He describes his attraction to Eunice in a letter reprinted in *AGDA*, April 25, 1817.

"The great art of pleasing" John Gregory, *A Father's Legacy to His Daughters* (Boston: James B. Dow Reprint, 1834), 26, 34.

According to the later testimony McNemar, *Other Side*, 116.

The decision to accept James Chapman. See Eunice Chapman, *Account of the Conduct of the People Called Shakers* (Albany: self-published), 46.

Marriage, moreover, was not a commitment to be considered lightly . . . one-third of the land he owned. The following discussion of marriage and marital expectations draws from the definitive source on the subject, Henrik Hartog's *Man and Wife in America.* Detailed citations follow. *marriage was both a public compact . . . could not be revoked* 29, 53, 54. *"By marriage, the husband and wife"* 106. *coverture* 115–122. *So wholly did the law . . . incest* 105–106. *Even in spiritual matters* 153. *In return for her submission a woman received* 156–157. *ground rules* 53. *"rule of thumb"* 105. *dower rights* 144–146.

"civilly dead" Elizabeth Cady Stanton made this expression famous in the women's "Declaration of Sentiments," delivered at the Seneca Falls Convention in 1848.

"By marriage, the husband and wife are one person in law" William Blackstone, *Commentaries on the Laws of England,* ed. William Carey Jones, vol. 1 (San Francisco: Bankcroft-Whitney Company, 1915), 625.

CHAPTER 2: ARDENT SPIRITS

never even fed his own pigs Chapman, *Account,* 24.

differences were generational . . . basis for a marital relationship See De Wolfe's analysis of a similar generational conflict within the marriage of Mary and Joseph Dyer in *Shaking the Faith,* 11. Also see Glenda Riley, *Divorce: An American Tradition* (New York: Oxford University Press, 1991), 55; and Michael Grossberg, *Governing the Hearth: Law and the*

Family in Nineteenth-Century America (Chapel Hill: University of North Carolina Press, 1985), 6–9. On women's changing roles in the period, see Nancy Cott, *Bonds of Womanhood, "Women's Sphere" in New England, 1780–1835* (New Haven: Yale University Press, 1997).

He expected total acquiescence James states his complaints in a letter to Eunice, printed in *AGDA*, April 27, 1817.

"Republican Mothers" The original source on republican motherhood is Linda Kerber's *Women of the Republic: Intellect and Ideology in Revolutionary America* (Chapel Hill: University of North Carolina Press, 1980).

guzzled hard cider . . . average American imbibed . . . more taverns than churches Jack Larkin, *The Reshaping of Everyday Life, 1790–1840* (New York: Harper and Row, 1988), 285, 286, 281.

Country bars . . . reeked of spilled spirits . . . buffalo hides This description paraphrases an eyewitness account quoted ibid., 157.

so much seemed uncertain Ibid., 286.

reflected badly on her, too See Hartog, *Man and Wife*, 53–54.

"respectable" Chapman, *Account*, 11.

"on the limits" Hawley, *The Hawley Record*, 533.

$6,000 Eunice gives the original figures in her *Account*, 11. For conversions I have used a calculator on the Economic History Services Web site: www.measuringworth.com/ppowerus.

They followed a common pattern . . . This was the precarious situation For this discussion of separation and divorce, I have relied on Hartog, *Man and Wife*, especially 6–39, 76–82; Riley, *Divorce* 24–25, 50–51; Nelson Blake, *Road to Reno: A History of Divorce in the United States* (New York: Macmillan Company, 1962), especially 48–79; Norma Basch, *Framing American Divorce* (Berkeley: University of California Press, 1999), 19–42.

"in bed with the said" Cock v. Cock, New York State Court of Chancery, J0064-82, New York State Archives (1818).

"Jane McManus with her clothes all up" Quoted in Hartog, *Man and Wife*, 66.

But such informal arrangements Norma Basch, *Framing*, 19–20; Riley, 50–51. Hartog discusses the dangers through the case of Abigail Bailey in *Man and Wife*, 39, 40–62.

CHAPTER 3: A BETTER MAN

failure in the eyes of the world . . . claim to manhood Hartog, *Man and Wife,* 101, 93, 193.

"I felt myself unfit" James Chapman, "Memorial," 3.

In the predominant Calvinist way of thinking . . . salvation was available to all This discussion benefits greatly from Applegate's lively treatment of these theological issues in *The Most Famous Man,* 36–38. Thanks, too, to Carol Ganz, at the Connecticut State Library, for her insights on conversion.

"The bow of God's wrath is bent" Jonathan Edwards, "Sinners in the Hands of an Angry God," *The Works of President Edwards in Four Volumes: A Reprint of the Worcester Edition,* vol. 4 (New York: Leavitt, Trow and Co., 1844), 318.

horrific example Harvey Chalmers II, *Tales from the Mohawk, Second Series* (Port Washington, NY: Ira J. Friedman Inc., 1968), 30–32.

Others, however, were starting to reject such hopelessness . . . Daniel W. Patterson, *The Shaker Spiritual* (Princeton: Princeton University Press, 1979), 84; Applegate, *Most Famous Man,* 38, 159.

"founded on fanaticism" . . . "never seen, in any country" Flo Morse, *The Shakers and the World's People* (New York: Dodd, Mead and Co., 1980), 77, 85–86.

"Here are no pampered and purse proud nobles" Quoted in Glendyne Wergland, *Visiting the Shakers* (Clinton, NY: Richard W. Couper Press, 2007), 64.

It was later . . . that Shakers preferred to introduce their more contentious views Those who left the Shakers commonly made this point. See, for example, Stephen Stein's discussion of the apostate Valentine Rathbun's experiences in *Shaker Experience,* 16.

he became overwhelmed James Chapman, "Memorial," 3.

He had experienced a powerful conversion James's acceptance into the covenant is documented in "Index to Records from the Old Saybrook Congregational Church, 1736–1935," typescript from the Connecticut State Library, 1961, 54.

a unique provision that some considered unfair See arguments in *Kingsbury v. Wells*, New York State Court of Judicature, J0147 Writs of Certiorari, box 31, New York State Archives (1815).

"Spiritual Wine" Patterson, *Shaker Spiritual,* 170.

recounted every sinful act There is no explicit account of James's confession, but other accounts describe the ritual. See, for example, Thomas Brown, *An Account of the People Called Shakers* (Troy, NY: Parker and Bliss, 1812), 31.

"by the laws of God and man" James Chapman, "Memorial," 3.

CHAPTER 4: A WOMAN ALONE

Men heading out . . . fend off the chill. Atkinson, *Not Only Ours,* 24.

Many nights, past midnight Chapman, *No. 2,* 10–11.

"skeleton" Ibid., 10.

needy as an infant Chapman, *Account,* 12.

delighted in caring for them and teaching them Eunice describes her feelings, but the examples are mine. Ibid., 12.

excommunicated for dancing Letter to me from Judith Rundell of the Greene County Historical Society, August 23, 2005.

"Damn you" Atkinson, *Not Only Ours,* 77.

Eunice lashed out . . . "unchristian" Eunice's conflicts with her church are documented in "The Record Book of the Durham Presbyterian Church," Vedder Collection, Greene County Historical Society, Coxsackie, New York, 77.

no longer had patience for social decorum Thanks to Robert Ferguson for sharing this observation.

"evil" . . . "unbridled tongue" "Record Book of the Durham Presbyterian Church," 71, 77.

"fingers" Edward Deming and Faith Andrews, *Work and Worship Among the Shakers: Their Craftsmanship and Economic Order* (New York: Dover Publications, 1982), 92.

pressed into little cakes Wergland, *Visiting,* 186.

refusing even to take change . . . walking away See Henriette Lucy Dillon's remembrance, printed in Ibid.

"go on like madmen" . . . *There was grace that day* Minton Thrift, ed., *Memoir of the Reverend Jesse Lee, with Extracts from His Journals* (New York: N. Bangs and T. Mason, 1823), 112–114.

The Chapmans traveled to Watervliet Eunice does not specifically recount her journey. What follows is my speculation.

CHAPTER 5: WATERVLIET

the first Shaker community, called Watervliet Eunice only briefly recalls her initial trip to the Shakers in her books, as does James Chapman in his "Memorial." To re-create her visit, I have consulted Shaker diaries (especially Freegift Wells, Series of Daily Journals, WRHS 45, IV:B-285–286) and used other documentation from the period to fill in the gaps—largely visitors' accounts as they appear in Wergland's *Visiting the Shakers*, especially those by the Marquise de la Tour de Pin (18–20), Jacques Milbert (28–30), Donald MacDonald (34–37), William Owen (36–43), and Anonymous (46–49).

roughly 150 Shaker souls Brewer, *Shaker Communities*, appendix B, 215.

The road grew smooth . . . calmly grazed Wergland, *Visiting*, 18.

The buildings were color-coded . . . everything was shared Robert P. Emlen, *Shaker Village Views: Illustrated Maps and Landscape Drawings by Shaker Artists of the Nineteenth Century* (Hanover, NH: University Press of New England, 1987), 6–8, 110–111.

waste management Larkin, *Reshaping*, 158,161.

Observing that firewood Wergland, *Visiting*, 119.

cherished orderliness as proof Emlen, *Shaker Village Views*, 9.

called a mounting block Thanks to Glendyne Wergland for providing the name.

the Shakers' homes featured many technological advances . . . the more time one had for God White and Taylor, *Shakerism: Its Meaning and Message*, 310–315. These anecdotes are popularly told on tours at Shaker villages.

They had washing machines The Shakers did not have a patented device until decades later, but they had washing machines in some communities by the time of Eunice's visit. See Edward Deming Andrews,

The Community Industries of the Shakers (Charlestown, MA: Emporium Publications, 1971), 14.

"milk-warm water" ... *abundance was overwhelming* Wergland, *Visiting*, 40.

Legend had it Nancy Blanchard Sanborn, ed., *Enfield, New Hampshire, 1761–2000: The History of a Town Influenced by the Shakers* (Portsmouth, NH: Peter E. Randall Publisher LLC, 2006), 85.

When Eunice finally stepped across the threshold My description of the meetinghouse interior is based on Marius B. Péladeau, "The Shaker Meetinghouses of Moses Johnson," *The Magazine of Antiques*, October 1970, 48.

The secret to this architectural marvel Emlen, *Shaker Village Views*, 8.

dining table Benson John Lossing, *An Early View of the Shakers: Benson John Lossing and the Harper's Article of July 1857*, ed. Don Gifford (Hanover, NH: University Press of New England, 1989), 5.

Pine spittoons Wergland, *Visiting*, 304.

faint copper glint Ibid., 19.

churches such as the one Eunice attended in Bridgeport ... *"tithing men"* Lucy S. Curtiss, *Two Hundred Fifty Years: The Story of the United Congregational Church of Bridgeport, 1695–1945* (Bridgeport, CT: Privately printed under the direction of Yale University Press, 1945), 27.

White muslin dresses ... *under their cloaks* I am grateful to Lynne Bassett for her description and analysis of early nineteenth-century fashion and color preferences, in an e-mail correspondence from March 2, 2008. This description relies on her comments.

"bean pole stuck" Quoted in Morse, *Shakers and the World's People*, 202.

"might as well be Shaker" Quoted in Wergland, *Visiting*, 23.

Elder Seth Wells, came forth Neither Eunice nor the Shakers document Elder Seth's presentation on this day, but it was his role to speak at public meetings. See Stephen Paterwic, *Historical Dictionary of the Shakers* (Lanham, MD: The Scarecrow Press, 2008), 234.

But the Shakers' central reason ... *only for God* Seth Youngs Wells, "Account of the Shakers" (1823), WRHS 56, VII:B-65, 13–15.

Shakers' rules of etiquette See Wergland, *Visiting,* 135.

"the whole assembly rose as one person" Ibid., 312.

lined up in ranks For the basic procedure I have consulted Patterson, *Shaker Spiritual,* 74–75.

"saved from the temptation" Wergland, *Visiting,* 110.

kind of jig Wergland, *Visiting,* 213.

never even close to touching Campion, *Ann the Word,* 97.

like clouds in a storm Testimony of Christ's Second Appearing Benjamin Seth Youngs, *Testimony of Christ's Second Appearing; Containing a General Statement of All Things Pertaining to the Faith and Practice of the Church of God in This Latter Day,* 2nd ed. (Albany, NY: E. Hosford, 1810), xxv.

"shaking off" Wergland, *Visiting,* 209.

with their hands flapping Ibid., 50.

"trained dogs" Quoted in Alice Felt Tyler, *Freedom's Ferment: Phases of American Social History to 1860* (Freeport, NY: Books for Libraries Press, 1970),157.

Eunice seems not to have been turned off James recounts that Eunice seemed pleased by her visit, while Eunice makes no negative judgments when she recounts her initial visit to the Shakers in her first book. (Notably, she omits her initially upbeat portrayal in her second book. To me, this suggests that she was not yet as critical of the Shakers as she later became.)

With substantial property holdings . . . unimaginable to most Wergland, *Visiting,* 186; Emlen, *Shaker Village Views,* 7; Tyles, *Freedom's Ferment* 163.

Believers faced the same difficulties as everyone else Glendyne Wergland, *One Shaker Life: Isaac Newton Youngs, 1793–1865* (Boston: University of Massachusetts Press, 2006), 28.

From 1810 to 1820 . . . grew even more Brewer, *Shaker Communities,* 215; Wergland, *One Shaker Life,* 28.

women's chores Brewer, *Shaker Communities,* 80–81.

Visitors often noted that the Sisters looked pale and tired See, for instance, Wergland, *Visiting,* 146.

Shaker women were accorded equal footing Scholars have discussed how gender norms nevertheless continued to prevail among the Shakers, as Humez observes in "Woman Mighty," 90. Another excellent source on Shaker women's lives is Susan Ruth Thurman, *O Sisters Ain't You Happy?: Gender, Family, and Community Among the Harvard and Shirley Shakers, 1781–1918* (Syracuse, NY: Syracuse University Press, 2001).

CHAPTER 6: ANOTHER MOTHER

Ann Lee entered the world For the following sketch of Ann Lee's life, I have relied on Shaker accounts, including Bishop, Wells, and Avery, *Testimonies*; Jean M. Humez, *Mother's First-Born Daughters: Early Shaker Writings on Women and Religion* (Bloomington: Indiana University Press, 1993); Richard Francis, *Ann the Word: The Story of Ann Lee, Female Messiah, Mother of the Shakers, the Women Clothed with the Sun* (New York: Arcade Publishing, 2000); Stephen A. Marini, *Radical Sects of Revolutionary New England* (Cambridge: Harvard University Press, 1999); and Campion, *Ann the Word*. As Stephen Stein has cautioned, documentation for this first phase of Shaker history is thin, and much of the available biographical material relies on the recollections of early Shakers (Stein, *Shaker Experience*, 8–9). There are also multiple, conflicting versions of some events, for example, Ann Lee's visionary conversion, which may have occurred in a prison or in an insane asylum (Francis, *Ann the Word*, 42). I have included a full description of Ann Lee's life, based upon the available sources, believing that her history as a Mother—and mother—inform Eunice's experiences with the society. Detailed citations follow.

most intimate business Francis, *Ann the Word*, 7.

arranged marriage Marini, *Radical Sects*, 76.

"loved his beef and his beer" Quoted in Francis, *Ann the Word*, 92.

extracted from her mother's body Brown, *Account*, 13.

"stir up his affections" Quoted in Humez, *Mother's First-Born Daughters*, 30.

"Shaking Quakers" The Shakers had no standing relationship with

the Quakers, although the group's founders may have originally been Quakers, and the Shakers shared some features in common with the Friends, such as their pacifism and spontaneous worship. See Stein, *Shaker Experience*, 5.

The Shakers were one of a number of radical sects . . . move or speak Stein, *Shaker Experience*, 3–5.

Church of England seemed woefully distant Campion, *Ann the Word*, 9.

"James and I lodge together" . . . "While I was in this labor" Quoted in Humez, *Mother's First-Born Daughters*, 31.

the Shakers became deliberately disruptive . . . only true path Stein, *Shaker Experience*, 5.

"out of breath" Bishop, Wells, and Avery, *Testimonies*, 42.

"by marriage, the husband and wife" Blackstone, *Commentaries on the Laws of England*, 625.

"I have been in fine valleys" Quoted in Campion, *Ann the Word*, 44.

"like men wounded in battle" Quoted in Francis, *Ann the Word,* 110.

"man is the first" . . . "absent husband" Both quoted in Jean M. Humez, "'Weary of Petticoat Government': The Specter of Female Rule in Early Nineteenth-Century Shaker Politics," *Communal Societies,* 11 (1991): 2–3.

At times she could be fearsome . . . no better Mother Stein, *Shaker Experience*, 22.

"God hates liars" Quoted in Brewer, *Shaker Communities,* 12.

"Midnight orgies" . . . "love children" Quoted in Wergland, *Visiting,* 14.

"Your Mother" Quoted in Mary Dyer, *A Portraiture of Shakerism* (New York: AMS Press, 1972), 55.

"I have seen her slap the men" Ibid., 91.

Many Americans . . . were deeply offended Campion, *Ann the Word,* 92, 104–105, 142–143.

"I see a vision" Quoted Ibid., 93.

"like melted lead" Quoted in Francis, *Ann the Word,* 90.

"some by their collars" . . . "little diversion" Youngs, *Testimony,* 91, 93.

"his back was a gore" Quoted in Campion, *Ann the Word,* 151.

"as they would the dead carcass" . . . *"a woman or not"* Bishop, Wells, and
Avery, *Testimonies,* 75.

animosity clouded her readings Eunice's reactions to this text appear
in Chapman, *Account,* 58–59.

"Youth and children, being under age . . ." Youngs, *Testimony,* 506.

"not eat with such a sinner" Chapman, *No. 2,* 11. In Eunice's account,
this routine behavior commenced before her trip to Watervliet.

the children would do their part . . . count on her son in her old age See
Chapman, *Account,* 18–20. Unfortunately, Eunice provides few details
about her children overall; what little she shares is mostly in these pages.

mother's admitted favorite Eunice remarks in several places of her special attachment to her youngest child; for example, ibid., 35.

A man was obliged . . . not her place to pick and choose Hartog, *Man and
Wife,* 100, 150.

"If a Woman be of so haughty" Quoted ibid., 159.

prospect of being publicly auctioned Glendyne Wergland discussed this
general possibility during her presentation, "Visitors' Changing View
of the Shakers, 1780–1897," at the Shaker Seminar in Enfield, NH,
July 23, 2009.

CHAPTER 7: GOD'S CHOSEN

witnessed a scene Chapman, *Account,* 46. I have inferred the Shakers'
reaction and the woman's calling.

"You have come, with your old carnal affections" Ibid., 48. There may
have been more to Catherine Bonnel's story than she let on. Shaker
diaries reveal that Elias Bonnel was a troubled soul and that Catherine
herself was a forceful personality. However, her despair over her family's
divided state is incontrovertible.

He hated the tight, mean look James Chapman "Memorial," 4–5.

"that there was no prospect" Chapman, *Account,* 15.

CHAPTER 8: HOMECOMING

glum, mean spirit These remembrances and the scenes to follow are
based on Sarah Hawley's deposition, printed in Chapman, *Account,* 44–

45, as well as on Eunice's descriptions, ibid., 16–17. All quotations, unless noted, are from these pages. The dialogue between Sally and James, while my interpretation, follows Sally's recollections.

unidentified local man Ibid., 17.

"I hereby forbid" Catskill Recorder, November 16, 1814.

A woman who left her husband . . . other such privileges Hartog, *Man and Wife*, 156–158.

CHAPTER 9: ELDER SETH

"Natural and Spiritual Relation" Christian Goodwillie and Jane F. Croswaithe, eds., *Millennial Praises: A Shaker Hymnal* (Amherst: University of Massachusetts Press, 2009), 210.

radically defined what it means to be family See De Wolfe's discussion of the tension between "conservatism and progress" in *Shaking the Faith*, 15, and Humez, "Woman Mighty," 92.

twenty-four out of the twenty-six members Wergland, *One Shaker Life*, 18.

the opposite was true . . . invested in their care Priscilla Brewer discusses these problems in *Shaker Communities*, 87–114, and "'Numbers Are Not the Thing for Us to Glory In': Demographic Perspectives on the Decline of the Shakers," *Communal Societies*, 7 (1987): 25–35.

"We could have a great many" Quoted in Brewer, "Demographic Perspectives," 31.

But the Shakers themselves recognized the trend Freegift Wells, Records of the Church at Watervliet, New York, February 20, 1817, WRHS 44, IV:B-279.

"restraining" Hartog, *Man and Wife*, 137.

"alienat[ing] his wife's affections" Ibid., 123.

"mother's feelings" Isaac Newton Youngs, "Narrative of various events . . ." (1814–1823), May 28, 1819, LC 3:42.

engaged to be married Details of Elder Seth's life are documented in Calvin Green, "Biographic Memoir of the Life, Character & Important Events in the Ministration of Mother Lucy Wright" (1861), WRHS 51, VI:B-27, 32.

"She is talking" Anna White and Leila S. Taylor, *Shakerism, Its Meaning and Message, Embracing an Historical Account, Statement of Belief and Spiritual Experience of the Church from Its Rise to the Present Day* (Columbus, OH: Fred J. Heer, 1905), 351.

"places of refuge" Quoted in Wergland, *Visiting*, 198.

Elder Seth's aunt Martha Wergland, *One Shaker Life*, 18.

visit her in her shabby quarters Isaac Newton Youngs, "Narrative of various events . . ." (1814–1823), May 28, 1819, LC 3:42.

abandoned Wergland, *One Shaker Life*, 20.

not blindly obsequious Brown writes of Elder Seth in his *Account*, 55. The Elder presents his own life history in Seth Youngs Wells, "Account of himself in July 1846," Unpublisht Testimonies Continued, WRHS 52, VI:B-43, 192–206.

suicidal The Shakers do not recall James's first appearance among them, but James's own recollections indicate profound despair, and as Peter Penfield (as well as Eunice) deposed, James later made suicidal threats. See James Chapman, "Memorial," 3; Chapman, *Account*, 46.

the states had learned Jabez Hammond, *The History of Political Parties in the State of New-York, from the Ratification of the Federal Constitution to December, 1840*, vol. 1 (Albany, NY: C. Van Benthuysen, 1842), 381–382.

he had been deeply moved Seth Youngs Wells, "Account of himself in July 1846."

CHAPTER 10: BOUND

"Cryed [sic] *and took on"* Chapman, *Account*, 45.

Christmas was not what it is today . . . with relish For a dramatic description of the contrast, see Applegate, *Most Famous Man*, 20.

Their observances of the day began This anecdote is excerpted in Campion, *Ann the Word*, 76–78. Shaker Christmas observances are also discussed in Patterson, *Shaker Spiritual*, 231, and Chapman, *No. 2*, 65.

In Shaker parlance Note that there is an inherent tension in the idea of the Shaker gift, as it signifies both a spontaneous revelation and a command. See Stephen Stein, "Shaker Gift and Shaker Order: A

Study of Religious Tension in Nineteenth-Century America," *Communal Societies*, 10 (1990).

"hoping to excite" Chapman, *Account*, 21.

As James himself was to attest James Chapman, "Memorial," 2.

Prime Lane Information about the case of *Wells v. Lane*, which appeared before the New York Supreme Court in 1811, is available in the "Legal Cases" binder at the Shaker Heritage Society in Watervliet, New York. Also see William Johnson, *Reports of Cases Argued and Determined in the Supreme Court of Judicature and in the Court of the Trial of Impeachments in the State of New-York*, vol. 8 (Albany: Banks & Brothers, Law Publishers, 1863), 462–463.

Officially, the Shakers did not yet require Julia Neal, *By Their Fruits: The Story of Shakerism in South Union, Kentucky* (Philadelphia: Porcupine Press, 1975), 59–60.

"the Irish . . . rose in a riotous manner" Freegift Wells, Records of the Church at Watervliet, New York, August 12, 1811, WRHS 44, IV:B-279. On the M'Dowle case also see Johnson, *Reports of Cases Argued*, 328–332.

nearly $350 Records of the Shakers' expenses are available in "Enfield, N.H., Records," MS 242, box 22, folder 11.

vulnerability threatened to become her source of strength See De Wolfe, *Shaking*, 88.

a mob had converged . . . "scene of horror" See Benjamin Seth Youngs, "Transactions of the Ohio mob," WM 466.

"with intent" Carol Weisbrod, *The Boundaries of Utopia* (New York: Pantheon, 1980), 46; Edward Deming Andrews, *The People Called Shakers* (New York: Dover Books, 1963), 207–208. While the act did not mention the Shakers by name, the law, Andrews says, "aimed directly at the sect."

Its law allowed . . . suspected of being hidden Charles Slaughter Morehead and Mason Brown, *A Digest of the Statute Laws of Kentucky, of a Public and Permanent Nature*, vol. 1 (Frankfort, KY: Albert H. Hodges, 1834), 124–126. Weisbrod, *Boundaries*, 46; Julia Neal, *The Kentucky Shakers* (Lexington, KY: University Press of Kentucky, 1977), 58–59.

CHAPTER 11: MOTHER LUCY

"single females without friends" Wergland, *Visiting,* 193.

"naturally handsome" . . . *"mild and placid"* Green, "Biographic Memoir of Mother Lucy," 73–74.

born with every advantage Frances A. Carr, "Mother Lucy's Sayings Spoken at Different Times and under Various Circumstances," *Shaker Quarterly,* 8, no. 4 (1968): 100–101. For the following account of Mother Lucy's life and leadership I have also relied on Green, "Biographic Memoir of Mother Lucy"; Humez, *Mother's First-Born Daughters,* 64–132; Humez, "Weary of Petticoat Government"; and Stein, *Shaker Experience,* 49–118.

could not have been more different from that of the Shakers' first Mother See Humez's contrasts between Ann Lee and Lucy Wright in *Mother's First-Born Daughters,* 65–66.

sky blue dress Isaac Newton Youngs, "Narrative of various events . . ." (1814–1823), May 28, 1819, LC 3:42, March 23, 1818.

"could not bear to spoil her" Green, *Biographic Memoir of Mother Lucy,* 7. Other sources report that Goodrich "told Mother Ann that it was out of the question for him to try to suppress his sexual desires." Campion, *Ann the Word,* 94.

The Shakers often swooped . . . eager to believe again Stein, *Shaker Experience,* 23–24; Francis, *Ann the Word,*168.

bright, pure man Humez, *Mother's First-Born Daughters,* 52.

never impetuous or emotional . . . "natural instincts" Carr, "Mother Lucy's Sayings," 101.

worrying that his wife . . . "We must save Lucy" Ibid., 102.

"visible operations" Mother Lucy recounts this moment in her testimony, quoted in Humez, *Mother's First-Born Daughters,* 52. All subsequent quotations, unless otherwise noted, come from here. Note that Lucy does not precisely describe the "operations": I offer examples based on common eyewitness accounts.

"wean" Chapman, *No. 2,* 58.

opposition to female leadership Stein, *Shaker Experience,* 92.

"Wimmin [sic] are fools" Quoted ibid., 53.

When Mother Lucy's rule began . . . "national communal society of Believers"
. . . envy of the world Stein, *Shaker Experience*, 113–118.

preferential feelings Wergland, *One Shaker Life*, 168.

"fountainhead of love" Humez, *Mother's First-Born Daughters*, 65.

Chapter 12: Believer

Eunice was coming unhinged This chapter is based on Eunice's recollections, as well as on Shaker diaries, including Jethro Turner, Daily Journal, WRHS 46, IV:B-297, and two by Freegift Wells, Records of the Church at Watervliet, February 20, 1817, WRHS 44, IV:B-279; Series of Daily Journals, WRHS 45, IV:B-285-286. All quotations, unless otherwise noted, are from Eunice's *Account*, 22–38.

"idle hatchers" Quoted in Stein, *Shaker Experience*, 33.

"I hate your fleshly lives" Ibid., 36.

"Carnal Professors" Goodwillie and Croswaithe, *Millennial Praises*, 248.

It was spare and neat Eunice does not offer a specific description of her room. This depiction is based on other eyewitness accounts.

At half past five the next morning Eunice does not describe the mundane aspects of her Shaker existence: I have filled in the details using Shaker manuscripts and secondary sources. For example, the sounding of a conch (or similar instrument) is noted in Paterwic, *Historical Dictionary*, xxxv.

hot mince pies This is an example cited by a later Shaker. Nicholas Briggs, "Forty Years a Shaker," *Granite Monthly*, 52–53 (1920–1921): 468.

All communication . . . against the rules Hervey Elkins, *Fifteen Years in the Senior Order of the Shakers: A Narration of Facts, Concerning That Singular People* (Hanover, NH: Dartmouth Press, 1853), 3.

seasonal work Stein, *Shaker Experience*, 153.

Mother Lucy feared Theodore E. Johnson, "The 'Millennial Laws' of 1821," *Shaker Quarterly*, 7, no. 2 (1967): 36. All subsequent references to the Shakers' laws are from this source unless otherwise noted.

Elder Seth managed to maintain a cache Stein, *Shaker Experience*, 188.

Spirit over the letter Isaac Newton Youngs, "Narrative of various events . . ." (1814–1823), May 28, 1819, LC 3:42.

"I may take up my cross" Isaac Newton Youngs, "Narrative of various events . . ." 1814–1823, May 1, 1818, LC 3:42. Youngs's life is richly depicted in Wergland, *One Shaker Life.*

"snare of Satan" Quoted in Wergland, *One Shaker Life*, 33.

singled out for humiliation Elkins, *Fifteen Years*, 22.

One later apostate Anonymous, "Fifteen Years a Shakeress," *Galaxy*, 8 (1872): 461.

alternating between the extremes of love and torture Chapman, *Account*, 27–28.

"a strong man could not hold him," Chapman, *Account*, 18.

"the most abusive and refractory" McNemar, *Other Side*, 34.

nothing if not resilient Nelson Blake remarks upon Eunice's "extraordinary ability to bounce back" in "Eunice Against the Shakers," 365.

CHAPTER 13: VENGENCE

asked to speak with Elder Seth Chapman, *Account*, 46. My account of this meeting is based on Penfield's testimony in Eunice's *Account*. I have separately recounted a meeting from February 5, based on Eunice's and James's writings.

"as soon commit suicide" Chapman, *Account*, 46.

"No coquetry or ostentation" This and other descriptions to follow, unless otherwise noted, are from Green, *"Biographic Memoir of Mother Lucy Wright,"* 73–74. I have relied on two slightly different versions of Mother Lucy's speech, recounted in Jethro Turner, Daily Journal, WRHS 46, IV:B-297; and Words of Mother Lucy, WRHS 56, XII:B-161.

"particular affections" Wergland, *One Shaker Life*, 168.

She once told the Shakers Humez, *Mother's First-Born Daughters*, 95.

"em" Brewer, *Shaker Communities*, 37.

Their pace had slowed Humez, *Mother's First-Born Daughters*, 69.

"solemn songs" Patterson, *Shaker Spiritual*, 73.

"extraordinary" Quoted in Humez, *Mother's First-Born Daughters*, 94.

Most of these Believers had never known . . . rather than spiritual ones Brewer, *Shaker Communities*, 85–88.

depended less on sudden revelation Humez, *Mother's First-Born Daughters*, 65.

Eunice was emboldened Accounts by James, Eunice, and Penfield differ. James's account suggests that Penfield and Paine were present when Eunice made her threats.

"able to command any assistance" James Chapman, "Memorial," 7.

"threw unwanted babies" Quoted in Neal, *Kentucky Shakers* 58–59.

"Barking up" Quoted in Neal, *By Their Fruits*, 50–51.

CHAPTER 14: A CONSECRATION UNTO GOD

chiseled the boy's name Manuscript of the Merwin S. Hawley Autobiography, box 1, series 1, folder 3, Merwin S. Hawley Papers, BECHS. For Elijah Hawley's biography see Merwin Hawley's "Memoirs of his father, Elijah Hawley, Dec. 1870," box 1, series 1, folder 4 of the same collection.

"consecrated [himself] unto God" The letter appears in *AGDA*, April 25, 1817.

By George Chapman's recollection George's version of these events appears in Dyer, *Portraiture*, 301.

"James Chapman, on account. . . ." Freegift Wells, Records of the Church at Watervliet, February 8, 1815, WRHS 44, V:B-279.

"James Chapman, with his three . . ." Jethro Turner, Daily Journal, February 8, 1815, WRHS 46, IV:B-297.

Shaker Museum . . . Elder Henry Blinn Henry Blinn, *Historical Notes Having Reference to the Believers in Enfield, NH*, vol. 1, 107, MS 761, CSV.

Although Mother Lucy was known to delegate many tasks Humez, *Mother's First-Born Daughters*, 75.

The Shaker Mother recognized that nothing good . . . "run down the society" See Paterwic, *Historical Dictionary of the Shakers*, 251; Calvin Green,

"Biographical Memoir of the Life and Experience of Calvin Green" (1861–1869), WRHS 55, VI:B-28, 266. My thanks to Stephen Paterwic for sharing his insights and pointing me to Green's memoirs.

Articles of Agreement. Book of Records, MS 13614, Emma B. King Library, Old Chatham, NY. Thanks to Mary Ann Haagen for sending me a copy of this covenant.

PART II: TRIAL

"Be what you seem to be" Bishop and Wells, *Testimonies,* 289.

CHAPTER 1: CAPITAL CITY

The highest point in Albany For the following descriptions of the capital, I have used David Zdunczyk, *200 Years of the New York State Legislature* (Albany, NY: Albany Institute of History and Art, 1978), 18; C. R. Roseberry, *Capitol Story* (Albany: New York State Office of General Services, 1982), 13–15; Douglas G. Bucher, W. Richard Wheeler, and Mary Raddant Tomlan, *A Neat Plain Modern Stile: Philip Hooker and His Contemporaries, 1796–1836* (Amherst: Distributed by University of Massachusetts Press, 1993), 97.

Yankee grocers Information about Albany's changing population appears in David G. Hackett, *The Rude Hand of Innovation: Religion and Social Order in Albany, New York, 1652–1836* (New York: Oxford University Press, 1991), 40.

"sharp cocked hats" Worth, *Random Recollections,* vol. 1, 25.

Previously, two large churches For street and city descriptions, I have consulted the New York State Museum's Colonial Albany Social History Project Web site: http://www.nysm.nysed.gov/albany/streets .html#court.

hundreds of wagons Hackett, *Rude Hand,* 57.

At the end of the recent war . . . "broken meats and vegetables" . . . imprisonment for debt John J. McEneny, *Albany: Capital City on the Hudson, an Illustrated History* (Sun Valley, CA: American Historical Press, 1998), 15.

among the most populous and prosperous cities Hackett, *Rude Hand*, 78.

commercial hub . . . "gateway to the West" Allison P. Bennett, *The People's Choice: A History of Albany County in Art and Architecture* (Fleishmanns, NY: Purple Mountain Press, 1995), 31.

Dutch province See Gorham A. Worth, *Random Recollections of Albany from 1800 to 1808* (Albany, NY: J. Munsell, 1866), 26. On Albany as a Yankee town, see Hackett, *Rude Hand*, 57–99; McEneny, 76–77.

Just about anything could be had The following descriptions appear in *AGDA*, March 18, 1816; October 7, 1816; May 10, 1817; April 1, 1817.

"new town" Dwight, *Travels in New-England and New-York*, 405.

Hogs McEneny, *Albany*, 119-120.

spirit of speculation Hackett, *Rude Hand*, 82.

For every grand mansion boasting . . . "good" streets McEneny, Albany, 77.

in growing numbers Hackett, *Rude Hand*, 82.

"gloomy pile of stones" AGDA, January 30, 1818.

"marble veneers" . . . "deception" These "deceptions" are described by nineteenth-century observers, quoted in Bucher et al., *Neat Plain Modern Stile*, 99–100.

"most judiciously stocked" AGDA, December 21, 1818.

"America's first superhighway" Christopher Maag, "Hints of Comeback for Nation's First Superhighway," *New York Times*, November 2, 2008.

"I wish the devil" Dorothy Kubik, *West Through the Catskills*, 26. Note that the original says "d—l."

The fact that Eunice even turned to the law . . . only recourse Eunice had This discussion of Eunice's options is based on Hartog's *Man and Wife*, especially 24–25, 108–110.

Fathers' rights were so much assumed Ibid., 194–195, 214–215.

a man could appoint Grossberg, *Governing*, 242.

Technically, it was possible Hartog, *Man and Wife*, 72.

James had committed adultery Chapman, *Account*, 14.

marriage was not simply an agreement . . . deserved each other Hartog, *Man and Wife*, 24–25, 54, 70–73, 84 *("a right")*, 108–110.

"formative period in the history of American divorce" Riley, *Divorce*, 34.

The Revolution had been popularly imagined . . . bigamy Basch, *Framing*, 24–30; Riley, *Divorce*, 31–33; Grossberg, *Governing,*19–21.

national divorce rate Grossberg, *Governing*, 238. As Grossberg states, "The exact incidence of marital dissolution in early nineteenth-century America is difficult to determine."

"pure" Hartog, *Man and Wife*, 72.

"partial divorces" See Hartog, *Man and Wife*, 34–39; and Riley, *Divorce*, 50–51.

"doubtful sex" This example from Pennsylvania appears in Hartog, *Man and Wife*, 99.

Evidence of wrongdoing was insufficient Ibid., 66.

"guilty mind" Ibid., 72–73.

western territories See Basch, *Framing*, 23.

transform the model of the republican family . . . instillers of virtue See the introduction in Grossberg, *Governing*, especially 6–9; De Wolfe, *Shaking*, 11; Larkin, *Reshaping*, 52–53.

transformation in custody law . . . carry weight in custody disputes Grossberg, *Governing*, 235–285.

"tender years" Ibid., 239.

"best interest of the child" Ibid., 237–254.

"money and lawyers" Quoted in McNemar, *Other Side*, 19.

and keep it going indefinitely Thanks to Michael Grossberg for this observation.

Such a bill had passed before Ross's case is discussed in Blake, *Reno*, 67–68.

Yet a fundamental problem remained Nelson M. Blake, "Eunice against the Shakers," *New York Historical Society* 58, no. 41 (1960): 367.

"privilege" This entire episode appears in Chapman, *Account*, 40–41.

CHAPTER 2: EVIL REPORTS

rumors that James was dead Chapman, *Account*, 53.

veritable network Elizabeth De Wolfe describes apostate "networks" or communities and offers a detailed analysis of "anti-Shaker activism" in *Shaking the Faith*, especially 7, 114, 185. Eunice's activities are described in Elder Seth to Elder Benjamin, July 19, 1817, WRHS 25, IV:A-77.

another kind of home See De Wolfe's discussion of "the apostate family" in *Shaking the Faith*, 7.

"The leaders of this dreadful catastrophe" Valentine Rathbun, *Some Brief Hints of a Religious Scheme, Taught and Propagated by a Number of Europeans, Living in a Place Called Nisqueunia, in the State of New-York* (New York: s.n., 1783), 35.

The more she heard and read of broken Shaker families I offer one interpretation of how Eunice's views on her mission changed between the 1815 and 1816 legislative sessions. My analysis is based on her published writings and letters, in which she refers repeatedly to the plight of other women and to her divine, heroic role. See, for instance, her comparison between herself and Abraham in *Account*, 37.

"wandering idiots" Chapman, *No. 2*, 24.

"instrument" Chapman, *Account*, viii.

sloop full of wheat Cuyler Reynolds, *Albany Chronicles: A History of the City Arranged Chronologically, from the Earliest Settlement to the Present Time* (Albany: J. B. Lyon Co, 1906), 417.

"purity" Andrew E. Norman, ed., *The Autobiography of Martin Van Buren* (New York: Chelsea House, 1983), 85.

impossible to dislike him Hammond, *History of Political Parties*, 455.

Much of this turnover was inevitable My thanks to Philip Lampi for the information on elections, as well as for the member tallies below. E-mail communications with the author, May 13 and 14, 2009.

nerve-racking for Eunice See Chapman, *Account*, 41. Eunice's enemies publicly upbraided her for bothering lawmakers at their residences (see, for instance, McNemar, *Other Side*, 19), and other records provide evidence of her leaving materials at boardinghouses.

"other poor distressed women" See Elder Seth to Elder Benjamin, July 19, 1817, WRHS 25, IV:A-77.

"evil reports" Jethro Turner, Daily Journal, March 9, 1817, WRHS 46, IV.B-297.

left arm so lame Ministry letter from New Lebanon, May 16, 1816, WRHS 20, IV: A-33.

bloodbath had taken place Kenneth Salzmann, "Voting Trends: Political Dirty Tricks in the Nineteenth Century," http://ezinearticles.com/?Voting-Trends—Political-Dirty-Tricks-In-The-19th-Century&id=857085.

"like so many hounds" Chapman, *No. 2,* 52.

CHAPTER 3: CIVILLY DEAD

"overcome the flesh" . . . "maintain his faith and station" These quotations appear in Seth Youngs Wells, "Account of Himself in 1846," Unpublisht Testimonies Continued, WRHS 52:VI:B-43, 192–204.

Joseph Hodgson, who was well equipped Green, "Biographic Memoir of Mother Lucy," 67.

The room was stuffy Roseberry, *Capitol Story,* 15; Bucher et al., *Neat Plain Modern,* 96–100.

"backsliders" Elizabeth A. De Wolfe, "Erroneous Principles, Base Deceptions, and Pious Frauds: Anti-Shaker Writing, Mary Marshall Dyer, and the Public Theater of Apostasy," (Diss., Boston University, 1996), 7.

"extraordinary" . . . celibate despite himself Bishop and Wells, *Testimonies,* 298–299.

"Nay" All quotations from this meeting, unless noted, are from a transcription that is reprinted in Chapman, *Account,* 49–52.

"whether it be right or not" Brown, *Account,* 55.

the Shakers took issue with this presentation . . . See Seth Youngs Wells, *Thomas Brown, and His Pretended History of Shakers. Correspondence between Seth Youngs Wells of Shakers, New York, and Professor Benjamin Silliman of Yale College* (New Haven: 1911), 4.

favored a limited education Seth Wells's views are quoted in Brewer, *Shaker Communities*, 76.

"much opposition from the prejudiced part" Freegift Wells, Records of the Church at Watervliet, March 22, 1816, WRHS 44, IV:B-279.

"unlawful and immoral" The committee's report is reprinted in Chapman, *Account*, iv–vii.

"not without analogy" There is a precedent for this equation in William Blackstone's *Commentaries on the Law*. The English jurist wrote of how prisoners and monks equally suffered a civil death. See Blackstone, *Commentaries*, 226–228.

"very threatening epistle" . . . *"crafty"* Elder Seth to Elder Benjamin, July 19, 1817, WRHS 25, IV:A-77.

CHAPTER 4: TORTURED IN THE WHIRLWIND OF AFFLICTION AND WOE

"the size of a musket ball" Freegift Wells, Records of the Church at Watervliet, April 20, 1816, WRHS 44, IV:B-279.

Wild winds raged See *Northern Whig*, May 21, 1816.

The hills around Albany J. Munsell, *Annals of Albany*, vol. 6 (Albany, NY: J. Munsell, 1856), 116.

light cloths froze Freegift Wells, Series of Daily Journals, June 6, 1816, WRHS 45, IV:B-285–286. Other Shaker incidents described below are recorded in this journal.

ecological oddities On the "year without a summer" see Wergland, *One Shaker Life*, 27; John Bailey, *The Lost German Slave Girl* (New York: Grove Press, 2005), 20–21.

had found new quarters See *The Albany Directory for the Year 1817* (Albany: Packard and Van Benthuysen, 1817).

vast covered market . . . smoke, gossip, and scheme This description paraphrases an anonymous eyewitness account: "Albany Fifty Years Ago," *Harper's Magazine*, March 1857, 460.

she could not help reflecting Eunice's reminiscences of her children appear in her *Account*, 18–20. Here she also describes how she dissolved into tears. Also see Dyer, *Portraiture*, 295; and Eunice Chapman, *An Account of the Conduct of the Shakers* (Lebanon, OH: Van Vleet and Camron, 1818), 80. (This book is not to be confused with Eunice's *Account of the Conduct of the People Called Shaker* of 1817.) Henceforth this source will be cited as *Account 1818*.

"long-lost babe" . . . *Eunice was painfully aware* See Dyer, *Portraiture*, 296. Eunice specifically comments on Julia's greater ease among the Shakers in her *Account*: her awareness of Julia's likeliness to forget is my speculation.

weeping Chapman, *Account*, 19.

For Eunice to choose to write Several studies have informed the discussion of Eunice's writing to follow: Miller, "Serpentine Advances in Sacred Space"; Humez, "A Woman Mighty"; and De Wolfe, *Shaking the Faith*. (Also see my thesis, "Rational Renegades: Antebellum Anti-Shakers, Shaker Apostates, and the Literary Imagination," Diss., Columbia University, 2004, 99–147.) These scholars discuss the plight of female anti-Shaker authors and the benefits of the captivity, sentimental, and other genres to such authors. Miller and Humez both analyze Eunice's exploitation of these genres, and while De Wolfe does not discuss Eunice's writings in detail, her readings of Dyer's works have provided a model for my analysis of Eunice's literary techniques. (See especially *Shaking the Faith*, 8–9, 12–13, 115–119.) As De Wolfe writes, Dyer, too, "employed sentiment—the affections of the heart—not simply to cause tears, but to provoke a response leading to action" (117). Detailed citations follow.

after the advent of the penny press See Basch, *Framing*, 147.

writing was her one chance . . . create an acceptable persona De Wolfe, *Shaking the Faith*, 5, 9; Miller, "Serpentine Advances in Sacred Spaces," 62.

Skeptics found it hard to believe Chapman, *No. 2*, v. Mary Dyer faced similar accusations, as De Wolfe notes in *Shaking the Faith*, 73.

Eunice had little help from the anti-Shaker writers. Ibid., 12.

narratives of Indian captivity De Wolfe, *Shaking the Faith*, 13, 118–19;

Humez, "Woman Mighty," 95–96; Miller, "Serpentine Advances in Sacred Places," 39–40, 62.

"If the reader should observe. . . ." Chapman, *Account*, iii.

especially the Sisters Humez discusses Eunice's particular animosity towards sisters in "Woman Mighty," 96.

"spiritual husbands and wives" Ibid., 26.

actions they may well have taken I thank Glendyne Wergland for this observation.

"As I sat weeping" Chapman, *Account*, 29.

Mother Lucy once issued a similar gift See Humez, *Mother's First-Born Daughters*, 72.

literary sentimentalism De Wolfe, *Shaking the Faith*, 13, 118–19; Humez, "Woman Mighty," 95–96; Miller, "Serpentine Advances in Sacred Places," 39–40, 62.

"But here I must drop my pen" Chapman, *Account*, 19.

America's first best seller Patricia L. Parker, "Charlotte Temple, America's First Best Seller," *Studies in Short Fiction*, v. 8 no. 4 (Fall 1976). Miller also mentions that Dyer's work is "pedagogical" in the manner of Rowson's work in "Serpentine Advances," 78.

"off the page" . . . participate in the action of the story . . . girls flocked to Charlotte's supposed grave . . . not until the appearance Susanna Rowson, *Charlotte Temple and Lucy Temple*, ed. Ann Douglas (New York: Penguin Books, 1991), xxi, x, xvi, vii.

the narrator of the tale coaches her readers' reactions Likewise, Eunice "coaches her readers' responses, by consistently calling the children 'little captives,'" as Humez writes in "Woman Mighty," 96.

told from a point of completion Or, as Douglas writes of *Charlotte Temple*, "this story is enacted from the viewpoint of its finish." Rowson, *Charlotte Temple and Lucy Temple*, xxxiii.

if only they will help her See De Wolfe's articulation of the relationship between sentiment and action in Mary Dyer's work in *Shaking the Faith*, 12–13, 117. De Wolfe focuses on sympathy as a moral agent.

"enslave[d]" Chapman, *Account*, 54.

"Do not women and children" Ibid., 56.

"the whole world must yet come under" Ibid., 55.

"Military Tax" Ibid., 60.

return to the home where she properly belongs See Miller's discussion of Chapman's "strategy of victimization" in "Serpentine Advances," 65, 68.

printing was muscle work Rollo G. Silver, *The American Printer, 1787–1825* (Charlottesville: University Press of Virginia, 1967), 11.

stacks of slim, freshly printed volumes . . . special binding My thanks to David Whitesell for taking a look at the copy of Eunice's *Account* at the American Antiquarian Society and speculating about the binding. The information in this description draws from his e-mail correspondence with me, August 3, 2009.

depositions For an interesting reading of how such depositions conferred legitimacy on female writers like Eunice, see De Wolfe, *Shaking the Faith*, 74.

"a number of respectable ladies" Chapman, *No. 2*, 36.

"Ladies Society" . . . Churchgoing women Hackett, *Rude Hand*, 86, 89.

thirty-seven and a half cents De Wolfe, *Shaking the Faith*, 94.

The Female Marine, AGDA, February 24, 1817.

Mrs. Taylor, Otsego Herald, January 9, 1817.

CHAPTER 5: INFAMOUS SLANDER

"the common people swallowed" . . . "all these effects" Elder Seth to Elder Benjamin, July 19, 1817, WRHS 25, IV:A-77.

Adding to all of this hostility . . . "season of scarcity" . . . not far from the Watervliet Shakers See Ministry at New Lebanon to Ministry at Harvard, July 2, 1818, WRHS 20, IV:A-33, as well as Freegift Wells, Records of the Church at Watervliet, January 1817 WRHS 44, IV.B-279.

In New York City AGDA, February 22, 1817.

a copy of Eunice's book arrived . . . "so watchful, so careful" Elder Seth documents the book's arrival and reception in Watervliet and New Lebanon in his letter to Elder Benjamin, July 19, 1817, WRHS 25,

IV:A-77. I have assumed that Mother Lucy received the book in Watervliet, since she arrived there on January 17.

"that filthy daughter" Seth Wells to Issachar Bates, July 26, 1817, WRHS 25, IV:A-77.

"never more to receive" Freegift Wells, Records of the Church at Watervliet, February 20, 1817, WRHS 44, IV:B-279.

charmer of the female sex John F. Marszalek, *The Petticoat Affair: Manners, Mutiny, and Sex in Andrew Jackson's White House* (Baton Rouge: Louisiana State University Press, 2000), 59.

"magic" McNemar, *Other Side*, 15.

Eunice's charms fell flat Elder Seth to Elder Benjamin, July 19, 1817, WRHS 25, IV:A-77.

the senators were as bored Ibid. The Shakers' "Remonstrance" appears in McNemar, *Other Side*, 30–37. All quotations to follow, unless otherwise noted, are from this source.

"the power of God" . . . fortunes seem to have reversed Elder Seth to Elder Benjamin, July 19, 1817, WRHS 25, IV:A-77.

CHAPTER 6: JAMES

"Memorial" All quotations to follow, unless otherwise noted, are from this source.

opposite of the supportive subservent wife De Wolfe writes of how Joseph Dyer depicted his wife Mary as "the opposite of everything a woman should be" in *Shaking the Faith*, 81.

"appeared to have a good effect" Freegift Wells, Records of the Church at Watervliet, New York, March 24, 1817, WRHS 44, IV:B-279.

subverted their claims to innocence Blake, "Eunice," 369.

CHAPTER 7: AN ACT OF RELIEF

"a half-grown and half-learned itinerant printer" Stone, *The Life and Times of Sa-go-ye-wat-ha, Or Red-Jacket*, 99.

"You write, my son" Ibid., 15.

"conservative" Ibid., 98.

puritanical father Ibid., 2.

"put an effectual quietus upon that extraordinary mania" Ibid., 73.

fascinating AGDA, January 29, 1818.

Pendleton was also famous Thomas Fleming, *Duel*, 60, 324.

"The case now before the committee" Pendleton's speech appears in *AGDA*, April 7, 1817.

How could they forget These names are not listed in *AGDA*. I pulled the cases from legislative records. On Hall, New York Assembly Journal (Early American Imprints 41619) January 30, 1817, p. 140; Griffen, February 17, 1817; Pardee, February 6, 1817; Barnum, January 22, 1817.

"enticing little woman" Elder Seth to Elder Benjamin, July 19, 1817, WRHS 25, IV:A-77.

"it would puzzle us to say" Thomas Jefferson, *The Works of Thomas Jefferson*, ed. Paul Leicester Ford, vol. 12 (New York: G. P. Putnam's Sons, 1905), 59, 73.

"very bad character" Ministry New Lebanon to Ministry Union Village, March 27, 1819, WRHS 20, IV:A-33. Most of what follows draws from Josiah Terry's deposition, Chapman, *No. 2*, 46–51.

"impetuity of passion" McNemar, *Other Side*, 146.

"walk by faith and not by sight" Chapman, *Account*, 48.

"more finished instrument of the devil than Eunice" Ministry New Lebanon to Ministry Union Village, March 27, 1819, WRHS 20, IV:A-33.

Eunice saw their efforts she became disenchanted De Wolfe, *Shaking the Faith*, 34–35.

Eunice saw their efforts Dyer, *Portraiture*, 338.

CHAPTER 8: MOTHER AGAINST MOTHER

picture of rustic reverie . . . "opportunities provided for sport" This description of New Lebanon paraphrases and closely follows part of a visitor's account from the period, reprinted in Wergland, *Visiting*, 177–181. I have interwoven details from other visitors' accounts, ibid., 131–187. Also see Lossing, *An Early View of the Shakers*.

"angled for husbands" Wergland, *Visiting*, 4.

When not enjoying the waters Ibid., 132, 155–156,

"the orgies of the evening crowd" Ibid., 187.

Shaker named Riley Chapman, *No.2*, 60

Eunice had heard other stories Ibid., 58.

"noble mountain terrace" Lossing, *An Early View of the Shakers*, 30. In the original description, it is the metal roof of the church that sparkles, but the meetinghouse that Lossing saw was different from the one in Eunice's time.

"of no use" Chapman, *No. 2*, 59. The following exchange appears in this source.

"smart, capable woman" Isaac Newton Youngs, "Narrative of various events . . ." (1814–1823), May 28, 1819, LC 3:42.

"renounced his faith" . . . *"other evils"* Ibid., September 1817.

"Mrs. Lucy Goodrich" Eunice Chapman to Lucy Wright, December 4, 1817, WRHS 25, IV:A-77.

Mother Lucy had faced repeated challenges on account of her gender The following discussion of Mother Lucy's leadership draws from Humez, *Mother's First-Born Daughters*, 64–77; Humez, "Petticoat Government," 1–17; Stein, *Shaker Experience*, 92; Brewer, *Shaker Communities*, 51–2, 57–58.

young men such as Angell Matthewson His words appear in Humez, *Mother's First-Born Daughters*, 67.

"petticoat government" . . . *"the lead being in the female"* Humez, "Petticoat Government," 8–9.

additional pressure on account of the newly published biography Stein, *Shaker Experience*, 83–85.

knew how to use her femininity to her advantage Humez, *Mother's First-Born Daughters*, 64–65.

"Eunice, I have received thy letter . . ." Lucy Wright to Eunice Chapman, December 12, 1817, WRHS 25, IV:A-77.

Ohio Shaker community . . . *Abraham Van Vleet* McNemar, *Other Side*, 115–129.

"check the ravages" This was said of Jonas Platt. Dixon Ryan Fox, *The Decline of Aristocracy in the Politics of New York* (New York: Harper Torchbooks, 1965), 242.

"American Blackstone" Thomas Fleming, *Duel: Alexander Hamilton, Aaron Burr, and the Future of America* (New York: Basic Books, 1999), 170.

" her own glosses" McNemar, *Other Side,* 116.

"dreadful bundle of trash" Ministry New Lebanon to Ministry Union Village, January 23, 1818, WRHS 20, IV:A-33.

"to be prepared" Dyer, *Portraiture,* 338.

Chapter 9: The Council of Revision

"We hope this subject is put to rest" AGDA, January 29, 1818.

"POSITIVELY HER LAST APPEARANCE" Ibid., February 18, 1818.

"some strange . . . magic" McNemar, *Other Side,* 15–16.

Eunice had finally released The precise timing of the publication is unknown.

"Think of it, here I am" John E. Raitt, *Ruts in the Road* (Delhi: John E. Raitt, 1982), 24.

"great fierce obstinate" Seth Wells to Ministry, March 14, 1818, WRHS 25, IV:A-77.

demagogue of the worst kind . . . man in his prime This character portrait draws from Raitt, *Ruts,* 15–24; Henry Van Der Lyn, Diaries, Vol. 1, 212–213, New-York Historical Society; *AGDA,* April 21, 1818; Fox, *Decline of Aristocracy,* 240; James Sullivan, ed., *The History of New York State,* book 12, chapter 3, part 5, available online at http://www.usgennet.org/usa/ny/state/his/bk12/ch3/pt5.html.

"back-woods members" AGDA, April 21, 1818.

"No matter what the bill" Ibid.

the council was unpopular Blake, "Eunice Against the Shakers," 370; J. Hampden Dougherty, *Legal and Judicial History of New York,* vol. 2 (New York: National Americana Society, 1911), 66–80.

democracy itself was on the line On Root and democracy, see Blake, "Eunice Against the Shakers," 371.

"The institution of marriage" The council's report appears in McNemar, *Other Side,* 7–12.

"We charge her with no crime" Quoted in ibid., 16.

"her only dependence for existence" Chapman, *No. 2,* 52.

CHAPTER 10: AN OBJECT OF DISGUST

Albany was awash . . . past a grown man's knees Munsell, *Annals of Albany,* 128.

"lady's turnpike" Albany Argus, January 20, 1818.

Packed to its capacity AGDA, March 14, 1818. All subsequent quotations (unless noted) are from here. I have reordered or summarized some points. My interpretations of the crowd's response and Eunice's reactions are based on the cadences of the speeches, the Shakers' observations, and Eunice's writing.

"modern enchantress" McNemar, *Other Side,* 18.

seventy-eight carriages Visitors' arrivals are documented in Jethro Turner, Daily Journal, March 1, 1818. WRHS 46, IV:B-298.

"idle" The Shakers' experience of the past few days are detailed in Seth Wells to Ministry, March 14, 1818, Watervliet, NY, Correspondences, WRHS 25, IV:A-77.

"the man who let his feelings" AGDA, April 7, 1817.

governor, DeWitt Clinton On Clinton, see Evan Cornog, *The Birth of Empire: DeWitt Clinton and the American Experience, 1769–1828* (New York: Oxford University Press, 1998).

despite his loyalties Clinton appears to have been conflicted about the Chapman case: A newspaper article reports that the governor "anxiously desired" Eunice's divorce. *National Advocate,* May 20, 1818.

"unschooled parliament" Thanks to Rachel Kousser for the translation. *Indoctum Parliamentum: A Farce in One Act and a Beautiful Variety of Scenes* (n.p. 1818).

"dizziness in the head" Quoted in Roseberry, *Capitol Story,* 15.

"If the mere privation of sexual intercourse" McNemar, *Other Side,* 9.

"set her face like a flint" Dyer, *Portraiture,* 338.

CHAPTER 11: AN ORNAMENT TO HER SEX

"brilliant but dissipated man" See "Chapter XXI: Town of Oxford," James H. Smith, *History of Chenango and Madison Counties* (Syracuse, NY: D. Mason and Company, 1880), 252–293.

Throop started off by announcing The following speeches appear in *AGDA*, March 13, 1818. See my explanation of "Sources," 353.

Erastus Root rose to speak Stone's presentation of Root's speech is less detailed than others. For parts of the speech, for instance where Stone refuses to provide specific language, I have referred to arguments attributed to Root in *Indoctum Parliamentum.*

"making love to the people" . . . *"Sham patrio" AGDA*, April 21, 1818.

"too indelicate—" AGDA, April 2, 1818.

"not only in this house" Ibid.

a Ciceronian saying This expression comes from Cicero's *Catilinom* i:2.

"Call him if you please" AGDA, March 13, 1818.

Eunice abruptly abandoned all sense of decorum. In what manner she expressed her pleasure was never recorded, though her behavior was apparently shocking enough to make some legislators wish to recall their votes. I offer an approximation, based on her other expressions to the Shakers, as well as on language she had used in prior conflicts.

"After the passage of the act" Anonymous, Domestic Journal of Important Occurrences Kept for the Elder Sisters at New Lebanon, March 1818, WRHS 32, V:B-60.

first and last to pass in New York State As Nelson Blake writes, "Eunice's was the only divorce ever directly voted by the legislature." "Eunice Against the Shakers," 359.

CHAPTER 12: O TEMPORA, O MORES!

"I have though I would not warn you again" Eunice's letter appears in McNemar, *Other Side,* 19.

"swallowed a barbecued Delaware" AGDA, April 2, 1818.

"arrogance and the malignity" . . . *"prostitute the name of the Almighty"* McNemar, *Other Side,* 17–18. Stone does not call Eunice a prostitute outright, but he implies as much.

"publicly insult the endearing affection" Chapman, *No. 2,* 82.

"were coaxed and flattered" Seth Wells to unidentified Shakers, September 2, 1818, WRHS 2, I:A-20.

"Mysterious providence" Dyer, *Portraiture,* 292.

PART III: REWARD

CHAPTER 1: CAPTIVE BABES

The Enfield Shaker community . . . *control the water's flow* These details appear in Sanborn, *Enfield,* 7, 13, 17.

sugar maples and butternuts Elkins, *Fifteen Years,* 11–12.

ranks of women lining up I thank Renee Fox at the Canterbury Shaker Village for sharing this anecdote with me.

"shook him as a dog would a woodchuck" Jane E. S. Blanchard, "A Sketch of Her Experience Previous to 1868," handwritten transcript from Mary Ann Haagen, 5. Also available in WRHS 52, VI:B-37.

children who were tardy Briggs, "Forty Years," 467.

"good manners" Isaac Newton Youngs, "A concise view of the church of God and of Christ on earth: having its foundation in the faith of Christ's first and second appearing, New Lebanon, 1856," 369, WM 861.

"usually consisted of good rich meat hash" Briggs, "Forty Years," 467.

"Love not self, that must be hated," Goodwillie and Croswaithe, *Millennial Praises,* 165.

"married" Briggs, "Forty Years," 471.

sneaky little girl Anonymous, "Fifteen Years a Shakeress," 32.

All that they knew . . . *"common and very base woman"* Dyer, *Portraiture,* 300–301.

Eunice made her preparations Eunice describes her journey and the adventure to follow in *Portraiture*, 291–309. All quotations to follow, unless otherwise noted, are from these pages.

passengers would be thrown about The hazards of stagecoach travel are detailed in Kubik, *West through the Catskills*, 65–67.

The town of Enfield was small Thanks to Richard Henderson for his insight into early Enfield geography.

Enfield was a resting stop . . . "lustily on his horn" . . . British guard Sanborn, *Enfield*, 167–168.

frontier of northwestern New Hampshire See De Wolfe, *Shaking the Faith*, 20 and following for details of Dyer's life.

"shoot them down in the street" Chapman, *Account 1818*, 80.

"dear little captives" Chapman, *Account*, 17.

CHAPTER 2: AN ELDER AND AN EMISSARY

On Monday morning, May 25 My primary source for this chapter is a wonderfully detailed statement by the Enfield Shakers. "A Statement Concerning the Mob at Enfield, New Hampshire," May 25, 1818. I thank Beth De Wolfe for her transcription of the original, now available at the Hamilton College archives. All quotations to follow, unless otherwise noted, are from this source.

she had Elder John in mind as her "mate" De Wolfe, *Shaking the Faith*, 80.

Two sisters of marriageable age . . . "fasten[ed] her with cords" Henry Blinn, Historical Notes Having Reference to the Believers in Enfield, NH, vol. 1, CSV 761, 310–312, 287–289.

"secured the services of a negro" . . . "shameful obscene and brutish" Ibid., 23. A general source on the history of Enfield's relationship with the Shakers is Peter James McShane, "The Shaker Religion and Its Effects on Enfield, NH" (Masters thesis, University of New Hampshire, 1977).

"come to drive the Shakers away" Blinn, Historical Notes, vol. 2, 115, CSV 762.

unusually mischievous group De Wolfe, *Shaking the Faith*, 196, note 54.

A separate lawsuit See Blinn, Historical Notes, vol. 1, 101–102.
unorthodox Methodist inclinations See Sanborn, *Enfield*, 138–139.

CHAPTER 3: LITTLE STRANGERS

The Believers were probably in the trustees' office I have speculated on
the Shakers' view of Eunice's approach. The two sides probably
squared off in the trustees' office, which was where the Shakers received visitors, as well as where Eunice awaited her children.

"Woe, woe, woe" (Original reads "wo." I have also changed some of
the punctuation in the quotations to follow.) The Shakers do not
specify when Eunice uttered these words, which appear in their
"Statement Concerning the Mob," but a likely guess is that they were
part of her greeting.

"modern enchantress" McNemar, *Other Side*, 18.

stood and stared at "the little stranger" Dyer, *Portraiture*, 294–295. The
dialogue and scenes to follow are derived from this source, the Shakers' "A Statement Concerning the Mob," or from Chapman, *Account
1818*, 80, unless otherwise noted.

"Would you not like to have me" Mary records her conversation with
her son in Mary Dyer, *The Rise and Progress of the Serpent from the Garden
of Eden, To the Present Day: with a Disclosure of Shakerism, Exhibiting a General View of Their Real Character and Conduct from the First Appearance of
Ann Lee. Also, the Life and Sufferings of the Author, Mary M. Dyer, but Now
Is Mary Marshall* (Concord, NH: printed for the author, 1847), 226.

Mary had tricked the child See De Wolfe, *Shaking the Faith*, 89.

Mary Dyer traveled back…relative weakness The Shakers describe this
incident in their "Statement Concerning the Mob." Eunice describes her
appeal among locals in Dyer, *Portraiture*, 294. De Wolfe analyzes Mary
Dyer's relative weakness and its evidence in her company in *Shaking*, 90, 93.

the initiative to move the children may have come from James himself Shaker
correspondence reveals that at least in the aftermath of this event,
James was adamant about the course he wished to pursue with his
children. I have offered one interpretation of his and the Shakers' mo-

tivations at this juncture. See Ministry New Hampshire to Ministry New Lebanon, July 30, 1818, WRHS 18: IV:A-11.

Chapter 4: Five Hundred Men

"wasting sickness" Thanks to Richard Henderson for this inscription from Mehitabel Cochran's grave.

Cochran asked to see James This exchange and all to follow, unless noted, are from the Shakers "Statement Concerning the Mob" and the Affidavit of John Lyon, copied in Henry Blinn, Historical Notes, vol. 2, 115, CSV 762, 112.

freight and passenger coaches traveling along the East Coast Sanborn, *Enfield*, 166.

word of Eunice's troubles spread quickly De Wolfe, *Shaking the Faith*, 94.

"sooner tie his children to a log" This quotation and all to follow, unless noted, appear in Dyer, *Portraiture*, 297–298.

they had no control Chapman, *Account 1818*, 81.

Sheriff Moses Johnson Johnson's testimony appears in Dyer, *Rise and Progress*, 125.

a whip and two pistols Hamilton Child, *Gazetteer of Grafton County, New Hampshire*, vol. 1 (Syracuse, NY: Syracuse Journal Company, 1886), 255.

"as though he had been taken captive" The following incident is recalled in Dyer, *Portraiture*, 299.

"flee . . . or lose" Chapman, *Account 1818*, 82.

"let them know what they might expect" Dyer, *Portraiture*, 299.

Chapter 5: Mother Again

"I trembled whenever he went out of my sight" Dyer, *Portraiture*, 290.

"strong iron cages" AGDA, August 28, 1817.

"astonishing feats" AGDA, May 21, 1818.

"one hundred square feet of Canvass" AGDA, May 5, 1818.

the leadership in New Hampshire wrote to Mother Lucy Ministry New Hampshire to Ministry New Lebanon, July 30, 1818, Enfield, New Hampshire, Correspondences, WRHS 18, IV:A-11.

The lawyer warned James Dyer, *Portraiture*, 303.

"should like to" Ministry New Hampshire to Ministry at New Lebanon, December 14, 1818, Canterbury, New Hampshire, Correspondences, WRHS 17, IV:A-3.

Cheapside See the New York State Museum's Colonial Albany Social History Project Web site: http://www.nysm.nysed.gov/albany/streets.html #southpearl.

"My son is now fourteen" Dyer, *Portraiture*, 304.

Eunice boasted to Mary Dyer Ibid.

"begging for a privilege" Ministry Union Village to Ministry New Lebanon, March 2, 1819, WRHS 24, IV:A-69.

spying for Eunice Ministry New Lebanon to Ministry Union Village, March 27, 1819, WRHS 20, IV:A-33.

One day in September Dyer, *Portraiture*, 305, Isaac Newton Youngs, "Narrative of various events . . ." (1814–1823), May 28, 1819, LC 3:42.

Eunice needed nothing more Nelson Blake writes that "on the basis of her new evidence" from George, Eunice secured "a formal New York court order granting her the custody of all three children," but I have not been able to confirm this. Blake, "Eunice Against the Shakers," 377.

"Much credit is due to this lady" Boston Commercial Gazette, September 27, 1819.

EPILOGUE

"best of her days" Eunice's letter is reprinted in McNemar, *Other Side*, 19.

she was able to legalize her claims Unfortunately, I have found no documentation of her final guardianship, though she is sure to have secured these rights in order to live safely in Albany.

"If all the members who voted" "From the *National Advocate*," *Albany Gazette*, January 10, 1820.

"rather odd" Caroline Hawley to Rhoda and Merwin Hawley, December 6, 1822, Hawley Family Papers, box 1, folder 1A, BECHS.

"I have this week received" Susan Chapman to Caroline Hawley, October 4, 1822, box 1, folder 1A, Hawley Family Papers, BECHS.

"I felt very gloomy" Susan Chapman to Caroline Hawley, June 24, 1824, box 1, folder 1A, Hawley Family Papers, BECHS.

When a circus caravan came Ibid.

became a belle Susan details her exploits in her letter to her cousin Caroline Hawley, May 2, 1826, box 1, folder 1A, Hawley Family Papers, BECHS.

"write with much sincerity" Susan Chapman to Caroline Hawley, May 6, 1825 box 1, folder 1A, Hawley Family Papers, BECHS.

"Shortly after my arrival in Troy" Susan Chapman to Caroline Hawley, May 2, 1826, box 1, folder 1A, Hawley Family Papers, BECHS.

modern incarnation of Henry VIII "At Eighty Wins Name and Right to Riches," *New York Times,* June 6, 1922.

"drunk in the streets" Ministry New Lebanon to Ministry Union Village, March 27, 1819, WRHS 20, IV:A-33. I have not found public records to confirm this charge, but the Shakers were accurate reporters and were not likely to make up such charges.

"She kept to her room" Ellis v. Kelsey et al., vol. 1, 321 (118 Misc. 763; 195 NYS. 126; 1922 NY Misc. LEXIS 1360).

"She was a light in the age in which she lived" Hawley, *Hawley Record,* 534.

"Declaration of Sentiments" . . . *not passed until 1860* Foner, *The Reader's Companion to American History,* 702, 981.

"incurable insanity" Blake, *Road to Reno,* 76.

"professional perjurers" Ibid., 192.

As for Eunice's act Correspondence regarding the withdrawal of this law is available in the "Legal Cases" binder at the Watervliet Heritage Society.

"another Eunice Chapman" Quoted in De Wolfe, *Shaking,* 204, n. 12.

"believing that the children could nowhere procure" Anonymous, "Giving Babies to the Shakers," *New York Daily Times,* August 4, 1855.

Her efforts helped expand the divorce laws De Wolfe, *Shaking the Faith,* 166.

"calm, patient, and resigned" "Mother's last visit to Watervliet," printed in *American Communal Societies Quarterly,* vol. 1, no. 1 (January 2007): 28.

Thereafter a group of four See Stein, *Shaker Experience*, 122–123.

"dropsical asthma" Alonzo G. Hollister, "Book of Remembrance," WRHS 58, VII:B-109, 166.

"difficult circumstances" Seth Youngs Wells, "Account of himself in July 1846," Unpublisht Testimonies Continued, WRHS 52, VI:B-43, 195.

listed as a shareholder Raymond Beecher, *Out to Greenville and Beyond: Historical Sketches of Greene County* (Coxsackie, NY: Greene County Historical Society Press, 1997), 123, Appendix B.

owing in great part Stephen Paterwic discussed how the Shakers owed their rising numbers to the children they received in his presentation, "Canterbury Takes the Lead," at the Enfield Museum's Shaker Seminar, held in Enfield, NH, April 4, 2009. The following discussion of the relationship between the incoming children and the society's decline, as well as Mother Lucy's warnings, relies on Paterwic's book, *Historical Dictionary*, xxviii–xxxi, 251.

Lucy Wright began actively counseling In addition to Paterwic, see Calvin Green, *"Biographical Memoir of the Life,"* WRHS 55, VI:B-28, 266.

deliberate effort to enlarge their ranks Ibid., xxviii.

One scholar has recently speculated Ibid., xxviii–xxxi.

"Era of Manifestations" On the "Era of Manifestations" and its aftermath, see Stein, *Shaker Experience,* 165–200; Brewer, *Shaker Communities,* 115–135; De Wolfe, *Shaking the Faith,* 165.

Other factors Brewer, *Shaker Communities,* 178–202; Stein, *Shaker Experience*, especially 338–358.

persecution actually invigorated them . . . they faltered See De Wolfe's analysis of how anti-Shakerism strengthened Shakerism in *Shaking the Faith,* 176, 185.

ACKNOWLEDGMENTS

My first thanks go to Robert A. Ferguson, whose literary lessons have been life lessons, and whose rigorous readings of all my writing—from my theses to this book—have shaped me as a writer. His ongoing mentorship and office hour sessions have meant more to me than he can possibly know. Other members of my doctoral committee at Columbia University, including Casey Blake, Andrew Delbanco, Eric Foner, and Robert O'Meally, also encouraged me to transform my dissertation chapter on Eunice into a very different sort of book.

My agent, Julie Barer, took me on when I had little more than a pile of research and an idea for a story. I want to thank her for guiding me through every stage of the writing and publishing process with such skill and flair. At Grove, Luba Ostashevsky set the book on its present course with her insightful, big-picture comments. I am deeply indebted to Alex Littlefield for editing countless drafts with great patience, sensitivity, and enthusiasm—and for naming this book. I also wish to thank Joan Bingham, her assistant Emily Cunningham, Jodie Hockensmith and Deb Seager.

Shaker scholars have provided me with a vibrant research community. Christian Goodwillie and Stephen Paterwic gave me vital leads, while Beth De Wolfe generously shared her expertise on anti-Shakers and encouraged me to pursue Eunice's story. I don't know what I would have done without Mary Ann Haagen's wisdom and counsel on all things Shaker. Time and again, she passed me invaluable manuscript pieces that fed into this story. Above all, she has taught me to see the Believers not simply as a historical society, but as real people. Glendyne Wergland, too, showed me a larger Shaker picture, both through her advice and through her scholarship. She shared priceless "tibits" with me, especially manuscripts regarding Seth Youngs Wells, and was always available to answer questions. I also want to thank legal scholars Norma Basch, Nina Dayton, and Michael Grossberg for their insights into the history of divorce and custody.

Numerous fellowships have supported my research, including the Larry Hackman Research Residency at the New York State Archives; the Helen Lehman Buttenwieser Fellowship at Columbia University; the Elder Henry Blinn Fellowship at the University of New Hampshire and the Canterbury Shaker Village; the Shaker Workshops' Scholarship Award; and the Faith Andrews Memorial Fellowship at the Winterthur Museum and Library. My time as a fellow at the American Antiquarian Society was especially fruitful, and I wish to give special thanks to Thomas Knoles, Philip Lampi, Diane Rugh, Caroline Sloat, and David Whitesell, as well as to fellow scholars Lynne Z. Bassett, Nina Dayton, and Cindy Lobell. I am grateful to Ken Fuld, David Watters, and Amanda Merrill for their hospitality at the University of New Hampshire.

I have benefited from the assistance of librarians, archivists, and other experts at historical societies, Shaker museums, and other collections across the Northeast. Particular thanks go to

Renee Fox at the Canterbury Shaker Museum; Carol Ganz at the Connecticut State Library; Jerry Grant at the Shaker Museum and Library; Trudy Hawley at the Hawley Society; Doug and Sancie Thomsen at the Durham Center Museum; Mary Boswell at the Enfield Shaker Museum; Christian Goodwillie and Randy Ericson at the Hamilton College Library; Lesley Herzberg at Hancock Shaker Village; James Folts at the New York State Archives; Starlyn D'Angelo, Lisa Granger, and Betty Shaver at the Shaker Heritage Society; Dee Forman and Mary Ellen Challenger at the United Congregational Church in Bridgeport; and Judith Rundell at the Vedder Research Library. Richard Henderson dug up wonderful details about early Enfield history.

I am grateful to the following individuals for reading chapters or drafts of my book: Robert Ferguson, Stephanie M. Griffin, Mary Ann Haagen, Mark Lamster, Joon Park, Meena Ramakrishnan, Glendyne Wergland, and Wonbo Woo. All errors of both fact and judgment are my own. Finally, I am deeply grateful to Donald Gibson, friend, teacher, and historian, who read through pages when I was ready to throw them all out, and sustained me with his courage, even through his illness. My great regret is that I could not put the completed work in his hands. Additional thanks go to Marcella Calabi, Peter Kafka, Mrs. Dong Ku Lee, and Sam Shin.

Friends and family nourished me through an over decade-long process. Special thanks to Vanessa Bauza, Rachel Kousser, Allegra Lowitt, and the Park family. Anna Kuchment, Dai Sil Kim-Gibson, Meena Ramakrishnan, and Allison Zmuda carried me through. My brother Wonbo offered his critical eye, as well as encouragement when I needed it most. My parents, Kyu Sung Woo and Jung-Ja Kim, who first introduced me to the

Shakers, are my inspiration. Kian and Oan, who were both born during the writing of this book, reminded me every day of what Eunice was fighting for. Finally, Joon traveled with me to archives across the country, on hunts for headstones and scraps of manuscripts in the unlikeliest places. I am truly grateful for his love, support, and wicked sense of humor.